Beyond Words

Beyond Words:
The Othering Excursion in Contemporary American Literature

To Margaret — in appreciation of your brilliance and warmth

By

Wendy Harding and Jacky Martin

Affectionately
Wendy

Cambridge Scholars Publishing

Beyond Words: The Othering Excursion in Contemporary American Literature, by Wendy Harding and Jacky Martin

This book first published 2007 by

Cambridge Scholars Publishing

15 Angerton Gardens, Newcastle, NE5 2JA, UK

British Library Cataloguing in Publication Data
A catalogue record for this book is available from the British Library

ISBN (10): 1-84718-370-0, ISBN (13): 9781847183705

TABLE OF CONTENTS

ACKNOWLEDGMENTS

Our work on this book began in earnest during a faculty exchange in 2002 at the University of Texas. We were able to use their superb library and also to present our work in its very early stages to members of the French Department and the English Department. We are very grateful for all the assistance we received during this exchange.

We thank our students and colleagues in France for the attention and support they have given us. We were given the opportunity to present an early version of Chapter One at the AFEA Congress in Lille in 2005. We much appreciated the constructive comments made by Marc Chénetier and Antoine Cazé on that occasion. We are particularly grateful for a special research leave awarded to Wendy Harding by the national university council (Conseil National des Universités) which gave us precious time to devote to our study. We spent part of this leave in Burlington, Vermont, where we enjoyed to the full the University of Vermont's library facilities.

Most of all we are thankful to the writers who have given us so much reading pleasure. We hope we have not betrayed them.

PREFACE

Le mot qui exprime le plus est le mot inexprimable.[1]
—Edgar Morin

The approach to contemporary American literature developed in this book is the result of our search for a methodology that would enable us to address the richness and complexity of current literary production. From the sixties onward and especially with the exhaustion of formalism, explorations of the determining forces of race, gender, and class in cultural productions have revitalized literary criticism, yet although ethnic, feminist, or materialist approaches have refined critical enquiry, they have also tended to underemphasize the interactivity of American writing. Though political factors motivate and energize literary texts, they in no way determine them. The heuristic hypotheses we have formed are rather that there are no pure or distinct identifications corresponding to social categories, that binaries are superseded by amalgams, and that the notion of conflicts between opposite entities (center/ periphery, ethnic/ mainstream, dominant/ subaltern) should consequently be supplemented by the perception of fusions, mutations, and cross fertilizations. By dividing literary production along the lines of gender or race, critics have neglected the aesthetic principles that American writers share in common. Yet, far from embracing the discredited ideal of universality, the texts that we consider in this study break through into unfamiliar terrain, leading us beyond the borders of the cultural system to open up zones of unpredictability where critical categories grounded in social polarities no longer apply satisfactorily.

Initially, we felt that certain features of contemporary American texts, such as their complex and indeterminate symbolism, their unconventional structures, and their mutating personae could be understood only by taking into account the imbrication of conflicting cultural factors. Our 1994 study of Toni Morrison's work developed the idea of a "cultural interface," a zone of semiotic complexity, open to writers across the political spectrum, where ideological representations could be subverted rather than reproduced.[2] Yet our concept of the interface did not account for our repeated impression that something in Morrison's texts resisted analysis; something was being signified that remained not only beyond the critics' reach, but also, intractably, beyond the range of the text itself, some "unspeakable thing unspoken,"[3] to quote the memorable phrase from *Beloved*. Certain poets, in discussing their craft, evoke this elusive remainder that resists critical tools and seems not only unexplainable but also unnamable, except through negation and paradox. Mark Strand speculates that: "Perhaps the poem is ultimately a metaphor for something unknown," and, speaking of the way in which paraphrase removes what is poetic from a text, he concludes: "It is for this reason that poems must exist not only in language but beyond it."[4] In a similar vein, Jorie Graham speaks of her "deepest resource" as a poet being her "not-knowing."[5]

Our impression that some writers try to signify something beyond the system of signification prompted us to explore the concept of hybridity that, in the late 90's, had become prevalent in the field of anthropological and cultural studies. Among those who have explored this concept in interesting ways are the French West-Indian writers Glissant and Chamoiseau, the Chicana author Gloria Anzaldúa, as well as post-colonial critics, like Homi Bhaba, and the anthropologist Laplantine in association with the philosopher Nouss.[6] In our own study of Toni Morrison's novels, we had occasion to appreciate its usefulness, particularly in challenging the classifications and binaries of more traditional critics. Though we have since discarded the concept in order to develop our definition of Othering, discussions of hybridity confirmed our impression that literature, while located within the socio-political arena, did not necessarily reproduce a carbon copy of its divisions and struggles. A text can evince a clear political bias or represent a recognizable social position and at the same time function *as text* in ways that bypass and often subvert these categories. Wherever they might be placed on the political spectrum, far from being limited to pre-established, pre-scripted positions, authors can address opposite factions and even amalgamate their themes and styles of representation in their own constructions. Over and above polemics or subversive strategies, many contemporary American literary productions evince a form of amalgamation that could be described as hybrid.

Yet, we realized that hybridity was perhaps a blocking or masking concept insofar as it was either too universal to be relevant or, worse, it might be conceptually flawed. Indeed, because of the impression it gives of bringing differences together in a syncretic fusion, the notion of hybridity tends to equalize them, and consequently annul the work of creators working through and in spite of differences. Homi Bhaba speaks of a "third space" beyond or between factions in which differences are cross-fertilized. This claim promotes the illusion of negotiation in privileged liminal or intermediary spaces, a conception that contradicts our conviction that all communities are at the same time socially affronted and ideologically embedded in one another. Moreover, hybridity does not escape the snare of binaries that it aims to avoid. It is difficult to conceive of an amalgam without, logically, at one point or another, positing pure substances that contribute to its making. Finally, though the concept of hybridity is useful politically as a riposte to the essentialist conception of culture, it is equally infiltrated by ideology. Essential "substances" and "binaries," as well as "hybrids," are discursive constructs—results not causations, observables not determinants. Hence they cannot be used as epistemologically reliable concepts. At the core of discursive production, both literary and non-literary, there is a form of energy but also vulnerability that is not accessible to the static concepts of either essentialism or *métissage*. Hybridity fails to recognize the performative force of the literary text. By "performativity" we mean that the cultural system is, if not transformed by literary texts, at least profoundly affected by them. In literary texts differences are not affronted or compartmentalized but reactivated, inflected, and addressed to readers. Reading is a matter of cultural awareness and disorientation well before it becomes the act of sidetaking that sometimes serves as a refuge from the responsibility opened by the Othering text.

All the formalizations that we have envisaged, serviceable and productive as they might seem, are flawed because they incorporate a blocking factor—the very notion of difference. Cultural differences are not objectively observable because they implicitly refer to a binary that is artificially treated as a single phenomenon. Yet it is clear that nothing is different in itself but always in relation to something else. When evoking differences two terms are always cited at the same time: an original reference term and something that differs from it, and implicitly also a hierarchy is often posed in the relation between the two. The dichotomous nature of cultural differences induces a number of critical attitudes centered on duality. Critics tend to side with one or the other of the two aspects involved in differences. They privilege either conformity with the dominant cultural system or deviations described as innovations. Cultural differences are either dichotomized in partisan terms, or the conflict between reproduction and innovation is related to outside determinants, as in the Marxist or Freudian systems, for example. Whether differences are considered in themselves or related to external sources, the cultural reference is in the best of cases divided and very often confrontational.

In order to change this paradigm the inherent duality of cultural artifacts has to be considered jointly as one global concept. We envisage the artwork as an organic structure combining the aspiration to reproduce the cultural system with the contrary aspiration to deviate from it. In creative artifacts at least, the desire to conform is inseparable from the will to deviate. Reproduction and innovation are always co-determined, what change are the proportions and modalities in which the two are brought together. We consequently exclude the two extreme situations that found the confrontational paradigm: no reproduction of the system is conceivable without a certain innovative component, and, similarly, no deviance can be achieved without some conformist reference. In that conception differences, positions, or oppositions count less than the manner in which the artwork combines the two aspirations.

We have chosen to name "Othering" the text's aspiration to signify beyond the cultural system in order to amalgamate what lies beyond its limits. The term calls for clarification since the gerund "Othering" could potentially designate exclusion (casting someone in the role of the Other) or empathy (putting oneself in the place of another), a contradiction that we see as the persistent ideological infiltration of the confrontational concept. We chose the term in spite of its limitations to capitalize on that contradiction. In our conception "Othering" refers to a process that precedes any ascription in ideological terms and thus annuls the contradiction. It describes the impact of the unknown upon the cultural system, or to put it differently, it refers to the various ways in which the system accommodates that which potentially denies it. The Othering factor, whose discursive status will be investigated in depth in our theoretical introduction, can, for the time being, be situated at the junction between that which can be said and that which cannot be said but nevertheless clamors for expression. It involves a new form of rhetoricity—the rhetoric of the inexpressible as opposed to the traditional rhetoric of optimized expression.

Consequently, our attention will focus on the tendency of certain texts to push the system beyond its expressive limits. This choice determines our critical orientation and the nature of the texts that we have chosen to study. Our book claims neither to propose new theory nor to apply a new critical method. It offers, instead, a new attitude to reading, characterized by an enhanced receptivity to textual phenomena that have received insufficient attention up to now.

Besides attempting to inscribe the Othering rhetoric in critical language, our book brings together a wide range of literary texts, selected mainly from the last three decades of the twentieth century, that seem to illustrate the Othering factor. Our collection of texts is obviously subjective, some will say arbitrary. It does not intend to be representative of contemporary American literature as a whole. As a matter of fact, it represents a very small segment of the profuse literary production of recent years. Yet we feel that the texts share a certain number of features that make them sufficiently remarkable to justify a full-length book study.

First, a number of them contain the Othering factor to a degree that makes them difficult to approach and, in some cases, engenders relative disregard. Nevertheless our prime motivation is not to propose a collection of lesser-known texts worth rediscovering, but, on the contrary, to show how the Othering factor is a vector of creativity in the American cultural system.

Second, our choice of combining short fiction and poetry will probably be found surprising by some. Nevertheless, we felt that this was the only way to study the Othering factor in all its various facets. Not only does it allow us to study similar structural effects in dense and loose forms, but also to discover the continuity between prose and poetry. Narrative patterns sometimes elucidate the enigmatic condensation of poems, and short stories gain by being compared to poetic expression. In fact in many instances the division between the two types of texts appears artificial.

The last noteworthy feature of our selection is our deliberate intention to ignore traditional groupings according to race, gender, ethnicity, and other social categories to show how, at least at a certain level, the productions of very different American authors can be fruitfully considered together. This is not the result of a naïve ecumenical intention but a direct consequence of our epistemological choices. Since the Othering factor occurs at the interface between reproduction and innovation, we want to show how the interchange, the permutation and the amalgamation of cultural signs precede and determine social or political ascriptions. We promote a vision of cultural activity as a relation of exchange and cross-fertilization rather than confrontation or exclusion. This does not imply denying the force of socio-political determinations but showing how they should not be aligned with a space of multilateral exchange in which signs are freely negotiated. Our ultimate aim is to assert the generative power of the Othering factor in the treatment of differences, in flagrant opposition to the blanking or compartmentalizing concepts that are sometimes offered in connection with them. Far from postulating a reduction, harmonization or neutralization of differences, the Othering factor forcefully illustrates their necessary proliferation, and their productivity in American culture.

Our aim in this book is not so much to criticize traditional approaches as to show that the Othering process in American literature opens new areas of investigation and demands new attitudes to texts. The texts that we have chosen cannot be said to be fully representative of contemporary

American literature, but they are indicative of an expressive trend that has become accentuated during these last decades. Recurrent in them is the "Othering excursion" or the desire to express in the words of the system what the system occults. In this new form of rhetoric readers are not called on to decode conventional constructions with predictable meanings, but to risk following the traces of excursions beyond familiar ground. This is the task that we have assigned to this book.

After outlining the theoretical bases of our approach in Part I, we will turn our attention to the range of rhetorical techniques that characterize the Othering excursion. In Part II, "The Rhetoric of Discordance," we examine the interplay between convention and disruption in Othering texts. The rhetoric of Othering that we identify in this section does not involve inventing a new language; instead writers employ recognizable grammatical features or rhetorical figures and distort or exaggerate them to make words and patterns work otherwise, to allow them to escape habitual formulae or modes of thought. Chapter Two deals with the way texts introduce uncertainty into the connection between referents and indexicals, thereby preventing us from reading in terms of pre-established conceptions and reconfiguring the subjectivity that the system holds to be single and unique. Words too are released from their attachment to subjects, so that discourse can have multiple centers and points of view. In Chapter Three, we examine texts that make plain their disruption or dispersion rather than striving for an impression of homogeneity. By deviating from rhetorical conventions simulating coherence, these texts open up the Othering process, creating new possibilities in which apparently incompatible discourses resonate against one another. Just as fragmentation permits the incursion of Othering, dilation has a similar effect. In Chapter Four, we show how repetition, amplification, and digression can serve to destabilize the text, forcing it to accommodate what seems not to belong. The rhetoric of excess overshoots the subject, seeming to miss the mark in the conventional sense, but aiming at something else outside the conventional. Divagations toward what seems to be peripheral or inessential lead us toward what remains unknown or unknowable.

Whereas Part II studies the disruptive forces working against convention, the main emphasis of Part III, "The Rhetoric of Integration," is on the problem of containing those forces within recognizable forms. Writers must choose between the temptation to impose closure along with the disorder that this entails and the lures of openness along with the risk of disintegration. Chapter Five, "Failed Attempts at Wholeness," examines a number of texts that center on the quest for totality or perfection only to illustrate that this very pursuit creates its opposite. The search for forms of wholeness raises the problem of how to deal with disruptive elements. Attempts to isolate absolutes and to shape icons of oneness, purity or permanence from the cultural magma produce instead contamination, ambivalence, or alienation. In Chapter Six, "Hybridizing Texs," bring heterogeneous elements into contact not to blend them into a new form of wholeness, but to leave them distinct and still recognizable. Movement energizes these distinct entities to produce new relationships, transforming static juxtapositions into dynamic relations characterized by irregularity, disruption, violence, and change. The final chapter in Part III, Chapter Seven, "Experimental Forms," deals with texts in which the Othering principle seems to have been given free rein. Yet the problem of form remains crucial. Since all these texts are ostensibly in flagrant defiance of traditional templates, they have to open new ground. Three strategies are examined: some texts evince deviant forms by reversing conventional patterns; others try to evolve original forms based on the disruption of traditional linear formats; still others seem to abandon conventional references completely, proposing alternative forms. These texts place the conventional categories of textuality in disarray, accumulating gaps, illogicalities and distortions, juggling a multiplicity of perspectives, alternating moments of clarity and confusion.

Finally, Part IV of our study, "Othering Nodes," shows how, beside delivering an identifiable meaning, Othering texts initiate a performative process through which readers are invited to generate meanings by occupying certain specific Othering "nodes"—imaginary stances on the confines of the system from whence they can assess the conflicting claims of what is within and what is beyond the system. In Chapter Eight, the archetypal images of a "hole" or "wall" or "edge" represent sites of liminality in which the subject-object relationship is completely redefined. The world is no longer available to the eye to be scanned and named, while the mind's categories no longer apply. Far from isolating subjects, these "Sites of Exposure" place them at an unstable place where the constraints of society are loosened up and new configurations can be envisaged.   Chapter Nine, "Objects of Disorientation," looks at how common objects can be positioned in such a way that they provoke intense disturbance in and among the people around them. They project farther outside the system than the sites of exposure. They become centers of disturbance that induce the Othering process. These tremors not only affect the situations in which the characters are placed but, more deeply, they destabilize the very norms through which they can be interpreted. Chapter Ten, "Mediators of Escape," looks at texts in which characters introduce disturbance into the text. The form of Othering induced by "mediators" in DeLillo's *The Body Artist* and in the other texts that we analyze in this chapter is doubly demarcated from the cultural system. It cannot be understood in terms of the system's norms, yet unlike the Othering processes considered up to this point, it cannot be placed in contradistinction to them. Mediators occupy the equivocal position of being at the same time focal points and blank spots in the narration. They stand as phantom images of the questing subject looking beyond his or her steadfast certitudes. They suggest, even through their very improbability, the possibility of another form of knowing.

As we insist in our conclusion to this study, our book does not aim to create a new form of dualism, discarding convention in favor of the Othering function, abandoning harmony and closure for disruption and openness. Instead by affirming the complementarity of the systemic and non-systemic, we hope to contribute to a fuller appreciation of the complexity and the harmonious imbrication of literary productions in contemporary American culture.

Notes

---

[1] This punning phrase suggests both: "The word which expresses the most is the word 'inexpressible'," and: "The most expressive word is the word that cannot be expressed."

[2] Wendy Harding and Jacky Martin, *A World of Difference: An Inter-cultural Study of Toni Morrison's Novels* (Westport, Connecticut: Greenwood, 1994).

[3] The phrase is from Toni Morrison's *Beloved* (New York: Alfred Knopf, 1987) 199, and is taken up in the title of her ground-breaking essay: "Unspeakable Things Unspoken: The Afro-American Presence in American Literature," *Michigan Quarterly Review*, 28 (Winter 1989) 1-34.

[4] Mark Strand, *The Weather of Words, Poetic Invention* (New York: Knopf, 2000) 74.

[5] Jorie Graham, "The Glorious Thing: Jorie Graham and Mark Wunderlich in Conversation," *American Poet*, 1996, available online at the Academy of American Poets Website (http://www.poets.org).

[6] See Édouard Glissant, *Caribbean Discourse: Selected Essays*, trans. J. Michael Dash (Charlottesville: University Press of Virginia, 1989); Jean Bernabé, Patrick Chamoiseau and Raphaël Confiant, *Éloge de la Créolité* (Paris: Gallimard, 1989); Gloria Anzaldúa, *Borderlands / La Frontera: The New Mestiza* (San Francisco: Aunt Lute Books, 1987); Homi Bhaba, *The Location of Culture* (London: Routledge, 1994); François Laplantine and Alexis Nouss, *Métissages de Arcimboldo à Zombi* (Paris: Pauvert, 2001).

PART I:

THEORETICAL BACKGROUND

CHAPTER ONE

READING BEYOND THE CULTURAL SYSTEM

> The task of aesthetics is not to comprehend artworks as hermeneutical
> objects; in the contemporary situation, it is their incomprehensibility that
> needs to be comprehended.
> —Theodor Adorno, *Aesthetic Theory*, 157.

Reading allows no objective vantage point, only varying degrees and modes of engagement. In interpretation the text cannot be distinguished from the reading, just as readers cannot be distinguished from their appropriation of texts. It is difficult to accept Jonathan Culler's perception of "a gap or division within reading,"[1] or of a chain of "dualisms: an interpreter and something to interpret, a subject and an object, an actor and something he acts upon or that acts upon him."[2] Instead, we find an interactive structure in which readers' expectations and texts' potentialities merge. The critical concepts that readers use offer no epistemological neutrality; they are an integral part of the relation they establish with texts. As Paul de Man has justly observed:

> Prior to any generalization about literature, literary texts have to be read,
> and the possibility of reading can never be taken for granted. It is an act of
> understanding that can never be observed, nor in any way prescribed or
> verified. A literary text is not a phenomenal event that can be granted any
> form of positive existence, whether as a fact of nature or as an act of the
> mind. It leads to no transcendental perception, intuition, or knowledge, but
> merely solicits an understanding that has to remain immanent because it
> poses the problem of it intelligibility in its own terms.[3]

The literary text is indissociable from the act of reading. According to the reader's particular field of enquiry—let us for example imagine a female or a minority reader "resisting" canonical Western texts[4]—the text will not be envisaged in its totality, whatever that word may mean in relation to texts, but reorganized—in effect recreated as "read" text—in accordance with the reader's specific interests. Conversely, texts' specific definitions—their spatial layout (as in cummings's poems), their rhetorical complexity (as in a Shakespearean sonnet) or their historical context—

become remarkable for a special category of readers or approaches. Instead of dealing with a secondary, adventitious or "supplemental" (in the Derridean sense of that word) activity, we consider critical interpretation as a co-construction whose terms cannot be observed in isolation.

The product of this co-construction is usually a "reading" whose function is to reduce the distance between text and cultural context. As a consequence, the strangeness created by the physical existence of texts is diminished but at the same time reasserted. To understand how this paradoxical result is achieved we can compare the reading process to translation. If the text translates completely into the codes of a different language, the chances are that its content is so general that it hardly requires translation. Similarly, if a text perfectly matches a critical stance, it is a mere exemplification of its postulates and loses all traces of singularity. Conversely, in translation just as in interpretation, what the act of reformulation cannot process exactly demarcates the text's specific contribution, the indeterminate "what" in Jacques Derrida's quibbling formulation, "what remains *untranslatable* is at bottom the only thing to *translate*, the only thing *translatable*. What must be translated of that which is translatable can only be the untranslatable."[5] It follows that, by encompassing their object, critical approaches inevitably fall short of its singularity, or to put it differently, critical readings generate an irreducible remainder.

Our claim is that the act of interpretation engenders an irreducible remainder that is the text's specific difference or its literariness. Paradoxically, the literariness thus engendered remains inaccessible to ordinary critical approaches. The main difference between pragmatic and literary texts consists in the way in which this interpretative remainder is considered. In pragmatic texts it is usually discarded as a residue, an informational "noise" that has to be reduced to a minimum, whereas in literary texts it is often deliberately created in order to suggest another dimension of meaning which we call the "Othering" experience. In that specific configuration, the text is doubly distanced: first, as we have shown, as the result of the process of reading, and second, when this distance, instead of being viewed as a liability, is requalified as an artistic choice. This is the process that we intend to illustrate now in a reading of Robert Hass's prose poem, "A Story About the Body"[6]:

> The young composer, working that summer at an artist's colony, had watched her for a week. She was Japanese, a painter, almost sixty, and he thought he was in love with her. He loved her work, and her work was like the way she moved her body, used her hands, looked at him directly when she made amused and considered answers to his questions. One night,

walking back from a concert, they came to her door and she turned to him
and said, 'I think you would like to have me. I would like that too, but I
must tell you that I have had a double mastectomy,' and when he didn't
understand, 'I've lost both my breasts.' The radiance that he had carried
around in his belly and chest cavity—like music—withered very quickly,
and he made himself look at her when he said, 'I'm sorry. I don't think I
could.' He walked back to his own cabin through the pines, and in the
morning he found a small blue bowl on the porch outside his door. It
looked to be full of rose petals, but he found when he picked it up that the
rose petals were on top; the rest of the bowl—she must have swept them
from the corners of her studio—was full of dead bees.

The poem's setting is a recognizable American institution—the artist's
colony. The narrative pattern is simple. After a first casual meeting
between a composer and a painter, a more intimate relationship begins to
develop. Potential sources of tension threaten to produce complications in
this conventional plot. Besides the opposition between man and woman,
there are also a number of other obstacles to be negotiated: he is a
composer and she, a painter; he is implicitly American, while she is
Japanese; finally, there is the misfit between their ages—he is described as
"young" and she is "almost sixty." Between these polarities, fields of
attraction can be imagined on the young man's side: the stimulation of
another creator working in a different field, the allure of oriental grace
with the additional seduction of experience and maturity. We note that all
these factors of attraction could potentially be reversed and become factors
of repulsion. The text's cultural values are clearly visible and readers
might expect its narrative development to bring the tensions induced by
the situation to a conclusion. This is what narration is about. The bias
induced by the focalization through the young man's point of view ("had
watched her for a week," "he thought he was in love with her," "the
radiance that he had carried around in his belly and chest cavity") leads us
to expect a resolution in the form of either seduction or disillusionment.
Indeed, the latter occurs—the young man's idealized desire does not
outlast the revelation of the woman's mutilation.

The narrative could stop at this point; yet, a gradual shifting of
perspectives complicates it. Initially, the Japanese artist is described from
the outside, from the male perspective, as a "body" in motion (the poem's
title is "A Story About the Body"). However, once the narrator reports her
speech, this inflects the narrative in an unexpected direction. Another
register of language enters the text when the woman pronounces a phrase
that the young man doesn't understand, though interestingly she speaks his
language. She needs to translate "double mastectomy" for him as, "I've
lost both my breasts." Finally, the story concludes with the ambiguous

gift of the "small blue bowl" that that she leaves on the young man's doorstep.

The description of the blue bowl that "looked to be full of rose petals" but which in fact hides "dead bees" stands as an unexpected coda. Rather than bringing the story to a satisfying resolution, it contributes to defuse and confuse the narrative situation. The discovery of the gift is carefully staged: first the composer finds the blue bowl sitting on the porch, then he sees the rose petals, then he discovers that "the rose petals were on top" and that "the rest of the bowl … was full of dead bees." The progression of the narration appears to replicate the stages in the young man's discovery, but it also follows a conventional narrative pattern of delay, withholding revelation in order to create suspense. What is unconventional, however, is that the denouement appears to increase rather than end the reader's perplexity. In shifting its focus from the young man to the woman and finally to "it," the text follows a schema that is different from, even opposite to, the usual narrative order. Far from answering the reader's questions, the open-ended conclusion produces uncertainty. The ending even draws our attention away from the couple's situation. The final sentence begins by placing "it" in the subject position, focusing our attention on something else, something that our critical discourse could class as a symbol. However, that would be another form of dismissal, when in fact, as we will see, involvement is needed.

Indeed, only by simplifying the potentialities of the blue bowl can we produce a well-defined interpretation. Does it represent a derisive love present, an ironic pot pourri, or an oriental talisman? None of these readily available readings satisfy, and the word "represent" may not even apply. Indeed, rather than the vehicle, the sign of something else, the bowl is something "left on the porch outside his door", that is, left unattended, apparently abandoned rather than addressed to anyone in particular. The narration moves from binaries (man/woman, young/old, West/East) to a form of hybridity, in that the blue bowl with its rose petals and dead bees seems to bring together masculinity and femininity, life and death. The text even seems to graft onto narrative something resembling haiku. Yet saying this does not settle the questions raised by the text. The ending resists decoding and in fact destabilizes our familiar system of representation constructed on binary differences. It is impossible to attribute values with certainty. Is the bowl a representation of the woman who offers it, a masochistic self-portrait of an attractive surface concealing secret mutilation? Or is it a representation of the young man whose apparent tenderness hides a meanness of spirit? Or does it project an image of their failed sexual encounter? Do the rose petals represent the woman's vulnerability, her mutilated femininity, or her disillusioned love? Do the dead bees stand for the exhausted and discredited potency of masculinity, the death of the woman's desire, or the transformation of either or both of the lovers into what is refused (the sweepings from the studio floor)? Are they a token of mortality? Or do they point to the failure of communication and the exhaustion of language—the dead *B*'s recalling the spurned *b*ody, the amputated *b*reasts? All of these seem to apply, but none exactly fit because they exclude one another.

The text's polyvalence produces a kind of semantic fission—the generation of endlessly multiplying and contradictory interpretations—that seems to defeat the very purpose of interpretation. Answering the questions generated by the text finally seems beside the point. The symbolism of the end is offered not as a solution but as a pathway leading to a different type of perception. In its representation of the painter's ambiguous offering, Robert Hass's prose poem reconfigures difference as Othering.

In "A Story About the Body" Hass employs the "Othering" perspective in order to gesture toward what might lie outside the system, that is, the predefined conceptions that make our world safe and predictable. His prose poem breaks away from familiar conceptual moorings while only vaguely indicating new ones. It confronts us with the multiplicity and the commutability of meanings rather than inviting us to extract a "reading" from the story. In this perspective differences are not organized into systems or binaries (as in conventional discursive formations) but they are given an organic relationship incorporating recognizable components but also jeopardizing the system and even invalidating the notion of system. The Othering orientation simultaneously defuses all expected interpretations based on conventional codes and promotes a new receptivity to a polysemous interpretation. Rather than coming to a conclusion, the story invites us to relinquish the quest for exhaustive comprehension. The renunciation of knowledge sanctions the indeterminacy in the reader's interpretation. Indeterminacy does not mean indecision or confusion, quite the contrary. It means accepting the share of non-definition that persists after the story's ending, accepting that it is part of its global signification, and above all that it should remain unprocessed. Meaning in the Othering perspective is not something one acquires, that can be defined and garnered to become part of the "known", the "identifiable" or the "predictable" but something that resists acquisition. The rose petals and bees offered in a blue bowl represent a perception of complexity rather than a thing known. The text is no longer simply a container for meaning but a pathway to a new form of consciousness. It aims at promoting "knowing" rather than just knowledge. This "knowing" should not be thought of as intuition or as mystical or esoteric understanding. The Othering perspective is complementary to the systematic or ideological perspectives in that it exposes their limits. Hence Western societies tend to depreciate it, even though they cannot eliminate it.

Conventional strategies of interpretation are designed to unriddle, elucidate, and finally eliminate the Othering process. They are based on deeply ingrained assumptions that are never clarified and hence never called into question. Most limiting among these assumptions is the apparently self-evident notion, derived from linguistics, that the text in association with its referent comprises all the signifying material that needs to be elucidated. Our claim strongly challenges that presupposition by positing that certain texts, particularly of a literary nature, appear to be unreadable according to that linguistic model. They ostensibly contain areas of indeterminacy—such as the bowl of rose petals and dead bees— that cannot be explicated according to cultural codes. These irregularities are specifically constructed in order to suggest another dimension of meaning that cultural codes, and even language, are unfit to express. Instead of considering the text as the only source of meaningfulness, we hypothesize that texts which evince the Othering process are divided between what can be assigned to pre-constructed codes—such as the narrative part of "A Story About the Body"—and what cannot be explicated—the poem's coda. Our conception of texts juxtaposes two orders of signification that both disqualify and strangely complement each other: on one hand, the traditional order is left open-ended, and on the other, the Othering mode remains enigmatic. In both cases, the possibility of expressing meaning in discourse is put into question.

In order to account for that apparent disorder in signification, we have to reconsider the seamless translation of "discourse as event" into "discourse as meaning" such as Ricoeur describes it:

> ...I propose to say that, if all discourse is realized as an event, all discourse is understood as meaning. What we wish to understand is not the fleeting event, but rather the meaning which endures.... Just as language, by being actualized as discourse, surpasses itself as system and becomes event, so too discourse, by entering the process of understanding, surpasses itself as event and becomes meaning.... If language is a *meinen*, a meaningful intention, it is precisely in virtue of the surpassing of the event by the meaning. The very first distanciation is thus the distanciation of the saying in the said.[7]

As opposed to Ricoeur, frequently in our reading of contemporary American literature, we do not see any "surpassing" of the text as discursive event in the production of meaning, or even a summation of the situation of enunciation in its linguistic expression. On the contrary, our whole approach considers the linguistic statement as a reduction of the situation's potentialities. From discourse as event to text, we posit an inevitable depletion of the original meaning potential contained in the enunciative situation. The difference is crucial insofar as the hermeneutical process of clarification established by Ricoeur becomes in our perspective a progression toward opacity. In Ricoeur's view the transition from event to meaning production permits a smooth elucidation of sense, whereas we believe that literary texts cannot be fully explicated. Consequently, it would seem that only pragmatic texts strictly adjusted to reference corroborate Ricoeur's proposition; imaginative texts, detached from immediate application, have to strike a balance between what can be formulated and what cannot be expressed within the linguistic and cultural codes.

In most literary texts the inexpressible part in the original situation is either reduced or carefully controlled. In fact, it could be said that a text's artistry depends in part on its capacity to make sense of that remainder. In the particular case of what we have chosen to call the Othering texts, the events to which the text is, or pretends to be, referring so far outreach the possibilities of discourse that the text's communication appears obstructed and its meaning seriously compromised. Yet it is precisely on that expressive disorder that writers stake their artistic statements. What is considered as an almost disposable remainder in other texts becomes in the Othering texts the all-important ground on which to inscribe another form of signification. In that paradoxical situation, discourse is obviously doubly invalidated: first, as a means of expression relying on pre-existing codes, and second, as an attempt to express the inexpressible through traditional means. It could also just as justifiably be considered as being enriched since in Othering the writer pits convention against disruptive strategies in order to make the cultural system outreach its limitations.

But what exactly can be expected beyond the limits of the cultural system? Is the notion of limits conceivable in a cultural system that is coextensive with our perception of the world? Is such a thing as the "inexpressible" conceivable once it is agreed that everything that can be couched in language is *ipso facto* expressible and what isn't simply does not exist? What kind of reference can be envisaged for what is denied expression within the system? Conscious of the limitations of cultural norms, a number of critics and literary theorists have tried to envisage what could be posited beyond the limits of the system. It is clear that these recent enquiries, like ours, were motivated by the general trend in contemporary American fiction and poetry to challenge the constraints of cultural codes, to reject closure and to discredit the expressive possibilities of language.[8]

In order to fill the gap between these dissident texts and their readership, three classes of propositions have been suggested. The cultural system is perceived by writers like French poet and essayist Yves Bonnefoy as a conceptual grid that favors empirical accessibility but obscures an original pristine state of reality—an "être-là d'avant la parole,"[9] in which things would not be differentiated and devitalized as concepts. Other analysts such as George Steiner see the inexpressible part of the artwork as the imprint of transcendence: "This essay argues a wager on transcendence. It argues that there is in the art-act and its reception, that there is in the experience of meaningful form, a presumption of presence."[10] Recently, writers like Gumbrecht have revived the notion of presence in the form of an immanent and very substantive transcendence: "Therefore, 'production of presence' points to all kinds of events and processes in which the impact that 'present' objects have on human bodies is being initiated and intensified."[11] Other critics have introduced the notion of alterity and its variants such as otherness or exteriority[12] that for the sake of simplification we intend to envisage together. Whatever the designation, the obvious references are Hans-Georg Gadamer's hermeneutical theory or the philosophy of Emmanuel Lévinas, whose systems are clearly founded on a duality between the circumscribed world of the Self and the appeal of the Other. The important notion that critics like Derek Attridge derive from their works is the perception that something unknown and unknowable might happen outside the sphere in which the Ego is confined, a space of infinite "exteriority" (the subtitle of Lévinas's *Totality and Infinity*[13]), which coexists and intersects with the ego's conception of totality. Although the philosophical possibility of such a dualism was clearly denounced in Derrida's famous "Violence et Métaphysique,"[14] Attridge conceives of "verbal creation" as "a handling of language whereby something we might call 'otherness,' or 'alterity,' or 'the other,' is made, or allowed, to impact upon the existing configurations of an individual's mental world."[15]

All these conceptions together with associated psychological processes such as epiphanies, visions or encounters in which otherness or presence are manifested are, from the strict point of view of literary analysis, either blurry concepts or screening notions that fail to illuminate the phenomena that we have associated with Othering.[16] Since we can only posit one commonly shared cultural system in which all our conceptions must be expressed, and, as Wittgenstein declared, "What we cannot speak about we must pass over in silence,"[17] we should refrain from conceptualizing alterity, presence or "Beingness" *as if* they could refer to something tangible outside the system. Any attempt at defining something beyond representation, and, what frequently amounts to the same thing, the very failure to do so,[18] automatically refers back to something known within the system, placed in relation with other notions that will identify its meaning. Thus "other" derives its meaning from "self," "otherness" from "sameness," "presence" from "absence" or "being" from "nothingness." There is quite literally *no* outside the system. It follows that although we can neither imagine nor even conceive of anything outside the system, we can nevertheless *aspire* to disenfranchise ourselves from its limits or imagine what the world would be like without the system. This is what the Othering literary text is about. As far as we are concerned, the reference to an exterior entity does not seem to be very productive in order to account for the perplexing irregularities that abound in contemporary American literature. It merely displaces the problem of interpretation from inside the culture where it should remain onto an improbable entity that not only deprives critics of their usual tools but also confronts them with an opaque concept.

If it is vain to associate literary texts with exteriority, we find infinitely more productive the aspiration to emancipate oneself from the system. Othering paradoxically corresponds to an excursion outside the system related within the limits of the system. Yves Bonnefoy, examining the function of poetry in the contemporary world, defines its specific communication poetically as a "negative theology" which exposes our aspiration to signify the "informe":

> L'aventure du sens pourra enfin commencer. *L'hypothèse du sens*, plutôt, notre furieux besoin, dans l'espace du poème, d'organiser notre connaissance, de formuler le mythe de ce qui est, d'échafauder le concept, pourra subir la diffraction de l'informe. Et cette poésie qui ne peut saisir la présence dessaisie de tout autre bien sera du grand acte clos la proximité angoissée, la *théologie négative*.[19]

In the "diffraction of the formless," we find the three basic elements that we associate with the Othering relation: the aspiration to signify, its distortion through its encounter with the "formless," and the text's resulting diffraction, which causes its orientation toward unity to be deflected and broken into a pattern of fragments. The meaning produced in the Othering process is at the same time interrupted and expanded, dislocated and enhanced.

This contradiction accounts for the strangeness and the deviance of the texts that we have chosen. The temptation is to dismiss them as merely anomalous, marginal or unimportant. Yet, for us, it is precisely these inexplicable passages, like the bowl of rose petals and dead bees in "A Story About the Body," that appear to concentrate the most energy and the most significance. Derek Attridge proposes an explanation that could be at the root of the Othering phenomenon; the irregularity of texts, which, in his view, results from the emergence of otherness, result from the repression of underlying conflicts:

> At any given moment, this complexity is a divided and contradictory one, its semblance of coherence sustained by the repression or exclusion of some elements or possibilities, subject to constant challenge from outside as well as to ongoing tensions within. . . . It is this instability and inconsistency, these internal and external pressures and blind spots, this self-dividedness, that constitute the conditions for the emergence of the other . . . (25).[20]

Indeed, both social criticism and psychoanalysis, to which Attridge is implicitly referring, have taught us to consider blocks, lapses or irregularities in the continuity of discourse as "symptoms" of underlying strategies of dissimulation, masking on the social plane the exercise of power, and on the psychological plane, the aftershock of childhood trauma, and often combinations of both. Yet, it is useful to make a distinction between these "symptoms" that signal the return of the socially or psychologically repressed and what we call, after Lévinas,[21] Othering "traces." Even though traces are bound to be culturally and psychologically inflected, their function should not be described as exteriorly motivated. They are neither dissimulative nor assignable to any decoding system. They are, on the contrary, exploratory, expressing (not deflecting) a desire to suggest new forms of meaning in denial of all pre-constructed norms and systems. They are experienced as "blocks" in interpretation, but they are at the same time "pathways" insofar as they indicate new dimensions of meaning.

What is the nature of the other meanings opened by the Othering process? What does it mean to signify beyond the "frontiers of consciousness" as T.S. Eliot would have it: "If, as we are aware, only a part of the meaning can be conveyed by paraphrase, that is because the poet is occupied with frontiers of consciousness beyond which words fail, though meanings still exist."[22] What are these plural meanings beyond the limits of common paraphrasable signification? Are we inevitably, from the moment we try to define them, brought back to the contradictions that we indicated earlier? If we exclude all references to an external reality, all relations outside the cultural system, there is still the possibility of using the system against itself—against its fundamental orientation to define and organize. In the Othering perspective, writers play the cultural system against itself. They turn the system on its head and examine the consequences. This does not mean that they place themselves outside the common system of reference. They try to submit the system to demands that it cannot meet. As a consequence, as we have observed, the system breaks down, but this collapse is not disastrous. It is the origin of Bonnefoy's "diffraction," of Eliot's plural "meanings," of diffracted images or optical illusions that the system engenders but cannot accommodate.

Although the socio-cultural causes that motivate the presence of the Othering factor in contemporary American literature lie beyond the scope of the present study, it is important to examine its genesis in discourse. The Othering process, as we understand it, is a consequence of the division established by Lévinas between the "saying," which designates the global experience that the text is testifying to, and the "said" corresponding to its textual expression in discourse. The linguistic component of discourse ceases to be the only definition of meaning and it incorporates the trace of an experience that predates (but can also follow or coincide with) its inscription in text. Since, as we remarked earlier, the context of discourse by far surpasses the possibilities of the linguistic system, the trace coincides with what we designated earlier as a remainder. The only difference is that this remainder does not reflect a failure in expression; it is the vestigial mark of an attempt to convey the inexpressible. The Othering text typically combines, on one hand, what we could call the substratum, i.e. what the text is about, its referential content, and, on the other hand, cryptic traces, indecipherable in themselves yet pointing to a signification lost but recoverable. The linguistic system is placed in a situation of total disarray; its specific resources are denied, while the emphasis is placed on opacity. Yet this situation should not be considered as a failure, it is, on the contrary, the sign of reinforced signification. This new experience is the amalgam between what is sayable and what is not, between known and unknowable. These two aspects of the Othering text cannot be separated because they support each other. The obscurity, the indeterminacy, the resistance to reading created in the Othering text is an appeal to readers to change their linguistic habits and to reconsider their expectations, to prepare themselves for another type of persuasion.

In order to provoke that conversion the writer must put in place a very special rhetorical strategy. It is at this point that we dissociate ourselves from the Lévinasian concept of "trace" as the imprinting of signification over simple tautology as a result of the command of the Other. In our conception of the relation between the referential substratum and the cryptic trace, they form a new signifying combination that the writer addresses to readers—an address which is not an exchange of meaning but an invitation to reconstruct. The writer (and the reader after him) has to build on the ruins of the system. The Othering trace is not the imprint of the other's presence as in Lévinas; it is a rhetorical construction devised by the writer in order to produce sense out of the fragments and in the interstices left behind by the failure of the system. But in order to appreciate the scope of that construction we have to revise our conception of the function of rhetoric while keeping in mind Adorno's reflection that "technique is the definable figure of the enigma in artworks, at once rational and conceptless."[23] Traditionally, the art of rhetoric is based on tropes, which, by deviating from standard expression, are supposed to enhance meaning. In Othering rhetoric, the figures created by the writer do not so much deviate from the system's linguistic norms as jeopardize the principles that underpin the system. They oppose figures of disruption to the figures of ornamentation of traditional rhetoric. They do not promote an embellishment of signification but rather its opening to other modes of comprehension. Instead of offering exercises in stylistic virtuosity, they stake everything on meaningful failures that depend upon the reader for their interpretation. The main body of our study will evince the two correlated aspects of that peculiar rhetoric of disruption: Part II entitled "The Rhetoric of Discordance" will explore some of the effects that can be created by the disruption of the text's fundamental elements of stability, and Part III, dealing with "The Rhetoric of Integration" will try to discover what alternative forms have been imagined to accommodate a text potentially reduced to the sum of its fragments.

Othering rhetoric is endowed with a performative force. Before it can be envisaged as a "process" (Adorno) or as an "experience" (Lacoue Labarthe)[24] involving the reader, the Othering text organizes a pattern of possible escape routes that are supposed to guide us after the dismantling of the cultural system. These itineraries are never clearly marked, nor are they exclusive of one another. The Othering text disappoints readers' anticipation of formal patterns and of meaning definition. Readers' expectations are doubly baffled insofar as the text fails to deliver a meaning along the traditional lines while it presents us with insoluble conundrums that appear to stand in lieu of conventional literary themes. It forces us to abandon our conception of texts as closed systems and to envisage the possibility that texts could be sounding boards for creative processes of interpretation. Besides, since the text is no longer geared to a main focus of interest converging on a central vision but crisscrossed by a network of scattered markers, a multiplicity of reading itineraries is conceivable.

Most importantly, the Othering text demands that we should no longer consider the text as an act of exchange between creator and reader but as an invitation to share and recreate an experience for which the written medium is only a protocol open to improvisation. We fully share Derek Attridge's view according to which the reading response "is not a matter of an act calling forth a wholly secondary and subsidiary reaction, then, but of a *reenactment* that, paradoxically, makes the 'original' act happen, and happen differently with each such response."[25] Further along in his study, Attridge refers to reading as "a *staging* of meaning and feeling: a staging that is realized in . . . a performative reading."[26] The Othering text is like a jumbled score or a garbled performance text that needs not so much to be corrected—the missing parts are lost and irretrievable—but reinvested and recreated in the reader's experience. And as Strand points out, speaking of poetry, the process can never be completed: "Perhaps the poem is ultimately a metaphor for something unknown, its working-out a means of recovery. It may be that the retention of the absent origin is what is necessary for the continued life of the poem as *inexhaustible artifact*."[27]

Finally, it appears that the aim of reading in its Othering (dis)orientation is simultaneously to defuse all expected interpretations based on convention and to promote a new receptivity to polysemous interpretation. The final outcome is an intellectual exercise in suspension of interpretation rather than an evaluation. This suspension of comprehension induces a further attitude in the reader that tends to promote a sense of indetermination, yet not indeterminacy. It means accepting the share of non-definition that persists after, for example, the ending of "A Story About the Body," accepting that this indetermination is part of the global signification. Meaning in the Othering perspective is not something one acquires, but something that resists acquisition. It coincides with the realization that beyond the situation and the characters in Hass's story, there is something in the human condition that resembles rose petals and bees in a blue bowl, that can be perceived through these objects—a composite perception rather than a thing known. The critic should try and emulate what Edgar Morin describes as "complex vision":

Or, dans la vision complexe, quand on arrive par des voies empirico-
rationnelles à des contradictions, cela signifie non pas une erreur mais
l'atteinte d'une nappe profonde de la réalité qui, parce qu'elle est profonde,
ne peut pas être traduite dans notre logique."[28]

More than a transgression beyond the system, Othering is an existential
experience that requires participation, involvement, and empathy rather
than understanding; it demands awareness rather than knowledge. It is
fundamentally an in-between experience uncomfortably placed on the
margins of the known world. Mark Strand expresses the same view but
places it before or beyond the advent of language:

It may be that something beyond 'meaning' is being communicated,
something that originated not with the poet but in the first dim light of
language, in some period of 'beforeness.' It may be, therefore, that reading
poetry is often a search for the unknown, something that lies at the heart of
experience but cannot be pointed out or described without being altered or
diminished—something that can be contained so that it is not so
terrifying.[29]

Taken as a whole this book is an introduction to Othering in the act of
reading. It asks critics to adopt a new attitude in relation to the complexity
of texts. Instead of being interpreters trying to unravel a text's intricacies
in order to produce an intelligible rendering of it, they should be prepared
to expose themselves to the text's polyvalence. The Othering approach is
neither a rhetoric of elucidation nor of indeterminacy, it is an exercise in
receptivity to the text's suggestions. If, once again, we may be allowed to
detach one of Lévinas's images from its original ethical context, the critic
should be "exposed" to the text, placed in its vicinity: "la proximité que
signifie la vulnérabilité."[30] Ricoeur says approximately the same thing:
"To understand is not to project oneself into the text but to expose oneself
to it."[31] The critic is vulnerable insofar as s/he is no longer at the source of
meaning but under the aegis and also under the sway of the text. Criticism
becomes an exercise in sensitivity to the suggestions of the text. Since it
engages the reader's personal experience it also contains a risk, the risk of
losing oneself through the text. Such a conception of reading as
disorientation does not imply that no meaning can be discovered, it means
that the Othering factor opens the text to areas of complexity concealed by
apparent illogicality. Othering certainly demands a relinquishment of
authority, a willingness to let oneself be absorbed by outside solicitation
that resembles the position of a theatrical audience. However, the critic's

receptivity also requires a particular vigilance. It is more a form of commitment than a dramatic immersion. The Othering critic is not passively receptive like a theatrical audience. Although in total submission to the Othering factor, the critic is actively responsible for preserving the complexity of its significations. This is the paradox of the Othering approach.

We finally need to consider the place of Othering criticism in the cultural context. We feel that once again the critical concept that we are observing is an occasion for reconsidering the underpinnings of the theories regulating the relations between text and context. Although they have been criticized, several times reconsidered, and sometimes profoundly reformed, a few fundamental preconceptions subsist almost ineradicably at the back of contemporary critical discourse: first we almost always find the idea that text and context are valid objects of observation; second that, as the resemblance between those two words suggests, a relation of contiguity exists between the two; third, that this relation is of a deterministic nature; and finally, that the reader/critic is placed at the interface between the two. Of course, we do not deny that artworks are submitted to socio-cultural forces on both the production and reception sides, but what seems more debatable is the idea that they should be the direct reflection of these forces. Our conception of the relations between text and context can be compared to the phenomena observed by psychologists or anthropologists looking at how children or members of non-Western societies define for themselves neutral spaces in which the conditions of their insertion in society can be "represented" to themselves and to the rest of the community. Winnicot, expanding Freud's reflection on the fort/ da logic of his grandson's play in *Beyond the Pleasure Principle*,[32] postulated the existence of "transitional phenomena."[33] Winnicot insisted on the cultural importance of an intermediary area: "an intermediate area of *experiencing*, to which inner reality and external life both contribute."[34] His claim is important for our consideration of the role of Othering. In the experience of playing, just as in reading literature, the subject, because (s)he is placed in an area of neutrality, experiments with rapidly changing combinations between the terms of the subject-object duality and so doing, learns how to balance the demands of both. Slightly later Clifford Geertz's description of Balinese cockfights characterizes them as the counterpart of play in the social field. He showed that, like the function of play in children's integration, and: "like any form of art, the cockfight renders everyday experience comprehensible by presenting it in terms of acts and objects which have had their practical consequences removed and been reduced (or, if you prefer, raised) to the level of sheer appearances, where their meaning can be more powerfully articulated and more exactly perceived."[35] This analysis of the anthropological context could be transferred nearly word for word to the Othering situation that we are trying to define. Because the cockfights are cut off from the routine of daily existence, they project the societal norms and themes in a domain outside the normal hierarchies, on the plane of "sheer appearances," where they can be freely exchanged by the members of the social group. In the same way, we believe that artworks select a number of themes from their contexts and display them in such way that they can be observed in reading. This metasocial activity is a very basic activity because, like the Balinese cockfights, it "makes us visible to ourselves by representing us and everyone else as cast into the midst of a world full of irremovable strangeness we can't keep clear of."[36] We believe similarly that, between the text as monadic linguistic entity and the socio-political context, there is room for an intermediary zone of literary representation in which, through the act of reading, the socio-political reality is diffracted into its components and made accessible for anyone concerned.

In that zone, the traditional categories of criticism are not abrogated but reshuffled: meaning ceases to be an exclusive quest; object and subject readjust to find overlapping zones. This area of "cultural liminality" could be compared to Homi Bhabha's "interstitial space that emerges as a structure of undecidability at the frontiers of cultural hybridity."[37] Yet, we find it restrictive in Bhabha's study to reserve that space for "the minority, the exilic, the marginal, and the emergent"[38] because, although it is to Bhaba's credit to have denounced the myth of subalternity, he is implicitly recreating a new zone of exclusion. Surely reading at cultural interstices derives its definition and specificity from the fact that ascriptions, although cited and exchanged, are deprived of their deterministic potential. The interstitial space is a free zone in which everyone, independently of his or her habitus, can access and manipulate the whole palette of societal signs. What some could consider as naïve idealism is in fact the precondition for all acts of creation and interpretation. How could anyone conceive of anything beyond the strict limits of his or her psychological or social habitus if there did not exist a space in which, as Bhabha justly observes, practices "exist beside each other, *Abseits*, in a form of juxtaposition or contradiction that resists the teleology of dialectical sublation."[39] This space is not a place of stability, nor can it be validly represented as Ziarek's *aphesis*, "a releasing, a letting be or a letting go...."[40] In the Othering space cultural forces are projected, made visible, and exposed; temporarily defused, they consequently become unstable, mobile and reversible. And because they are no longer determined by society, they become accessible and exchangeable among all concerned. Although this space is ephemeral and inevitably infiltrated by external forces, it is vital to both creation and interpretation.

While we feel that readers should remain as long as possible in this in-between space, their major preoccupation has recently been described as that of responsibility: "All creative shapings of language (and any other cultural materials) make demands that can, in this extended sense be called ethical."[41] Hillis Miller pursues: "each reading is, strictly speaking, ethical, in the sense that it has to take place, by an implacable necessity, as the response to a categorical ground, in the sense that the reader must take responsibility for it and for its consequences in the personal, social, and political worlds."[42] Nevertheless, even in the restricted sense that Hillis Miller has of ethics as the necessity to read responsibly a work of art, we find it difficult to share his position. Can one be validly responsible to a text? Can a text determine an ethical response? It seems that the notion of responsibility has been illicitly transported from the interpersonal to the hermeneutic relation. Texts are not presences, they are just fields of possibilities, so that we do not need to confront them, only to find our place in them.

The Othering text calls readers not so much to responsibility as to relinquishment, a position made up in equal parts of disorientation at and awakening to the text's solicitations. The critic's attention should be devoted to both the text's structure and the de-structuring potential that the Othering factor always convokes simultaneously. In Part Four of our study, we will describe the critic's role as espousing and demarcating the text's "stance," always poised in an unstable position between structure and destructure. The critic's position should be one of receptivity and reactivity to the text's field of possibilities. Charles Simic expresses a similar position from the creator's point of view:

> To be 'capable of being in uncertainties' is to be literally in the midst. The poet is in the midst. The poem too, is in the midst, a kind of magnet for complex historical, literary and psychological forces, as well as a way of maintaining oneself in the face of that multiplicity.[43]

"Being in the midst" is certainly part of the task of the Othering critic, but it is only second to his task of "maintaining [him]self in the face of that multiplicity" which is more difficult to achieve because it implies receptivity but also steadfastness.

As Wolfgang Iser has justly recalled, "Each theory...functions as a divining-rod for the historical need that it is called upon to cope with."[44] This is why we feel the Othering principle can be validly applied to the contemporary American cultural context in which conflicting cultural worlds are bound together interdependently without losing their original characteristics. Our initial intuition was that the socio-political binaries that are often convoked in order to describe the American cultural life are insufficient to account for the specific phenomenon of literature. We consequently formed the hypothesis that literary discourse is one of the ways in which systems and subsystems can be evoked without being either lumped together in a general conception of culture or distributed according to socio-political categories. Side by side with the traditional means of decoding reality that contribute to confirming the system, there is another way of appropriating the cultural world which consists in putting it into question. Our conviction is that reconfirming the system goes hand in hand with the Othering perspective that envisages what lies beyond the system. It is one of the basic functions that individuals have at their disposal: they can take sides within the system or think "beyond" it. In so doing they encounter what is outside not as something alien but as an imaginary zone of experience that has to be taken into account. In this view of culture, the notions of margin and center lose their pertinence and need to be replaced by intersecting zones of merging and interaction that the Othering principle explores preeminently.

Notes

[1] Johnathan Culler, *On Deconstruction: Theory and Criticism After Structuralism* (Ithaca: Cornell University Press, 1982) 67.

[2] Culler 75.

[3] Paul de Man, "The Rhetoric of Blindness: Jacques Derrida's Reading of Rousseau," *Blindness and Insight: Essays in the Rhetoric of Contemporary Criticism,* Theory and History of Literature (Minneapolis: University of Minnesota Press, 1983) 107.

[4] For examples of this type of reading see Judith Fetterley, *The Resisting Reader: A Feminist Approach to American Fiction* (Bloomington : Indiana University Press, 1978) and Toni Morrison, *playing in the dark: whiteness and the literary imagination* (Cambridge, Mass. : Harvard University Press, 1992).

[5] Jacques Derrida, "Ulysses Gramophone: Hear Say Yes in Joyce," *Acts of Literature*, ed. Derek Attridge (London: Routledge, 1992) 257-8.

[6] Robert Hass, "A Story About the Body," *Human Wishes* (Ontario, Canada: The Ecco Press, 1989) 32. Subsequent references will be included parenthetically in the text. We will adopt this convention when quoting all other literary texts.

[7] Paul Ricoeur, *Hermeneutics and The Human Sciences*, ed. & trans. by John B. Thompson (London/New York: Cambridge University Press, 1981) 134.

[8] See Lyn Hejinian, *The Language of Inquiry* (Berkeley: University of California Press: 2000).

[9] Yves Bonnefoy, *La Vérité de parole et autres essais* (Paris: Mercure de France, 1992) 51. "A being-there of before speech." [Our translation.]

[10] George Steiner, *Real Presences* (London/Boston: Faber & Faber, 1989) 214.

[11] Hans Ulrich Gumbrecht, *Production of Presence: What Meaning Cannot Convey* (Stanford: Stanford UP, 2004) xiv.

[12] We will not consider the more or less personalized "other" or *alter ego* that is often parasitically embroiled with otherness. As for Derrida's intentionally punning "tout autre" ("wholly/altogether/indefinable other"), we tend to consider it as supporting our conception since, in at least one of its possible readings, it refers to the impossibility of conceiving otherness as paradoxically generating texts. Cf. "Psyche" in *Acts of Literature*, 341-43.

[13] Emmanuel Lévinas, *Totality and Infinity: An Essay on Exteriority*, trans. Alphonso Lingis (Pittsburgh: Duquesne University Press, 1969).

[14] Jacques Derrida, *L'Écriture et la différence* (Paris: Seuil, 1967).

[15] Derek Attridge, *The Singularity of Literature* (London/New York: Routledge, 2004) 19. We discovered Derek Attridge's work through his early articles and hoped that his book would concur with our approach. Its publication revealed some points of intersection but also large of areas of divergence.

[16] We should credit Attridge for his pertinacity in wrestling with the complexities induced by this conceptual dark spot in his subchapter entitled, "The encountered Other." Yet his attempt to dissociate the other as "relation," a proposition that we totally endorse, from the other as substantial entity fails to convince, maybe because of the ambiguity induced by the surreptitious personalization of otherness.

[17] Ludwig Wittgenstein, *Tractatus Logico-Philosophicus*, tr. D.F. Pears and B.F. McGuinness (London: Routledge and Kegan Paul, 1961) 7.

[18] Thus Steiner curiously founds transcendent presence on the existence of indetermination in man's intellectual constructions: "There is no mind-set in respect of consciousness and of 'reality' which does not make at least one leap into the dark (the a priori) of the unprovable." Steiner 214.

[19] Yves Bonnefoy, *L'Improbable et autres essais* (Gallimard, Folios Essais, 1992) 127-8. "The adventure of meaning can begin at last. *The hypothesis of a meaning*, our furious need thereof, in the space of the poem, to organize our knowledge, to formulate the myth of what is, to construct a concept, will be submitted to the diffraction of the formless. And this poetry that cannot seize Presence dispossessed of all other compensation will be placed in the anguished proximity of the great closed act, the *negative theology*." [Our translation.]

[20] Attridge 25.

[21] Our relation to Emmanuel Lévinas's thought, particularly in *Otherwise Than Being: or Beyond Essence*, is tangential, some would say heretical, insofar as our explorations derive from its inspiration but eventually diverge onto different trajectories. Emmanuel Lévinas, *Otherwise Than Being Or Beyond Essence*, trans. Alphonso Lingis (Pittsburgh: Duquesne UP, 1998).

[22] T. S. Eliot, "The Music of Poetry," *On Poetry and Poets* (New York: Farrar, Strauss, Cudahy, 1957) 22-23.

[23] Theodor W. Adorno, *Aesthetic Theory* (New York: Continuum, 1997) 279.

[24] See Theodor Adorno, *Aesthetic Theory*, Chapter Ten "Toward a Theory of the Artwork," 232-260, and Philippe Lacoue Labarthe, *La Poésie comme experience* (Paris: Christian Bourgois, 1986).

[25] Attridge 91.

[26] Attridge 109.

[27] Mark Strand, *The Weather of Words, Poetic Invention* (New York: Knopf, 2000) 74.

[28] Edgar Morin, *Introduction à la pensée complexe* (Paris: ESF, 1980) 92. "Now, in complex vision, when one meets contradictions by empirico-rational means, that does not indicate a mistake but that one has reached a deeper layer of reality which, because it is deep, cannot be translated into our logic." [Our translation.]

[29] Strand 498-49.

[30] Emmannuel Lévinas, *Autrement qu'être et au-delà de l'essence* (Paris: Gallimard, Folio Essais, 2001) 92. "The proximity that vulnerability signifies." [Our translation.]

[31] Ricoeur 94.

[32] Sigmund Freud, *Beyond the Pleasure Principle*, translated and newly edited by James Strachey (New York: Norton, 1961) 14-15.

[33] Donald W. Winnicot, *Playing and Reality* (New York: Basic Books, 1971) 102.

[34] Winnicot, 102.

[35] Clifford Geertz, *Selected Essays* (New York: Basic Books, 1973) 443.

[36] Clifford Geertz, *Available Light – Anthropological Reflections on Philosophical Topics* (Princeton: Princeton University Press, 2000), 84.

[37] Homi K. Bhabha, "DissemiNation: time, narrative, and the margins of the modern nation," *Nation and Narration* (London/New York: Routledge, 1990): 299, 312.

[38] Bhabha 300.

[39] Bhabha 312.

[40] Krzysztof Ziarek, *The Force of Art* (Stanford: Stanford University Press, 2004) 12.

[41] Attridge 130.

[42] Joseph Hillis Miller, *The Ethics of Reading* (New York: Columbia UP, 1987) 59.

[43] Charles Simic, "Negative Capability and its Children," in *Poetics: Essays on the Art of Poetry*, eds. Paul Mariani and Gorge Murphy (Green Harbor, Mass.: Tendril, 1984) 51.

[44] Wolfgang Iser, *How To Do Theory* (Oxford: Blackwell, 2006) 170.

PART II

THE RHETORIC OF DISCORDANCE

CHAPTER TWO

THE ENUNCIATION OF OTHERING

In order to address the first aspect of the rhetoric of Othering, discrepancies in enunciation, we will briefly consider the much debated relationship between textuality and orality, for the two forms of discourse are not completely detached from one another, and Othering texts play with the resulting ambiguity. The conventions of literary interpretation implicitly connect speech and writing. Critics habitually characterize the discourse of poetry and fiction as belonging to "speakers" or "narrators" whose "voices" emerge from the words of the text. Perhaps this convention of associating texts with enunciative situations betrays the imperfect transition from oral to written culture or the nostalgia for a speaking "source"; certainly though, it governs the way texts are both received and written. Readers try to imagine speaking subjects as their eyes follow the black marks on the white page. Apprentice writers are urged to create consistent and credible "voices." One of the ways for writers to point beyond the confines of the system is to refuse to produce the unified and coherent voice that readers expect. To challenge literary decorum in this way is, on the one hand, to expose as a construction what might otherwise be taken as self-evident in the written text, and, on the other hand, to call into question the received ideas about the nature of the speaking subject that lie behind our expectations as readers.

What readers expect of voice in texts is above all that it provide one or more centers of consciousness to give credibility and consistency to the represented world and to stabilize heterogeneity, flux, and difference by creating oppositions between subject and object in a Cartesian paradigm. Either stable and potentially nameable first person speakers or more magisterial third person voices seem to channel and, to a degree, control the inherent polyphony of language.[1] In focusing on the constitution of the subject in discourse, we are thus dealing with one of the mainstays of our cultural system. Individuals assert their own coherence and declare their relation to the world through their consistent use of personal pronouns (I, you, he) and demonstratives (this or that), which work to organize or even repress the confusion of preexisting voices. In writing, where there is no visual referent for these indexicals (so called because of their function of indicating or pointing to the referent),[2] consistency becomes even more essential.

When, in a process of destructive creativity, writers break with the conventions of the discursive system they permit the incursion of the Othering process and indirectly readmit a host of repressed voices. By introducing uncertainty into the connection between indexicals and their referents, the texts we will look at in this chapter shake the cultural system at its foundations. Though the poems and short stories considered here employ similar discursive strategies, we have chosen to consider them individually rather than collectively in order to appreciate the diverse trajectories of their departures from enunciative conventions. With their shifts and inconsistencies in enunciation, these texts prevent us from reading in terms of pre-established conceptions, suggesting instead other ways of conceiving subjectivity, or, in the most extreme cases, calling into question the very concept of subject. In breaking with the conventions that make discourse cohere, writers run the risk of having their work rejected for what appears to be a lack of clarity or comprehensibility. However, when the Othering function succeeds, they elude pre-existing categories and accomplish the vital function of allowing us to perceive something beyond the already constructed. These Othering departures from enunciative conventions reawaken the Bakhtinian perception that we enter into an ongoing dialogue rather than initiating discourse, and they disrupt the Cartesian division between the self and what is external to it.

Since it is widely known, Elizabeth Bishop's poem, "In the Waiting Room,"[3] provides a good starting point for considering some of the aspects of the Othering function as it operates through voice. The poem begins with a conventional I-centered discursive situation and then disrupts it, showing how the subject can be made and unmade in discourse. The opening sentence places the speaker at the center of the represented world: "In Worcester, Massachussets,/... in the dentist's waiting room" (159). The paratactic series of verbs that locate the speaker in this setting seems deliberately banal: "I went ... and sat ... and waited...." The redundancy of the echoes of the poem's title in lines 4, 5 and 7 emphasize the clichéd nature of the scene. Indeed, the Othering process develops from an almost hyper-conventional representation of an ordinary subject in a very quotidian setting.

Discursively speaking, in the first lines of the poem everything is in its conventional place according to the Cartesian construction of self. The "I" provides the central organizing focus and occupies the grammatical function of subject, in opposition to the other constituents of the scene, whose grammatical position is subordinate, whether they are people

("Aunt Consuelo," "grown-up people") or objects ("arctics and overcoats,/ lamps and magazines"). Everything outside the self lends an illusion of materiality to the scene and thereby indirectly imparts consistency to the "I." In employing this conventional discursive model, the speaker situates herself within the system that founded modern science, allowing a detached position for the subject to observe and define an objectified world. Indeed, the precocious young reader "carefully/ studie[s]" the *National Geographic* magazine, in which objects of geological and anthropological interest are displayed (159).

This conventional world of discourse is upset by a new form of expression: the "*oh!* of pain" (160), described in the second stanza. This spontaneous cry introduces a new voice"—Aunt Consuelo's voice—" (160) that undoes the opposition between the "I" and the things hitherto described as exterior to it. The two voices are confounded; inside and outside are confused. In fact, the "*oh!*" reminds us of a state anterior to the "*I*," a state of existence that is undifferentiated, pre-verbal, pre-subjective, even animal. The division between locutor and allocutor in the enunciative situation is undone, and differences recede in a discourse that has become destabilized, giving rise to progressively stranger enunciations: "it was *me*"; "I was my foolish aunt"; "you are an *I*/ you are an *Elizabeth*/ you are one of *them*" (160). The cry radically decenters the subject, moving her outside herself. The italicization creates parallel forms, suggesting that "an *oh!*" also produces "an *I*," giving birth to a new kind of subject that is both distinct and joined, single and multiple, as implied in the punning question: "*Why* should you be one, too?" (160). The poem thus questions the stability of identity, transforming the "I" into someone else ("my aunt"), and the self into others ("you"; "an *Elizabeth*"; "one of *them*").

No longer aloof from and discursively in control of the world she describes, the speaker has become both connected and diminished. The "*oh!*" is therefore an ambiguous expression of both empathy and horror. The involuntary exclamation produces, on the one hand, disorientation and loss: "the sensation of falling off/ the round, turning world/ into cold, blue-black space," and, on the other hand, a sense of union, a feeling that something "held us all together/ or made us just one." The waiting room, normally the place where patients anxiously await treatment for tooth decay, mutates into a "weighting" room, where "Elizabeth" painfully acquires a new consciousness of the arbitrary and empowering separations imposed in language between "I," "you" and "them."

By breaking discursive molds in this way, Bishop's poem points beyond the conventional confines of subjectivity. Such improbable statements as "you are an *I*" (similar to Rimbaud's "je est un autre," though with the pronouns in reverse order) cannot simply be dismissed as a child's faltering experiments with language and with autonomy. The poem does not allow readers this distance. After first situating us "in the waiting room," the excursion into estrangement leads us through the paradoxically familiar (because clichéd) oddities of the *National Geographic* to the wholly new "sensation of falling off/ the round, turning world /into cold, blue-black space." This excursion takes us beyond the merely foreign to an encounter with the disturbing "unlikel[iness]" (161) that borders the familiar. By upsetting our sense of what is sayable, making language "stutter," as Deleuze would say,[4] the poem also works to extend the limits of what is thinkable.

Although the other texts we will examine depart from enunciative conventions in different and sometimes more radical ways, the implications of these departures have already been suggested in "In the Waiting Room." Othering enunciations convey dual, paradoxical states: for example, a sense of dispersion or even loss of subjectivity coupled with a sense of expansion or connection. Ultimately, these anomalies question the assumptions that ground communication, challenging the rules but also, potentially, liberating us from them.

As we have seen in Bishop's poem, the subject's displacement from centeredness to Othering is represented through the destabilizing of what linguists call "indexicals" or "shifters." These are words whose interpretation depends on the conditions accompanying utterance; some examples are expressions of time (now, tomorrow, yesterday), of place (here, there), of person (I, you, he), or deictics (this, that). These grammatical words are of interest because, although they are context-bound and are themselves devoid of reference, they are often called on to support claims to truth and logic. In oral communication they are underwritten by gesture or presence: *this* can be pointed to; *I* is the person speaking. In literature, indexicals serve as focal points around which the reader imaginatively constructs the "world" of the text, even though, paradoxically, they no longer have visible referents. Indeed, the lack of such referents means that grammatical conformity becomes all the more necessary to coherent literary discourse. Breaking with convention to the point of introducing a measure of incoherence necessarily interferes with our habit of taking for granted language and its pretension to construct subjectivity and represent reality.

In his short story "The Blizzard,"[5] Russell Banks turns what might otherwise be a fairly conventional account of marital infidelity into a highly disturbing and unpredictable adventure in reading by interlacing two different forms of narrative address. "The Blizzard" begins

conventionally enough with a descriptive paragraph representing a typical
New England scene:

> A low, mottled grey sky, smooth and unbroken in texture. The man stands,
> hands in pockets, next to the neatly stacked, headhigh woodpile, looking
> first up at the sky, then down to his feet, and he smiles beneath his thick
> moustache and shakes his head, as if remembering something that had been
> funny long ago and only to him. (21)

The opening paragraph introduces the voice of a third person or
"heterodiegetic" narrator,[6] who, in what narratologists term "external
focalization,"[7] seems to observe the newly introduced character from the
outside. "The man" is not named, but introduced anaphorically, in the
middle of a situation. According to the conventions of narrative realism,
we might expect that his name will be introduced later on in a
conversation, and that the time of the story will be made to extend back
analeptically to the "long ago" incident and forward at least to the blizzard
introduced in the title and suspended above the scene in the first line. In
switching in the next paragraph to the first-person, the narrative becomes
derailed from this predictable track. Abruptly, without any of the
discursive conventions signaling a change of speaker, an "I" describes a
habitual response to the cold. The reference to "my moustache" (22)
recalls the "thick moustache" (21) belonging to the "he" of the opening
paragraph, even though the personal pronouns seem to indicate two
different subjects.

   In fact "The Blizzard" is split rather than shared between a
heterodiegetic and an autodiegetic narrator.[8] Their alternating and
incompatible representations create an unstable effect. External
focalization represents the male protagonist as a philandering bully, while
the explanation and self-justification of the first person narrator produce a
more sympathetic character. However, nothing accounts for the alternation
of the two voices. A simple way to recuperate the narrative through
interpretation, to bring it back into the realm of the conventional, would be
to explain the split discourse as the schizophrenic disjunction of the
narrator's personality. However, the narrator anticipates and annuls this
strategy by giving both that diagnosis and its opposite: "It occurred to me
that he was insane. It occurred to me that he was not insane" (33).
Multiplying the indexicals makes the text point in two different directions,
"on both sides of his eyes" (33). Revealing both perspectives at once
exposes the way in which point of view determines judgment, thereby
laying bare the arbitrariness of claims to truth.

Finally, calling attention both to its own fictiveness and to the ways in which fictional devices serve the construction of identity, the short story concludes with a logical proposition that underpins constructions of self: "If this indeed was the city of Portsmouth, New Hampshire .... then, I must have been the person who was standing in the street, the tall man with the tiny icicles in his moustache" (33). Indexicals like "this" serve to attach the subject to the world to which he is able to point, but, at this stage in the story, the city has been effaced by the blizzard, indicating the defeat of any hope of certainty and the opening of a host of other possibilities in which fixity no longer counts in the interpretation of discourse.

In poetry the contradictory or paradoxical occurrence of indexicals functions somewhat differently from narrative. In the lyric tradition, rather than being responsible for relating a situation, the speaker normally describes an intense feeling or perception which readers are invited to share. Claims to truth in poetry lie not so much in the creation of a recognizable world as in the representation of a credible emotional state. In Amiri Baraka's poem, "An Agony. As Now,"[9] the proliferating indexicals both fragment the speaker's persona and trouble readers' attempts at relating to it.

Although the first stanza of the poem seems to be describing something like self-hatred—"I am inside someone/ who hates me. I look/ out from his eyes" (60)—the simplistic interpretation that the speaker suffers from schizophrenia or a split personality induced by racial division does not hold up in front of the ever-increasing complexity of the poem. Consider, for example, the speaker's various ways of representing his outside as both a kind of protective armor, "Slits in the metal for sun" (60), and an instrument of torture, "It burns the thing/ inside it" (61). In addition to metaphor, idiosyncratic punctuation creates ambiguity, so in the phrase—"Flesh,/ white hot metal" (61)— where a noun is separated by a comma from another nominal group, flesh and metal could be one and the same, or the first substance could be opposed to and in painful contact with the other. Most disturbingly, with the I's free appropriation of pronouns, the self scatters, as the speaker claims possession of what is "mine," "his," "its," and even "yours": "if you are the soul I had/ and abandoned when I was blind" (60). At the same time, the "I" seems also to dispossess itself and to become an object: "(As now, as all his/ flesh hurts me) It can be that" (60). The unconventional, unrestricted use of shifters makes the speaker both possessor and possessed. The conventional construction of identity is abandoned in the search for something other, something that would necessarily be difficult to define because it seems to destabilize cultural oppositions, somehow exculpating and inculpating the speaker at the same time. Reducing the poem to its racial determinants, although they are relevant, would certainly diminish the complexity of its interpretive possibilities. Baraka's poem is not a tract against racism; instead, it shows how oppression can be transformed into an exploration of the self's multiple positions and identities.

Shifters give a paradoxical sense of contact and immediacy to something that is only vaguely defined: "It can be that" (60). The organizing feature of the poem is not the integrity of the speaker but the intensity of the discourse, as suggested by the repetition of the word pain at the center of the poem, by the final word, "screams," isolated in the last line, and of course, by the title, "An Agony. As Now." If intense emotion ("Agony") and immediacy ("Now") conform to our expectations for lyric poetry, the indefinite article "An" and the conjunction "As" produce a kind of conundrum. "An" implies that agony can be counted, that it is one among many, while "As Now" suggests that pain is both personal and immediate—the one referred to at this very moment—and yet somehow comparable to many others. Moreover, beyond mere sense, the words produce sound and feeling, a rhythmic and alliterative cry of pain that, like music, invites participation more than interpretation.

The problem with language, in particular in the Cartesian use of it as a tool for acting on the world, is that it creates distance between subject and object, between the I and everything else. By taking liberties with language writers show the risks and stakes involved in its use, and through the Othering function point beyond it, indicating what Deleuze and Guattari would call "lines of flight."[10] The "stuttering" occurrences of incompatible indexicals in Bishop, Banks, and Baraka multiply the points of reference that map subjectivity. Rather than using language to fix a stable "I" at the center of the world, these writers employ indexicals to create trajectories of transformation and mutation. Constituted through mobile and unstable shifters, the subject is ungraspable, but also freed.

In Othering enunciation the subject relinquishes the central and magisterial position of conventional discourse, exchanging agency for some form of contact with the world. So far this exchange has been represented as accidental or imposed; in two works we will now examine, Barry Lopez's short story "Winter Count 1973: Geese, They Flew Over in a Storm"[11] and Jorie Graham's poem, "I Was Taught Three,"[12] it is willingly undertaken.

Midway through Lopez's short story, the narrator identifies the as yet unnamed protagonist by recounting his search for his own name on a conference program:

He was due—he thought suddenly of aging, of illness: *when our children, they had strangulations of the throat*, of the cure for *any* illness as he scanned the long program—in the Creole Room. Roger Callahan, Nebraska State College: "Winter Counts from the Dakota, the Crow and the Blackfeet: Personal Histories." Jesus, he thought, why had he come? (56-57)

This disjunctive revelation of self through the impersonal medium of print suggests a cause for the protagonist's malaise apart from his discomfort in the impersonal and alien surroundings of the Convention hotel. A teacher of American history, Callahan has been invited to present his research on Native American winter counts, which are defined as "personal views of history, sometimes metaphorical, bearing on a larger tribal history" (61). The expectation induced by the setting is that he will perform this professional role with "the definitive, the awful distance of reason" (61).[13] However, as the passage quoted above reveals, Callahan has given up distance for empathy. Winter counts infiltrate his thoughts, so that an account of tribal suffering harmonizes polyphonically with his own thoughts of mortality. The collective expression *"our children"* undermines the discourse of science that controls through detachment and generalization. At the end of the short story, the protagonist chooses connection and even identification, as we see from the adoption of the first person plural in his final affirmation: "That is all that is holding us together, stories and compassion" (62). Lopez's unconventional teacher figure rejects objectivity for feeling, giving up science in favor of stories.

Without a master discourse to give them a spurious coherence, the winter counts that emerge through free indirect discourse in the narrative may seem too elliptic, too enigmatic, and too strange to make "sense"; nevertheless, the short story indicates a new construction of sense at its borders. At the end of the story, in a gesture that effaces the boundaries between outside and inside, Callahan throws open the windows of his hotel room and exposes himself to the outside world, allowing himself to be invaded by the storm that "roared through his head" (63). Then he hears "In the deepest distance, once, ... the barking-dog sounds of geese, running like horses before a prairie thunderstorm." This poetic ending exemplifies the language of connection that takes the place of the rejected master discourse. Through metaphor, it links three species of animal in an unscientific collation very different from the usual taxonomies. At the same time, it breaks down distinctions between here and there, bringing the prairie into the New Orleans hotel. Finally, in a disturbance of conventional relations consistent with this volatility in nature, the historian adopts a subaltern discourse, and the story's title turns out to be Callahan's own winter count.

Jorie Graham's "I Was Taught Three" goes even further in divesting the subject of the Cartesian position of mastery and detachment. In contrast to the "I" of *cogito*, her speaker assumes a role that is passive and only superficially primary. While the poem's title, "I Was Taught Three," positions the subject as the originator of thought, the first line of the poem gives primacy to language instead: "names for the tree facing my window." Though the passive verb form in the title emphasizes the role of the "I," it effaces the agency of the teacher(s), giving importance to "names" instead. It reminds us that rather than being responsible for naming (the Edenic myth of origins), we are born into language. The speaker does not control words; words shape her perceptions of things. Language creates the subject, rather than the contrary. Each of the three names "for the tree facing my window" captures a particular network of associations. Thus, in naming the tree either *"Castagno," "Chassagne," "chestnut"* (6), she enjoys multiple possibilities of being. At the same time, through the multiple designations that map its existence through time and its expansion in space, the tree gains the status of subject, enjoying a reversibility of positions with the "I":

No, this
was all first person, and I

was the stem, holding within myself the whole
bouquet of three,

at once given and received ... (6)

Rather than a means to mastery, naming becomes a process of reciprocal construction; names are "given and received" mutually, so that finally the "I" is just "a name among them." In this poem, subject and object are no longer split, for in relating to the tree outside her window, the speaker becomes a "human tree/ clothed with nouns," and the tree takes shape inside her. No longer threatening, the fluidity of indexicals—the "I" merging with the "this," and the "them"—has become the sign of a new potential. The "I" takes on a vegetal quality, becoming a "stem" for its "bouquet" of words. Endowed now with language, the tree represents a pledge of coherence through connection rather than separation: "promising more firmly/ than can be/ that it will reach my sill eventually" (7).

Implicit in all the works that we have examined so far is their tendency to chafe against language as a system. Not surprisingly many of the texts that experiment with discrepancies in enunciation take language as their main subject. Rather than presenting situations to be resolved or states to be exposed, discourse itself becomes the issue. This tendency culminates in L.A.N.G.U.A.G.E. poetry where words are seemingly divested of meaning and become materials diverted from their usual (communicative) function in order to construct new works of art. Our investigation of the ways in which the Othering function works through discrepancies in enunciation ends, then, with a brief examination of some highly un-representational works. Working with some of the clichés of discourse, Charles Simic's poem, "Two Riddles," and Donald Barthelme's "The Rise of Capitalism" abandon meaning for playfulness and humor. Clarence Major's prose text, "An Area in the Cerebral Hemisphere," and one of Linda Hejinian's poems from *The Cell* free words from their representational function in a more radical attempt to extend the limits of what is sayable.

Charles Simic's "Two Riddles"[14] takes language in two different directions; on the one hand, the poem restores some of the literal sense to a pair of clichés, and, on the other hand, it invests dead metaphors with unexpected meanings. The first of the two riddles evokes the absurdity of human life in a post-Cartesian, post-Nietszchean world, where the beliefs that once anchored the subject and assured the meaning of language have disappeared:

Hangs by a thread—
Whatever it is. Stripped naked.
Shivering. Human. Mortal.
On a thread finer than starlight.

By a power of a feeling,
Hangs, impossible, unthinkable,
Between the earth and the sky.
I, it says. I. I.

And how it boasts,
That everything that is to be known
About the wind
Is being revealed to it as it hangs. (56)

This riddle links two indexicals, "I" and "it" in a perplexing partnership. The "it" in line 2 is, first of all, a reference to a subject that is elided. Something that is not named—implicitly the answer to the riddle—"[h]angs by a thread. " However, rather than resolving the question and defining the "it," as is customary in discourse, the poem's second line draws attention to the imprecision of the pre-constructed cliché and to the free-floating indeterminacy of language. Moreover, although the linguistic system allows speakers to designate a subject as either "I" or "it," the use of both pronouns at once places the system in crisis. When Simic's "it" speaks, its use of the first person appears nonsensical: "I, it says. I. I" (56).

Rendering literal the cliché, [his life?] "hangs by a thread," the poem envisions the subject hanging "impossible and unthinkable,/ Between the earth and the sky" (56). The image evokes Renaissance representations of man positioned at the center of creation, between angels and apes, heaven and hell. It also recalls Jonathan Edwards's famous sermon, comparing sinners to loathsome spiders suspended in God's hands over the pit of hell.[15] However, the thread by which the subject hangs—"Shivering. Human. Mortal."—is perhaps nothing more than a line made of language, in other words, the phrase itself, that posits an actor, an action, and a context. Demoted from the start from the status of self by the pronoun "it" ("Whatever it is."), the grammatical subject has the temerity to call itself "I" and to imagine "that everything that is to be known/ About the wind/ Is being revealed to it as it hangs." Refusing to grant man full status as an "I" positioned in opposition to an "it," the poem exposes the fragility of subjectivity, leaving "it" suspended between dignity and futility, humanity and non-humanity, being and non-being. This state of indeterminacy and inbetweenness is exactly what "normal" communication seeks to avoid or clear up and what Othering communication explores.

Simic's second riddle continues the job of demonstrating the arbitrariness of the system, drawing our attention to the semantic emptiness of pre-constructed expressions by taking a phrase that paradoxically uses four words to say that words are not necessary:

> It goes without saying . . .
> What does? No one knows.
> Goes mysterious, ah funereal,
> Goes for the hell of it.
>
> If it has an opinion,
> It keeps it to itself.
> If it brings tidings,
> It plays dumb, plays dead.
>
> No use trying to pin it down.
> It's elusive, of a retiring habit,
> In a hurry of course, scurrying—
>
> All that's known about it,

> Is that it goes
> Without saying. (56-57)

After the introductory cliché, "It goes without saying," we would expect an ensuing clause to state what is felt to be obvious. Instead the poem takes as its subject the cliché itself, or more precisely, in the manner of the first riddle, the semantically empty "it": "It plays dumb, plays dead" (56). The impersonal pronoun normally fills in for a subject that is subsequently (or sometimes previously) defined by a statement's context. The first riddle stages a battle for definition, pitting the "I" against another speaker who refuses "it" the status of a person. In the second riddle, the impersonal "it" gains an agency of its own through sentences that expand the neutral "goes" into a more descriptive lexical field: "In a hurry of course, scurrying" (57). The connotations that link actions like playing dead and scurrying with small animals give the words of the cliché a ludicrous, cartoonish animation. By making them the subjects of his poem, Simic revives dead metaphors, but they become comic puppets. Associating the phrases with actions exposes the emptiness behind the masks of language. At the same time, playing with empty phrases liberates the creative potential of words that have become lifeless and exposes the strangeness behind the apparently obvious.

Obviously, to be credible systems of language and thought have to suppress ambiguity and eliminate contradiction. In "The Rise of Capitalism,"[16] Barthelme undermines the pretensions of master narratives to coherence by playing incompatible discursive fields against each other in a comic conflict. The title of the short story suggests that what follows may be a treatise on political economics; indeed, some of the phrases from the text could reasonably belong in that context. Take for example the opening of the second paragraph: "Capitalism places every man in competition with his fellows for a share of the available wealth" (205). The abstract nouns from the lexicon of economics create the impersonal tone that conforms to the expectations produced by the title. However, the text's opening lines seem to be drawn from a different, much more personal discursive field. A first person narrator admits to "mak[ing] a mistake" (204), to "assum[ing] an attitude—melancholy sadness—toward it" (204). The language of romance is placed in nonsensical proximity to that of economics. A clichéd love note is interpreted as a "critique of my attitude toward capitalism" (204). Subsequently, theological discourse from Christianity and Hinduism infiltrate the text. The voice of the first-person narrator in the opening paragraph is submerged by the discordant clash of master discourses that seem to speak all by themselves. If the resulting incongruities prompt laughter, they also draw attention to the potential for nonsense that underlies all established discourses, simply because they vehicle ready-made concepts that are beyond the control of those who wield them.

Nevertheless, saying that beyond sense lies nonsense merely represents discourse in terms that are ideologically compatible with the system. Though laughter mocks order, it also potentially abets it by reconciling us with incongruities in the system. Comedy exteriorizes contradictions in order to exorcise them through laughter. Simic and Bartheleme prevent such easy recuperation by also venturing into the realm of the absurd, which works in the opposite way to comedy, interiorizing contradictions by creating anguish. Thus, Simic's first riddle, while deriding what might simply be a ready-made expression, also suggests the anguish of existence. The hanging phrase becomes uncomfortably like a hanging man, suspended and doomed. And after parodying all the master discourses, Barthelme's text leaves us without any of the confident assurances that authority provides. The alternatives to capitalism listed at the end cancel one another out: "A knowledge of European intellectual history ...; Passion ..., especially those types of passion which are nonlicit; Doubt ... [and finally] Fear..." (208). Finally, words refer to nothing tangible, and the texts confront us with that nothing. However, in both texts, along with the disquieting sense that beyond language a gaping void beckons, there is also a suggestion of the totality that discourses vainly try to approximate. With the problems of existence raised but not resolved, these texts leave humanity suspended between subject and object, interiority and exteriority. This state of suspension characterizes the Othering experience. The comic absurdity found in Othering texts does not mark a loss of transcendence but rather a promises a new field of possibilities.

In the texts we have looked at so far, the reliance on familiar literary features like character, situation, or theme has progressively diminished, as the Othering process operates increasingly on literariness itself. We will now consider two final texts, a prose piece by Clarence Major ("An Area in the Cerebral Hemisphere")[17] and a poem by Lyn Hejinian (one of the entries for November, 13, 1986 from *The Cell*),[18] which abandon all pretensions to be "about" something and use language as the raw material for creation rather than a vehicle for meaning. In attempting to abandon meaning altogether, these texts seek to escape the trap of reproducing pre-established discourses.

Language is the subject, one might even say the target, of these writers who force words to work against the system. They make statements that are anomalous, irregular, abnormal, and illogical. (Naturally, the negative prefixes of these terms are designed to convey the judgment of upholders of verbal law and order.) They take liberties with punctuation: Hejinian's poem uses capital letters and one dash, but no commas or periods; Major's prose text uses punctuation to produce grammatically incomplete structures such as: "Come on in and close the." or "I got my fan going but." (Major 2175). The two writers play fast and loose with indexicals: "she" "I" and "he" float free from referents; "yesterday" is divorced from time and set in motion, so that it "rolls under and/ holds its information up and/ forward for long ..." (Hejinian 31). These writers place words in disjunctive configurations to short-circuit logic, for example Hejinian's "blunt November summer" or Major's "swift traffic was known to move through her living room." Language becomes the protagonist of these texts: "Red and yellow language coming/ with the tongue" (Hejinian); "These little thoughts that slide back down narrow, worn paths" (Major 2175).

If in reading these texts we struggle to make sense of them, we experience a sense of frustration and loss, for sense constantly escapes through the anomalies in enunciation. However, if we embrace the irregularities, we can enjoy the freedom won by the writers' work: "Anything can happen," Major's text proclaims. Abandoning logic, his text opens up possibility. The "she [who] is behind fieldglasses" in the first paragraph can be both watched and watching. For the friend who "sat on the sounds of her own voice" (2175), words are tangible as well as audible. The subject is opened up, so that the "she" seems to be at once thinking and thought. The title "An Area in the Cerebral Hemisphere," designating an unspecified mental space, could be referring to the minds of the protagonist or the voyeur, the speaker or the reader. It draws attention to the way in which the text works not on the world, but on the mind. The text floats between points of view. In this dispersed construction of subjectivity, being is not simply decentered or scattered; it is both nowhere in particular and everywhere.

In Major's text we discover not the absence of meaning but a kind of shimmering infinity of meanings. The opening sentence places a female protagonist between non-existence and limitless possibilities: "She is not absolutely anything." Stressing the words "not" and "anything" negates being, while emphasizing "absolutely" refuses to essentialize it. New possibilities for existence seem to hover at the edge of each successive sentence: "She is something naked, skin and thought but so hot today" (2175). The subject wavers between states of oppression and excitation, between body and mind. The subsequent clause, "Because the walls are pressed" (2175), apparently explanatory, since it begins with the word "Because," provides perplexity rather than clarity. Yet, we persist in our efforts at interpretation because, as Mephistopheles observes in Goethe's Faust, "As long as man keeps hearing words / He's sure that there's a meaning somewhere."[19] The Othering process leads away from the reassurance produced by the singularity of meaning.

When the pretence of attaching words to referents is abandoned, using language liberates us from the material world. "I could have only said so," Hejinian's poem claims, after producing the sequence, "The blunt November summer...." These writers give a whole new sense to the idea of doing things with words.[20] Rather than using performative language, they make language perform. Their texts produce the incredible special effects of signs freed from the task of signifying; nevertheless, as Hejinian observes in *The Language of Inquiry*, "words [are] attractive, magnetic to meaning" (51). We might say that we bring meaning to them, but Hejinian puts it differently, giving agency to the words themselves. For her, words have "reach": "The meaning of a word in its place derives both from the word's lateral reach, its contacts with its neighbors in a statement, and from its reach through and out of the text into the outer world..." (50). So rather than falling into meaninglessness, lines like "The year is thick and / long and thrust ..." give us a new way of imagining time. Growth becomes luxuriant and aggressive, phallic and erotic. At the same time, in their proximity to the preceding lines ("Red and yellow language coming/ with the tongue"), the statement draws attention to the act of speaking, to the sensuous action of the tongue in sounding out *the*, *th*ick and *th*rust.

The departures from the system found in these texts surprise us; they are pleasing and unsettling at the same time. The reaction of the young Elizabeth of "In the Waiting Room" might fittingly describe the experience of reading them: "How—I didn't know any word for it—how "unlikely" . . . (161). Necessarily, each text is very different, for no rules can be fixed if Othering is to follow its emancipatory impulse. As opposed to grammatical structures, lines of flight, once opened up, must be continually drawn anew. These texts celebrate a world in transformation, where the self is not only malleable, but engaged in endless metamorphosis. Language is no longer fixed in an unchanging system, but available for experimentation and mutation.

In conclusion, these texts reconfigure the subjectivity that the system holds to be single and unique. They disrupt coherent, subject-centered discourse to produce a subject that is multiple and ductile. The center is abandoned in favor of in-between spaces. No longer pinned in place through the consistent use of indexicals, the subject is free to float, to disperse, to multiply. Finally words are released from their attachment to subjects, so that discourse can have multiple centers and points of view.

Notes

[1] We accept Bakhtin's thesis that each enunciation draws on a profusion of already uttered and placed voices: "In language, there are no 'neutral' words and forms—words and forms that can belong to 'no one'; language has been completely taken over, shot through with intentions and accents. For any individual consciousness living in it, language is not an abstract system of normative forms but rather a concrete heteroglot conception of the world. All words have the 'taste' of a profession, a genre, a tendency, a party, a particular work, a particular person, a generation, an age group, the day, and hour. Each word tastes of the context and contexts in which it has lived its socially charged life; all words and forms are populated by intentions." Mikhail Bakhtin, "Discourse in the Novel," *The Dialogic Imagination: Four Essays by M.M. Bakhtin*, ed. Michael Holquist, trans. Caryl Emerson and Michael Holquist (Austin: University of Texas Press, 1981) 293.

[2] See Gottlob Frege, "Thoughts," in *Collected Papers on Mathematics, Logic, and Philosophy*, ed. B. McGuiness, trans. P. Geach and R.H. Stoothoff (Oxford: Blackwell, 1984) 351-72.

[3] Elizabeth Bishop, "In the Waiting Room," *The Complete Poems: 1927-1979* (New York: Farrar, Straus and Giroux, 1979) 159-161.

[4] Gilles Deleuze, "*Bartleby*; or, the formula," in *Essays Critical and Clinical*, trans. Daniel Smith and Michael A. Greco (Minneapolis: University of Minnesota Press, 1997) 68-90.

[5] Russell Banks, "The Blizzard," *Searching for Survivors* (New York : Fiction Collective, 1975) 21-33.

[6] See Gérard Genette's chapter on "Voice" in *Narrative Discourse: an Essay in Method*, trans. Jane E. Lewin (Ithaca: Cornell University Press, 1980) 212-268.

[7] See Genette 189-194.

[8] The autodiegetic narrator speaks in the first person and is "the star" in the story, see Genette 245.

[9] Amiri Baraka, "An Agony. As Now," *Transbluesency, The Selected Poems of Amiri Baraka/LeRoi Jones (1961-1995)* (New York: Marsilio, 1995) 60-61.

[10] See in particular in Gilles Deleuze and Felix Guattari, *A Thousand Plateaus*, trans. Brian Massumi (Minnesota: University of Minnesota Press, 1987) 21. We have used the English translation where possible, though we also make reference to the French, *Mille Plateaux* (Paris: Minuit, 1980).

[11] Barry Lopez, "Winter Count 1973: Geese, They Flew Over in a Storm," *Winter Count* (New York: Simon and Schuster, 1981; Vintage, 1999) 51-63.

[12] Jorie Graham, "I Was Taught Three," *The Dream of the Unified Field. Selected Poems 1974-1994* (Hopewell, New Jersey: The Ecco Press, 1980) 6-7.

[13] Examples of this distant, professional discursive stance are given in the descriptions of the papers that Callahan listens to while he waits to present his own.

[14] Charles Simic, "Two Riddles," in *Selected Poems, 1963-1983*. Revised and Expanded edition (New York: 1990) 56-57.

[15] "The God that holds you over the pit of hell, much as one holds a spider, or some loathsome insect, over the fire, abhors you . . . .." Jonathan Edwards, "Sinners in the hands of an angry God," Enfield, Connecticut, July 8, 1741.
[16] Donald Barthelme, "The Rise of Capitalism," *Sixty Stories* (New York: Putnam, 1981) 204-08.
[17] Clarence Major, "An Area in the Cerebral Hemisphere," first published in *Statements: New Fiction from the Fiction Collective*, ed. Jonathan Baumbach, (New York: G. Braziller, 1975); reprinted in *The Norton Anthology of American Literature*, Fifth Edition, ed. Nina Baym (New York: W.W. Norton, 1998) 2175-78.
[18] Lyn Hejinian, "November, 13, 1986," *The Cell* (Los Angeles: Sun and Moon, 1992) 31.
[19] Johann Wolfgang von Goethe, *Goethe's Faust*, Part One, tr. Randall Jarrell (New York: Farrar, Straus & Giroux, 1976) 137; quoted in Lyn Hejinian, *The Language of Inquiry* 52.
[20] We evoke here the title of J.L. Austin's book on speech act theory, *How to do Things With Words* (Oxford, Clarendon Press, 1962).

CHAPTER THREE

DISRUPTIONS AS OPENINGS

The preceding chapter explored how Othering emerges when texts deviate from the model of subject-centered discourse. Organizing the text around a coherent "voice" is one way to lend consistency and authority to discourse, but it is not the only way. By employing reiterations, logical sequences and transitions, as well as predictable lexical collocations, texts produce the sense of unity and coherence that corresponds to aesthetic norms and cultural values. Nevertheless, as Hans-Jost Frey has argued, the impression of wholeness in the literary text is "only human fiction.... and all ordering is a vain attempt to make fragments into parts."[1] The compulsive search for wholeness displaces or occults fragmentariness. The aesthetic ideal of unity is always superimposed on the perception of dispersing fragments, and any vision of coherence is produced through dissimulation. By readmitting disruption, Othering alleviates and possibly capitalizes on the lingering suspicion that fragmentation lies behind unity. Rather than striving for a fictional wholeness, the texts that we will examine in the following two chapters make plain their disruption or dispersion. We will explore the ways in which, by deviating from rhetorical conventions simulating coherence, Othering texts open up to possibilities beyond the restrictions imposed by unity.

One of the metaphors linguists use to describe the structure of a text is that of a net.[2] Indeed, textile or weaving metaphors have been applied to texts since at least the Greeks.[3] Representing the text as a woven fabric proclaims its consistency as well as its status as finished object. A comparable aesthetic preference for wholeness probably underlies Cleanth Brooks' adoption of Donne's metaphor of the "well-wrought urn" to describe poetry.[4] In this chapter we will explore instead an aesthetic of incompletion which allows for holes, tears, or gaps in the textual fabric. These gaps disrupt lexical, thematic, and temporal continuity, creating various forms of disjunction or fragmentation. They create the conditions for the appearance of the Othering process, so that gaps become breaks, that is, interruptions that are both fissures and spaces of liberty.

Implicit (but usually ignored) in the textile metaphor is the recognition that texts are formed out of both continuities and discontinuities. Examine a tapestry carefully, and the individual threads can be distinguished. Turn it over, and the knots and seams may show. The literary text weaves words into phrases, lines, and sentences, linking them together into stanzas or paragraphs. Collocations or recurring combinations of words provide a sense of coherence and a measure of thematic predictability.[5] Punctuation and spacing mark the breaks necessary to breath, thought or memory. Transitions create continuity in logic or chronology. Normally, all these conventions give an impression of order and cohesion. They are the stitches that bind the text together. Nevertheless, they can also be used as marks of discontinuity signaling ruptures in the text, drawing attention to its incompleteness and disabling the conventional operations of language in order to make space for the Othering process.

Before looking at disruptions in texts, we shall briefly recall some of the visual, grammatical and rhetorical features of wholeness. With the introduction of print, conventions for the layout and typography of poetic and prose texts developed, in turn, shaping readers' expectations. Set forms in poetry generally conform to fixed visual models. For example, the quatrains of a ballad are separated from each other by blank spaces; sonnets are generally arranged either in fourteen line blocks or in stanzaic patterns. Because of such conventions for spacing, we expect that books of poetry will contain more blank space than books of fiction. Spacing draws attention to form and hence to the craft involved in shaping language. In free verse, spacing is less predictable, and can appear more natural and closer to prose. Short stories normally follow the typographical conventions for prose; in other words, they are organized into thematically coherent blocks or paragraphs. Direct discourse can be an exception to this practice, often imitating conventions for theatrical texts in setting each character's speech apart on a new line. If describing these conventions seems like an unnecessary statement of the obvious, it is because they have come to seem natural. They go without saying; we notice them only when they are breached.

Space in the text might be compared to silences or pauses in musical composition. When used conventionally, it produces harmony and thematic coherence. Nonetheless, in the texts we will examine, anomalous spacing (whether between blocks of text or within individual lines) violates the aesthetic of wholeness, opening up or drawing attention to lacunae. The same observation could be made concerning marks of discontinuity in syntax. Periods, semi-colons and commas normally mark the end of a logical unit and provide breathing spaces or moments of rest when the text is read aloud. When they are used anomalously, they rupture the normal rhythms of language, making the text's silences appear strange. Other, less frequently used marks signal slightly more unusual disruptions of continuity. Quotation marks, used to signal direct speech or citation, indicate the boundaries of oral expression or the interruption of one voice by another. This discontinuity affirms the system by proclaiming the integrity of the individual, even upholding notions of intellectual property. Dashes indicate breaks in thought, even as they join the intrusive idea to the sentence as a whole. Ellipses, from the Greek word for omission, indicate that something is missing from the text; three dots indicate the excision or the incompletion of a word or thought. Though ellipsis might be taken as the most obvious sign of rupture, the linguists Halliday and Hasan list it among the cohesive ties in discourse.[6] They refer not simply to the typographical marks, but to the more general use of omission in discourse to signal the absence of what is obvious (a perfect example of what goes without saying!). The unspoken confirms the system, working to create complicity among members of the same culture who are able to reconstitute systemic thought even through the gaps in discourse: in the case of the implicit, it affirms shared knowledge and customs; in the case of the unspeakable, it marks out what is taboo, beyond social limits.

Having reviewed the conventions for creating a sense of textual wholeness, we can now look at some of the tactics for disrupting the system. Disjunction can operate both within the sentence and within the larger structure of the text. By interfering with formal, thematic and chronological coherence, they violate the boundaries of the sayable and thinkable. The processes we will look at here are fissuring (creating formal ruptures), patchworking (creating thematic disjunction), and interrupting (creating chronological anomalies). These processes are interrelated and often work together in texts, but for the purposes of analysis, we will examine them consecutively.

To differing degrees, all the short stories we will look at in this chapter use blank spaces to fissure the text. J.D. Salinger's "A Perfect Day for Bananafish" [7] and Barry Lopez's "The Woman Who Had Shells"[8] are composed of three sections of uneven lengths, separated by spaces. "Persona," by Gayl Jones,[9] and "Extinctions," by Barbara Kingsolver,[10] are made up of five sections marked off from one another by spaces and, in the case of "Extinctions," by a centered dash. The prevalence of this type of organization might suggest that the texts are following a fictional convention, and that these breaks are comparable to chapter breaks in the novel. Indeed, if they simply followed the convention of eliding the unnecessary, the irrelevant or the obvious, they could hardly be called fissures. Nevertheless, in these texts, the spaces generally signal unexpected ruptures in the narrative.

Indeed, these gaps draw our attention to anomalies that not only confound efforts to fit the short stories into recognizable interpretative molds, but also frustrate the urge to ascribe meaning. Consider, for example, the gap that separates Muriel's telephone conversation with her mother in "A Perfect Day for Bananafish" from the dialogue between Mrs. Carpenter and her daughter Sybil. This blank space draws our attention to an abrupt shift in character and mood. In the first section, Muriel's remarks suggest that her young husband, Seymour Glass, is alarmingly deviant or deranged. The second conversation transforms him into something completely different through Sibyl's punning game: "See more glass," said Sybil Carpenter .... Did you see more glass?" (10). Rather than the initial binary separation of normal and abnormal, this new departure introduces double vision into the text. The new variant on Seymour's name could apply both to the sybilline child and to the imaginative young man, announcing the complicity that develops between them. Bracketed by gaps in spacing, the middle section of the text represents a brief interlude of acceptance and play, a space of mobility and ambiguity in contrast to the oppressive reign of normality inside the hotel.

More evidently and consistently fissured, Susan Minot's "Lust"[11] and Kimiko Hahn's "Afterbirth"[12] separate many short sections of various lengths from one another by blank spaces, so that the texts create a visual impression of discontinuity. The blank spaces make it obvious that the texts are patched together from heterogeneous scraps. "Lust" juxtaposes reminiscences that are thematically linked, but chronologically scattered. The fissures in "Afterbirth" separate fragments that are both thematically and chronologically divergent. Finally, looking more like the pages of a textbook than a short story, William Gass's "In the Heart of the Heart of the Country" is organized into 36 sections, set off from one another by titles in block capitals surrounded by blank spaces.[13] Though, at first, this gives the impression of a hyper-organized, heavily normative textual space structured on division and classification, this sense is soon dispelled by the recurrences of the same headings. For example, "EDUCATION" appears three times (196; 205; 216), as does "BUSINESS" (197; 207; 223) suggesting rather a lack of method and preparing us for the increasing strangeness of the observations contained within each section. These recurring and sometimes mutating titles—for example, "MY HOUSE" (192; 193) becomes "MY HOUSE, THIS PLACE AND BODY" (197), then "MY HOUSE, MY CAT, MY COMPANY (201), and finally, "HOUSE, MY BREATH AND WINDOW" (213)—suggest something very different from conventional ways of ordering a prose text. In fact, they recall the revolving gyres of Yeats' poetic universe, evoked in the opening sentence of "In the Heart of the Heart of the Country." However, in Gass's text, the spiral of history becomes splintered, demented, and unpredictable, veering neither toward doom nor salvation.

In poetry, gaps are much more expected than in prose; they even help to summarily distinguish the two forms of writing. Thus, to offer an immediate visual impression of fissuring, poems have to depart significantly from conventional stanzaic models. Such is the case of Adrienne Rich's "Nightbreak."[14] Split down the middle by blank spaces like a ragged fault line, the poem weaves together three different attempts to respond to the same event: the speaker's traumatized remembering of the massive American bombings in Vietnam; her attempt to cope with the emotional aftermath of the event; and the difficult search for a means of expression. The poem's first words—"Something broken"—suggest, in a fragment of syntax, all three, as if the violence had made coherence in language impossible, breaking the normal correspondence between vision and expression. Trauma lies at the very heart of the poem, yet it seems not to bear mentioning. It pulses like a magmatic core beneath the gaping fissure. The speaker herself is split between empathy for the victims ("something broken"), and American complicity with the aggressor ("by someone/ I love"). She seems to be associated with the bombers ("I go on/head down into it") and with the bombs being dropped ("Into the oildrum   drops/ the ball of fire". The poem's split form is the visual trace of the intensely traumatic positions that the speaker is trying to come to terms with in retrospect. The poem appears as a scattering of fragments testifying to the explosion of a center that can no longer be retrieved. It is an open wound ("The crack weeping") that resists the selective and cohesive tendencies of ideology.

Sonia Sanchez's poetic tribute to Billie Holliday, "for our lady,"[15] also appears to carry the process of fissuring to extremes. The language Sanchez organizes on the page is reduced to a kind of informal shorthand in which style counts less than urgency and intensity of expression. The English language is made a subject of derision, as if the writer was using a medium that she despised. Grammatical cohesion is deliberately broken and marks of punctuation misused as if sentences had to be fragmented in order to shed their unwanted connotations. The purpose of this linguistic refurbishing is of course, as with Rich, the expression of a visceral rejection of the discourse of the dominant community. Hence, Sanchez dispenses with capitals at the beginning of sentences and names (billie); she fractures the text grammatically with non-standard punctuation; she trivializes grammatical words by using the abbreviations of the want ads (u, shud, wud); she reproduces in her spelling the inflections of black dialect (tellin, tellen, gainst, yo); she introduces slashes that divide adjectives or pronouns from nouns (blue / nites, blk / man, yo / songs), thereby flagging problematic associations; she uses reductions to express contempt or doubt (wite, blk); or, on the contrary, phonetic spelling to mark special emphasis (reallee, permanentlee). Too often the innovations of Sonia Sanchez and of the other Black Arts movement poets have been dismissed as little more than typographic quirkiness. However, in keeping with our assumption that fissuring opens up the work to Othering, we take Sanchez's demo(li)tion of discourse as a struggle to make a rival form of expression emerge through the fractures made in conventional discursive structures.

Although we have looked at the way spaces and typographical marks fragment texts, it is important to bear in mind that as well as creating discontinuities, fissuring also produces new forms of coexistence (though never exactly of coherence). Hence the second tactic of piecing together disjunctive discourses is related to the first, since the gaps help make visible the edges of juxtaposed pieces of text, and the fragmentation and dissociation of discourses permit the construction of new combinations.

The patchworking process is both visually and linguistically obvious in Anne Carson's poem, "Sumptuous Destitution."[16] The poem's typographical layout creates a regular pattern out of textual fragments; its 25 lines alternate normal print with italicized quotations, followed by parenthetical references to the quotes. A contemporary critical discourse on Emily Dickinson has been segmented and fragments of Dickinson's correspondence with Thomas Higginson are interpolated between the segments. If the words in normal print are read alone, they produce conventional sentences, the first of which sounds like a line from a seminar paper:

"Sumptuous destitution"
Your opinion gives me a serious feeling: I would like to be what you deem me.
                    (Emily Dickinson letter 319 to Thomas Higginson)
is a phrase
You see my position is benighted.
                    (Emily Dickinson letter 268 to Thomas Higginson)
scholars use
She was much too enigmatical a being for me to solve in an hour's interview.
                    (Thomas Higginson letter 233 to Emily Dickinson)

of female
God made me Sir Master—I didn't be—myself.
                    (Emily Dickinson letter 268 to Thomas Higginson)
silence.

However, the poem's insertion of fragments from the letters electrifies the measured declaration that: "'Sumptuous' destitution' . . . is a phrase . . . scholars use . . . of female . . . silence," allowing readers and poets from the past and the present to enter into conversation. A contemporary woman's voice summons the dead poet, and Emily Dickinson's voice replies with all its passionate urgency.[17]

In the second half of the poem, the speaker exhorts her foremother to save her poems and letters, "threads" of discourse for future readers and writers:

Save what you can, Emily.
....
Save every bit of thread.
....
One of them may be
....
the way out of here.

Evoking the Cretan labyrinth, the poem refers both to itself and to previous discourses. The poem resembles a labyrinth, and one of Dickinson's lines may guide us through it; at the same time, since the labyrinth was a construction built to hide the evidence of forbidden female desire, the speaker seems to join with Emily Dickinson in a quest to break out of the confining patriarchal system. After all, the oft-quoted oxymoron from one of Dickinson's poems that Carson uses for both her title and first line shows that the writing that has not been recognized as language is, in fact, a new idiom made from and imbricated in the juxtaposed pieces of the old one. In Dickinson's poem negation communicates the impracticability of conventional terms: "Without a Name," "a Joy— Reportless."[18] Then in a form of verbal patchworking, the oxymoron "a sumptuous Destitution" conveys something beyond common experience through the violence of juxtaposed opposites. Dickinson's unconventional expression makes language opaque and difficult rather than transparent and obvious. It may evoke responses like that of Thomas Higginson quoted in Carson's poem: *"She was much too enigmatical a being for me to solve in an hour's interview."* Yet only by being broken and remade can language be prevented from simply reproducing more of the same.

Something comparable to this patchworking process operates within the linguistic system through compound structures. This conventional means of word formation can become an othering process. Two words can join to suggest a non-systemic phenomenon, like the word *Bananafish* from Salinger's short story. This paradoxical creature, at once whimsical and tragic, serves to express the young man's contradictions. Once a compound enters the system, though, it takes on a coherence of its own and often the two words are fused. Such is the case with the word "afterbirth," a compound noun designating the placenta and foetal membranes expelled from the uterus after a baby is born. However, this fusion does not necessarily fix the concept; Othering tactics can serve to destabilize it. The heterogeneous juxtaposed fragments of Kimiko Hahn's "Afterbirth" work against applying a single definition to the title, and the text activates other possible readings of the word.

In Hahn's text the sense of "Afterbirth" fractures and recomposes to include potentially infinite after-birth experiences. Even in the opening sentence, the limited denotation of the title mutates into something much more: "In some societies, women eat the placenta after that final stage: the expulsion of the afterbirth when the belly heaves a great sigh and lies on the pelvis like a nostalgic sack" (132). There is an "after" beyond "that final stage", not only a ceremony involving the placenta, but also the body's reaction, the belly's "great sigh" of relief after and immediate nostalgia for pregnancy. The fragment that follows this poeticized anthropological observation seems to belong to a completely different order of discourse: "Rose missed something when she moved from the small town of her childhood to the city near water. Not the farms, though the smell of hay did become nostalgic" (132). This seems like the beginning of a narrative, but no coherent story develops. Though there are other fragments involving Rose and subsequently her sister Hazel, "Afterbirth" pieces them into a textual crazy quilt that includes further anthropological observations (133-4; 135; 136), a dictionary definition of the word "pla.cen.ta" ((137), a recipe for bread (137), and descriptions of incidents concerning other, apparently unrelated characters (Monica, 134; Eleanor, 134, Anne 138). There is even a journal entry that could serve as a metanarrative description: "July 5, 1990. I can't seem to finish Wittig. The progression is so non-linear I cannot hold onto the narrative thread" (138).

The narrative threads of "Afterbirth" have been deliberately severed to create non-linear discursive patterns. Juxtaposed to the first fragment of text, Rose's move from country to city in the second fragment is not the beginning of a short story but a rite of passage, like the ones described in the initial fragment, an instance of birth after birth. The word "nostalgic" links the two contrasting pieces of text together like a quilting thread.

In "Afterbirth" forgotten associations are recovered and reactivated. For example, the etymological note for placenta traces what seems to be a specialized medical term with its Greek root to its source in a homely metaphor: "flat cake, fr. Gk plakount-, plakous" (137), and this definition resonates through the text, reconnecting typically American women (having babies; baking cupcakes; reading books) to mothers in other cultures. We are tempted to borrow Deleuze and Guattari's term from *A Thousand Plateaus* and to say that associations spread rhizomatically in the text, except that this organic metaphor occults the impression of cutting and piecing that is also at work. Nevertheless, the text illustrates the rhizomatic capacity of words to reach out in many directions, allowing meaning to flourish and proliferate even after the connection to their sources has been severed.

The new compound "Nightbreak" from Adrienne Rich's eponymous poem is also an example of the patchworking process binding disparate experiences in equivocal conjunction. In commuting day into night, the poem's title manages to conjoin two normally opposed periods of time in one liminal moment. In the new compound the noun "break" is associated with opening as well as disruption, beginning as well as ending: "What breaks   is night / not day" (99). "Nightbreak" also suggests a nighttime feeling of anguish on the model of "heartbreak." It holds together disjunctive but related experiences in ambiguity. The poem is both an experience in dislocation and an effort at reconstruction, an attempt to accomplish both at the same time. The text is the outcome of a struggle to reach a compromise between antagonistic forces.

These patchworked texts have in common an attention to subjects or discourses that normally tend to be elided. They attempt to find a way to speak the unspeakable. In the aftermath of the Vietnam bombings, a different language is needed, one that in its otherness will disavow the "master" discourse. Describing the silence after the attacks on Vietnamese villages, "Nightbreak" adopts a discourse of negation:

> The enemy has   withdrawn
> between raids   become invisible
> there are
>   no agencies
>   of relief (99)

The words, "withdrawn," "invisible," "no agencies," point to an abandonment of responsibility that contradicts all possible ideological justifications. America can no longer claim to be a shining example: "the darkness becomes utter." Nevertheless, in this last affirmation, we can hear the trace of a new possibility, besides expressing complete obscurity, "darkness becomes utter[ed]," finding expression in the poem. "Nightbreak" thus announces a temporary end to silence and occultation.

Before new ways of existing can be envisaged, the dominant discourses have to be cracked open and exposed, as Salinger's short story also suggests. In "A Perfect Day for Bananafish," stereotypes are derided in the flippant title of the young woman's magazine article, "Sex Is Fun—Or Hell" (3), and in the dismissive reference to psychoanalysis, "They have to know about your childhood—all that stuff" (8). In their place, Seymour's story of the bananafish who swim into holes, gorge themselves on bananas, and finally die of banana fever seems to offer other insights into his malaise. Although in some ways it suggests an allegory, the story is too opaque, quirky, and difficult to tally with the elliptic account of the young man's life and death. In representing desire and greed, and linking them to a comically hyper-evident phallic symbol, the bananafish story refuses ready-made explanations or solutions.

The texts we have examined so far illustrate how patchworking permits a critique of standardized discourses. A final example, Robert Creeley's "The Movie Run Backward," will illustrate how the technique of juxtaposing scraps of text can make language reflect on itself, exposing both the familiarity and the strangeness of the words we take for granted. Deviating from the post-Romantic tendency to disavow the influence of models,[19] Creeley's poem exemplifies the dialogic nature of language. Since all discourses are composed of previous discourses, words do not belong to living speakers but seem to take on a life of their own: "just words. The people/ who wrote them are the dead ones." As speakers use and recycle words, they reappear in texts like: "birds returning,/ the movie run backward." Thus, the words of the poem we are reading are due to reappear in their turn: "The words will one day come/ back to you...." In fact, Creeley accelerates the process by quoting his own text, cutting the first stanza in pieces to create new lines:

"birds returning."

You can "run the movie
backward" but "the movie run
backward." The movie run backward.

Thus, the poem is haunted by its own discourse, rendering the normal, usually hidden processes of intertextuality both hyper-evident and strange, giving a dual meaning to the statement: "Nothing so strange in its talk,/

just words." For the poem insists that words are both not strange (because familiar, recurrent) and extremely strange (because they are the words of others, returning and lodging in different places). Excerpted from the first stanza and re-quoted in isolation in the third, the title phrase of the poem suddenly becomes ungrammatical and bizarre, giving a kind of autonomy and agency to an object. In patchworking his own text, Creeley renders what had seemed natural uncanny or *unheimlich*. The German word better expresses the way in which displacement produces Othering; nevertheless, the poem illustrates that words have no home, they are nomadic, always displaced from somewhere else and always in perpetual movement. Actually, mobility is shown to be another, unacknowledged component of meaning.

In addition to the discursive discontinuities we have considered so far in fissured and patchworked texts, another way of working against textual coherence is by interrupting chronological continuity. By disrupting the linear unfolding of a story or the temporal unity of a poem, writers can set in motion the Othering process. For Othering to occur, these interruptions have to do more than simply provide a disjointed but ultimately reconstructible form. They must work to undo conventional assumptions about temporality and so ultimately question the very notion of time as chrono-logic.

The fragments of Barbara Kingsolver's "Extinctions" may at first seem to use markers of time quite conventionally, but almost imperceptibly, suggestions emerge that time has stalled. The story opens with the protagonist, Grace, watching television with her husband Randall the evening before her departure for a family get-together at Easter. Prolepsis points forward to the main event of the story: "Tomorrow she and the boys have to drive a hundred miles to have dinner and go to church with her relatives" (169). Analepsis shifts back to earlier moments in the couple's past, giving a sense of their differences as characters, and of a problem in need of clarification:

> Ten years ago, when they were babies, she argued with Randall that crib death was real, that something really could happen. Now she knows it isn't rational to need to see, half a dozen times every night, the slight movement of their chests under the covers. Randall calls her a worrier. (169-70)

Already, this passage hints at an anomaly in time, although Grace's obsessive surveillance of her sleeping sons as if they were still babies, as if the ten years since their birth had not elapsed, could simply be dismissed as a nervous mother's over-anxiousness. Ellipsis could initially be seen as conventional in the story too; the two boys' ten years of infancy are elided in this passage simply because they are uneventful, as are the myriad details of quotidian life omitted in the gaps between the story's sections.

Once Grace arrives at her cousin's house, however, the problematic nature of time in the story becomes obvious. On the one hand, Grace seems to be suffering from an acute form of amnesia: "Large parts of her childhood just seem to erase themselves quietly while she's not looking" (171). On the other hand, for her relatives the past is so immediate that deictics are used in impossible ways to describe it: "There is some secret *here*" (174; my italics). The discrepancy centers on the return to the community of Nestor Beltrain, a childhood acquaintance. The family has collaborated in a conspiracy of silence that begins to break at the holiday dinner table:

'What do you mean, hung me.'
'From that old mulberry tree out *there*,' he says, pointing toward the window as if it were still there. *But this is a different house.*
....
'You two wasn't living *here* yet. I'm the one seen it....' (174-175 [our italics])

It emerges from the conversation that there are family stories connecting Nestor Beltrain to Grace, retold in such a way that they seem present to everyone except her, even to those who were not witnesses. The family's silences fit into a predictable cultural pattern of collaboration, of the tacit condoning of violence against women. After the first revelation, the past returns to Grace with a chilling immediacy: "The memory comes down on her like an ice storm, stiffening her to the center with cold rage" (179). This metaphor that conflates and confuses inside and outside illustrates the complexity of the story's representation of time. For victims of trauma, the past is not over and done with, neatly consigned to history; it is either elided or intensely present. Because chronology has become irrelevant, recollections of past horrors return to Grace in disordered fragments. Though these are incomplete and will probably never be completely recoverable, what seems important instead is for her to experience the immediacy of anger and to act accordingly. On Easter Sunday, Grace seems to realize that redemption is not to be found in the hypocritical observance of conventions, but in the refusal of false simulacra of harmony. Abruptly departing before the Easter service, she "braces herself for the road and drives for the light" (181).

Thus the protagonist of "Extinctions" remains in a liminal state at the end of the story, with mystery not fully revealed and resolution deferred. This is not simply the kind of open ending that projects an undisclosed but predictable conclusion (the rejection of the values of the family for those represented by the husband, for example); instead, the character remains in the dark, poised on the brink of discovery but not able to achieve it. The story substitutes an alternative temporality of Othering, as the disturbance of linear chronology opens up new connections across time. For example, Grace's tormentor, Nestor (named for a Greek general), is recalled as himself a victim of his military father's violence. Moreover, Grace's returning memories of childhood victimization are juxtaposed to images of endangered species—the pandas on the television program described in the story's opening paragraph and the whales decorating the walls of the elder son's room. The title "Extinctions" thus becomes polysemous: it refers to violence and its occultation; it associates dinosaurs, whales, and pandas with the cruelties both exercised and sustained by human beings. Values are no longer ranked and sorted and thereby dismissed; instead, light coexists with darkness, sorrow with illumination, forgetting with remembering. Finally, the central character seems to be moving toward a form of knowing that has not yet been defined, and that we can only rightly conceive of as Othering.

As in Barbara Kingsolver's "Extinctions," the treatment of time in Barry Lopez's "The Woman Who Had Shells" demonstrates both the conventional and Othering processes of interrupting. The narration begins in the present tense, describing the beach at Sanibel Island on a day in July: "The light is blinding" (79). In an unsurprising retrospective movement, "Here at dusk, one afternoon ..." (80), the narrator shifts back in time to the memorable event that triggers the story: his vision of a woman picking up shells. Though he does not speak to the woman, she remains in his thoughts, so that in the second segment of the text, after a six-month gap in narrative time, he recalls the vision in a very different setting: "That winter, on a beach frozen to stone I stood staring at the pack ice of the Arctic Ocean" (82). In the third segment of the text, he sees her in yet another setting: "In one of the uncanny accidents by which life is shaped, I saw the woman the following year in New York" (82). As sketched out so far, this resembles a fairly conventional love story in which the man could be expected to seduce the woman who is the object of his fascination. However, other indications of time and space in the story bring the usual linear, goal-oriented movement to a standstill.

First of all, since the story begins in the present at Sanibel Island and then describes an episode that occurred in the same place but at an earlier moment, the narrative seems to have a circular movement of arrival, departure and return. Nevertheless, the narrator describes a setting that denies the progression of time: "shells lying in such profusion that people unfamiliar arrive believing no one has ever been here" (79). When he describes his first vision of the woman, an event that would be at least two years earlier if mapped on a timeline, his words conflate past and present. The past becomes immediate, through the choice of the deictic "this": "It was into this moment ... that the woman stepped" (80). Time becomes something that can be sloughed off: "The afternoon trailed from me" (80). Similarly, in the second segment of the text, when the narrator evokes a second vision of the woman, chronological progression becomes blurred, as the present and past tenses refer to the same moment: "We carry such people with us in an imaginary way, proof against some undefined but irrefutable darkness in the world. The nimbus of that moment remained with me for months" (81-82). Finally, in the concluding lines of the story, as dawn breaks in the woman's New York apartment, two distinct times and places become one: "In that stillness I heard her step among the shells at Sanibel and heard the pounding of wings overhead and imagined it was possible to let go of a fundamental anguish" (86). Moments that would ordinarily be sharply differentiated and placeable—summer at Sanibel Island, winter in the Arctic Circle, as well as a subsequent winter in New York—become, in the narrator's hands, a single, enduring occurrence that not only precludes narrative development, but also calls into question the desirability of progression that is the fundamental premise of narrative. Paradoxically, the story moves forward only to celebrate stasis, centering on liminal moments and places, but not seeking to advance beyond these thresholds. Pictured at dusk or dawn, at the border between land and water, the woman becomes a mysterious figure whose effect on the narrator is inexplicable: "My respect for her was without reason and profound. I lay for hours unable to move. Whenever the urge to rise and dress welled up, a sense of the density of the air, of one thought slipping irretrievably off another into darkness overwhelmed me"(81). Poised between the "blinding" clarity and "darkness" that characterize the same moment, the narrative seems to be becalmed in unexplainable zones of mystery.

Even after a night of conversation with the narrator, the woman remains enigmatic and unnamed. Perhaps part of her attraction is suggested in the verb choice in the title, "The Woman Who Had Shells." She is not the one who collects shells, for any desire to possess is relegated to the past in the title. Indeed, when the narrator first sees her: "she had gone to pick up a shell, turn it in the white tropical light, feel the cusps and lines, and set it back" (84). On the beach at Sanibel Island she "took nothing and disappeared" (81). Apparently relinquishing possession, orientation toward a goal, and everything associated with time in a linear sense, she inspires the narrator's conclusion at the end of the story that "it was possible to let go of a fundamental anguish" (86).

In "The Woman Who Had Shells" time appears to be both interrupted and stationary, producing effects of both obscurity and overexposure. This paradoxical aesthetic quality is mirrored in the last shell the woman hands to the narrator: "like an egg, as white as alabaster and as smooth, save that its back was so intricately carved that my eye foundered in the detail" (86). Handled "like an egg" the shell promises to give birth to new understanding. Perhaps too, the description of the object offers a lesson in reading. The short story is like this dual object: timeless and inscribed in time, resistant to questioning in its circularity, and, at the same time, inviting scrutiny with its complexity. Rather than analysis, it asks for contemplation, perhaps even wonder.

By interrupting linear time the Othering text relativizes or disqualifies it and thus permits non-teleological configurations that allow the emergence of new values. For example, in Kimiko Hahn's "Afterbirth" the failure of linearity enhances the sense of collectivity and community in post-partum experience. A similar re-patterning occurs in Susan Minot's "Lust," whose non-linear configuration of fragments relays a personal perception of time and also parodies conventional characterizations of female sexuality. Time retracts into an infinitely repeatable cycle of "before" and "after," in which women are first visible and desirable then absent: "Then comes after. .... They turn gradually to look at you, distracted, and get a mild distracted surprise. You're gone. Their blank look tells you that the girl they were fucking is not there anymore. You seem to have disappeared" (17). In this new configuration, women occupy the typically masculine position of invisible viewer, but the associated privilege vanishes with the subject's erasure.

We have shown how interrupted narratives deny the linear time usually associated with (his)story, choosing to suspend time in order to suggest other modalities of existence, including living both in and out of time. The Othering narrative can even arrest time by interrupting it; indeed, Barry Lopez's "The Woman Who Had Shells" achieves the stillness usually associated with lyric poetry. As a matter of fact, there is a kind of inversion of generic expectations at work in the Othering process of interrupting, so that in poems, it can work against the lyric tendency to arrest the moment.

The title of John Ashberry's poem, "And I'd Love You To Be In It,"[20] seems to promise that the text will describe a space and a moment for the addressee (the beloved?) to inhabit. However, the poem moves forward in three disjunctive stages, and then backward, so that neither space nor time cohere. The first two stanzas describe "the wall" in the past tense; next, the third stanza describes "the floor" in the present tense, so that it seems disconnected from the wall; then, the final stanza shifts to the future, describing an undetermined, hypothetical space—"In what skyscraper or hut I'll finish?"—before coming back to the present and ending in the past: "And we are swiftly inside, the resurrection finished." Though this temporal fragmentation frustrates the longing for presence suggested in the title, it makes possible something else: a movement into the unknown that is hinted at in the title, which, with its shift in pronouns, transfers the speaker's longing for a person ("You") onto an unspecified "It."

In Ashberry's poem, the disjunction of time goes hand in hand with the fragmentation of space. The speaker does not employ language to relay a recognizable image of the world; the wall he evokes in the opening line— "Playing alone, I found the wall."—fails to cohere into a credible description:

> One side was gray, the other an indelible gray.
> The two sides were separated by a third,
> Or spirit wall, a coarser gray. The wall
> Was chipped and tarnished in places,
> Polished in places.

Colors that hardly seem different or even differentiable are contrasted: "gray," "an indelible gray" and "a coarser gray." Then the past participles—"chipped," "tarnished," and "polished"—seem to apply more to metal than to stone. Moreover, the line break after "third" seems to create a geometrical aberration—a wall that has three sides—until the remainder of the sentence depicts an even more bizarre entity, a wall haunted by "a spirit wall." The wall also seems endlessly long and at the same time short enough to touch "the two ends." Readers cannot be satisfied with a definite image; instead the imagination is left to search restlessly for something that resists conceptualization.

To add to the scene's complexity, in the second stanza, when the speaker, who initially seems to be a child amusing himself alone, outside, describes being "forced to lie on the floor." In this new position, he is both constrained ("There is still no freedom,") and exhilarated with a new sense of possibility: "excitement/ Turns in our throats like woodsmoke." The turning suggests that a new phase of movement has begun to transform a blocked situation. Almost imperceptibly another person has joined the speaker. The wall seems to give way to an open trellis supporting new growth, signs of Dionysian fertility: "there are tendrils/ Coming through the slats, and milky yellow grapes ..." Without allowing readers to find their bearings or fix a location, the poem ends: "A mild game to divert the doorperson/ And we are swiftly inside, the resurrection finished." It is as if the familiar world had to be erased or broken down, in order for change to occur. The "doorperson" (an avatar of Cerberus?) suggests the keeper of rational order who has to be tricked into dropping his guard so that the speaker and his companion (potentially the reader) can be admitted into some new state.

Both Kingsolver's "Extinctions" and, to a much more radical extent, Ashbery's "And I'd Love You To Be In It" illustrate the liberating potential of the rhetoric of disjunction. By interrupting the conventional structures of history, founded on time, space and continuity, writers create structures that shake the established order of things. In the Othering process, gaps metamorphose into breaks in the sense of openings onto other possibilities of existence. New meanings emerge from the spaces and fissures in texts.

Breaks permit the seepage of discourses other than those that can be suggested through the conventions governing implication. We can see the difference between the implicit of the system and the Othering breakthrough in Gayl Jones's short story "Persona." The story deals with a subject that was unspeakable in American culture before the Gay Liberation movements of the late sixties. The text contains an elliptical discourse about sexuality that circulates at the girls' college where the narrator teaches: "It seems as if some man would marry Miss King. She's a nice woman" (85), or: "Many young girls thought they were ... worried about their sexuality but ... they should not worry. Things would even out" (86). These coded statements deal with deviations from the norm, but only to reinforce conventional ideas about sexuality. The first instates marriage as the natural condition of "nice women." Thus, there is an unspoken suggestion that Miss King has some invisible flaw or vice. The second statement, from a psychiatrist's speech at a freshman orientation lecture, suggests that women's unspeakable desire for women represents only a temporary imbalance that will be corrected over time.

Correspondingly, ellipses in the conversations of the female characters match those in official discourse. Throughout the story, even the narrator speaks banalities or allows her conversation to trail off into silence:

> I wanted to say something, to get her talking, but . . . (88).
> I started to say something, but didn't (90).
> I said nothing (91).
> I wanted to say something. I still did not know what (91).
> I said nothing. She looked at me a moment smiling. She told me I looked tired. I smiled, but still said nothing (93).

I didn't answer. I felt far away (94).

This insistence on her own silence, and on the yawning gaps that it creates in conversation, makes the narrator seem almost autistic. The exaggerated repetition of negations and of the word "nothing" opens gaping holes in the text. As a counterpoint to the narrator's pregnant silences, a discourse of lesbian desire, strangely unattached to any speaker, filters from time to time through the gaps in the text. A passage in italics recounting arousal at a woman doctor's touch floats free:

> *And ... I couldn't help the way I felt when she put her hands there. A dark-haired lovely woman. She was pregnant. That made me feel tender toward her. She was very gentle and I ... It was so strange.* (86)

This discourse could be the narrator's own recollection or a fragment of an overheard conversation. Like another passage describing the only named character, a distant, beautiful student, it is strikingly different from the rest of the text: "Gretta? That's a strange name for a girl from the South. She's a violet. Or a sunflower. Or a chinaberry" (87). Poetic imagery and intensity of feeling flow out from these isolated lyric passages, permitting a welcome release from the strained reserve characterizing the rest of the text. A woman's desire for women breaks though the heavy silence, but it is never appropriated nor claimed by anyone; it floats free in the gaps and silences in discourse.

The voices that emerge in "Persona," and in other women's texts we have studied here are not simply subaltern borrowings from the discourse of the master; instead, they can be seen as another idiom or perhaps another form of being in language. This is most evident in Sanchez's "for our lady," which is built on hypothetical structures, conditional clauses, indirect questions and modal statements: "if someone," "if some blk/man," "what/kinds of songs," "what kinds of lyrics," "u/shud have been loved," "u wud have swung,", etc. It is as if the text of the poem were a question addressed to the blanks in the structure troping Billie Holliday's unfulfilled destiny. Twice in the poem the speaker uses the exclamation "yeh," one of the few linguistic segments that is end-stopped by a period, signifying that it is self-sufficient. This "yeh" could be a mark of approval or resignation; it is also, because of its repetition, a mark of perplexity. It could mean anything that the poet does not wish to consign to language. The blanks in the poem are spaces of compassion, but also intervals of incertitude and doubt; "ain't no tellen", with its revealing change in spelling (the –en superscripting the values of "told" on those of the former "tellin") sums up the impression of incompletion produced by the poem.

Yet this declaration does not conclude the poem. The last two segments signal a new direction for interpretation: "Where the jazz of yo / songs./ Would have led us." The poem could be perceived as a continuation of the songs that Billie sang, not just a homage to her art, but an accomplishment of her destiny.

The poem "for our lady" introduces a new form of music into the English language, a jazz melody signaled by the opening line: "yeh." Since it is one of the poem's few end-stopped lines, it marks a significant pause, yet this break, coming so early in the poem, seems to disqualify the flow of words before it starts, as if speaking were not so important as marking a form of assent to the music that precedes words. What follows is a forceful jazz-like composition that combines short, syncopated sequences with the interposition of brief, intensely charged pauses in which sound reverberates. Sanchez's poem recharges discourse through the infusion of rhythm, for example, the syncopation of the spondees: "blue / nite"; blk / man"; or through intertextual citations of jazz lyrics: "blue / nites"; "ain't no tellin"); or through choric refrains ("yeh. / billie." "yeh. billie."; "ain't no tellin," "aint no tellen"). The poem's gaps create silences that not only allow the reverberation necessary for the appreciation of the phrasing, but also open up space for readers' responses, claiming full participation.

In fact, one of the ways in which textual breaks demand participation rather than semantic appropriation is through the inroads they make into other artistic forms. We have just shown how poetry approaches jazz in "for our lady." Earlier we discussed how narrative crosses over into the lyric mode through temporal interruptions. Other works suggest parallels with the visual arts. Carson's "Sumptous Destitution" resembles the art of collage or patchwork, cutting and pasting texts to form a visual pattern as well as a new configuration of sense. Rich's "Nightbreak" with its evocation of "The frail clay lamps/ of Mesopotamia/ row on row under glass" creates a parallel between the poet's retrieval of buried fragments of memory and the archeologist's art of assemblage. Only Rich refuses to conserve or reconstitute shattered forms: "I don't/ collect what I can't use I need/ what can be broken." The poem is a broken and reshaped object that means more than a deceptive whole. With its highly unstable piecing together of expressionistic gaps and enhanced words, the poem becomes a verbal talisman against the threat of oblivion. Salinger and Kingsolver create diptychs in which the representation of one space or experience is juxtaposed to another. In "A Perfect Day for Bananafish," the oppressive atmosphere inside the hotel contrasts with the expansive freedom enjoyed on the beach. In the opening segment of "Extinctions," the television program on the destruction of pandas sets one form of violence in complex relation to another. In an equivocal mixing of values, Nestor Beltrain is linked with both the endangered species and their persecutors. He is both Grace's torturer and the victim of paternal abuse. Though as an adult he still afflicts others, his tyranny seems somehow obsolete. Endowed with the privilege of the pulpit, he addresses his congregation in the dead languages of the patriarchs (Hebrew and Latin). This complex identification suggests both the strength and brittleness of patriarchy, its persistence and its extinction. The story conveys a contradictory message of grief and hope: it mourns the damage done by "an attitude" (181) and, at the same time, represents a victim's refusal to drown "this rage .... Like an orphaned cat" (180). Of course, in literary texts, a significant difference from the visual model of the diptych emerges. The "reach" of words means that separate parts refuse to remain distinct, giving rise to limitless connections and crossovers in open and mutable patterns.

Meaning becomes intensely volatile in these fragmented texts, perhaps nowhere more than in Gass's parody of systems. Though the layout of "In the Heart of the Heart of the Country" suggests an orderly row of juxtaposed boxes or jars, each labeled with its contents, this neat arrangement turns out to be illusory. The first section entitled "MY HOUSE" deals not with the interior, but with the trees outside, "headless maples," whose tall stumps serve as a lookout post for observing the surrounding countryside (192). A subsequent section entitled "WIRES" elaborates on how the outdoor observation point is in fact enclosed by electric wires which "cross like a fence in front of me, enclosing the crows with the clouds. .... I am on my stump, I've built a platform there and the wires prevent my going out." Presented from the narrator's peculiar angle of vision, the outdoors becomes the indoors and vice versa, for in the subsequent section on the house: "Leaves move in the windows" (193). In this Othering text, normally separate categories blend and mutate, undoing conventional oppositions. In the two segments entitled "THE CHURCH," the sacred is gradually taken over by the profane; at first the church simply "has a steeple like the hat of a witch" (193), but when the same category reappears it contains a description of a gymnasium in which "the whole community" has gathered to celebrate not a mass, but "a basketball game" (222). In Gass's travesty of encyclopedic thinking, the Midwest is no longer an area on a map, but a place in the mind where anything becomes possible. In a telling example of how fragmentation works to create openings, the narrator concludes one description with the words: "And I live *in*" (198). On the one hand, the truncated sentence reactivates an earlier intertextual reference to Plato's *Phaedrus,* so that the narrator's placement marks a demotion to "the sixth sort of body, this house in B, in Indiana" (197); on he other hand, *in* suggests a privileged place allowing pure interiority, giving new significance to the text's title. Most important of all, the sentence places the reader in front of a kind of abyss, demanding a leap into the unknown.

In different ways, and in contrast to the ideal of wholeness that is promoted in conventional critical discourse, these texts use fragmentation in order to disrupt the system and to make openings for other values. Rather than disturbing some anterior state of wholeness to propose a new order, they expose the fictitiousness of completion. The authors studied here may employ devices such as punctuation, spacing, or ellipses, formal conventions that can be used to compensate the sequential nature of language and bring order and unity to writing, but they divert them from their usual purposes in order to fissure the text and to disrupt expected collocations. The resulting fragments are then pieced together in unfamiliar conjunctions, not to restore a sense of wholeness, for the ruptures are not concealed, but to create new possibilities in which apparently incompatible discourses resonate against one another. Finally, chronological continuity is radically interrupted, calling into question not only the linearity of time but also the values associated with it. Gaps in the text function both as holes that belie the system's pretensions to be all-encompassing and as openings onto Othering. Unlike tapestries, these texts do not bind textual strands together in a stable picture; instead their cut and broken threads suggest multiple potential patterns in which subject positions become exchangeable and meaning can circulate and mutate instead of being formulated and arrested. Genres no longer remain distinct; texts can hybridize with music or painting. Categories cease to remain fixed, as these fragmented texts destabilize the hegemonic beliefs about gender, time, or being that seem to be cultural givens. In these texts, form no longer contains, as in the model of the well-wrought urn; instead, it releases, allowing the advent of multiple and contradictory meanings.

Notes

[1] Hans-Jost Frey, *Interruptions* (Albany: State University of New York Press, 1996): 27-28. Frey arrives at this conclusion in a tightly reasoned argument: "Wholeness is the order in which everything has its place and in which nothing is missing or excessive. Inside the order of the finite whole everything is a part, which means that everything is recognizable in its relationship to the whole and is therefore read as a metonymy for the whole. But this storing of the parts in the whole is as satisfactory as the position of the whole is disquieting. The whole, if it is finite, is not all-encompassing and remains surrounded by everything that has no place in its order. As soon as this unmastered remainder against the claim to closure made by order is perceived, the question arises whether the finite whole is again, in its turn, part of a higher whole" (27).

[2] See for example Chapters 5 and 6 in Michael Hoey, *Patterns of Lexis in the Text* (Oxford: Oxford University Press, 1991).

[3] Ovid's *Metamorphoses* describes how in the Greek legend of Philomela, after Tereus has raped her and cut out her tongue, Philomela weaves the story of her violation onto a cloth that she sends to her sister Procne, who unrolls the cloth (like a scroll) and reads her sister's fate: "suae fatum miserabile legit."

[4] John Donne, *Poems of John Donne*, vol I. E. K. Chambers, ed. (London: Lawrence & Bullen, 1896) 12-13 ; Cleanth Brooks, *The Well-Wrought Urn: Studies in the Structure of Poetry* (London : Dennis Dobson, 1949).

[5] This is Michael Hoey's main thesis in *Patterns of Lexis in the Text*.

[6] M.A.K. Halliday and R. Hasan, *Cohesion in English* (London: Longman, 1976); quoted in Hoey 4-6.

[7] J. D. Salinger, "A Perfect Day for Bananafish," *Nine Stories* (Boston, Little, Brown, 1953) 3-18.

[8] Barry Lopez, "The Woman Who Had Shells," *Winter Count* (New York: Simon and Schuster, 1981; Vintage, 1999) 77-86.

[9] Gayl Jones, "Persona," *White Rat* (New York: Random House, 1977; Lawrenceville, New Jersey: Northeastern University Press, 1991) 83-94.

[10] Barbara Kingsolver, "Extinctions," *Homeland and Other Stories* (New York: Harper & Row, 1989) 168-181.

[11] Susan Minot, "Lust," *Lust and Other Stories* (Boston: Houghton Mifflin, 1989) 1-17.

[12] Kimiko Hahn, "Afterbirth," *Charlie Chan is Dead: An Anthology of Contemporary Asian American Fiction*, ed. Jessica Hagedorn (New York: Penguin, 1993) 132-140.

[13] William H. Gass, "In the Heart of the Heart of the Country, ." *In the Heart of the Heart of the Country, and Other Stories* (New York: Harper & Row, 1968).

[14] Adrienne Rich, "Nightbreak," *The Fact of a Doorframe: Poems, Selected and New, 1950-1984* (New York: W.W. Norton, 1984) 98-99.

[15] Sonia Sanchez, "for our lady," *The Norton Anthology of African American Literature*, eds. Henry Louis Gates Jr. and Nellie Y. McKay (New York: W.W. Norton, 1997) 1904.

[16] Anne Carson, "Sumptuous Destitution," *Men in the Off Hours* (New York: Alfred Knopf, 2000) 13.

[17] Though we do not agree with Wolfgang Iser's claim that all instances of intertextuality have this destabilizing effect, his description of the semantic polysemy arising from appropriations or rewritings of other texts certainly applies to Carson's poem: "Such a rewriting is a transgression of boundaries, and the fragments brought back from the inroads made into other texts are pitted against one another, thus erasing their contexts, canceling their meanings, and telescoping even what may be mutually exclusive." "What is Literary Anthropology," *Revenge of the Aesthetic: The Place of Literature in Theory Today*, ed. Michael P. Clark (Berkeley: University of California Press, 2000) 174.

[18] Emily Dickinson, "In many and reportless places" (Poem 1382), *The Complete Poems of Emily Dickinson*, ed. Thomas H. Johnson (Boston: Little, Brown, 1997) 593-94.

[19] See Harold Bloom, *The Anxiety of Influence: A Theory of Poetry* (New York, Oxford University Press, 1973).

[20] John Ashbery, "And I'd Love You to Be In It," *As We Know* (Harmondsworth, Middlesex: Penguin Books, 1979) 89.

CHAPTER FOUR

THE RHETORIC OF EXCESS

Our examination of fissured and fragmented texts in the preceding chapter showed how, in refusing the illusion of wholeness and making the gaps in discourse evident, writers create perplexing but suggestive disjunctions and heterogeneous juxtapositions. Thus, as well as drawing attention to gaps in meaning, the lacunae in the texts give, paradoxically, an impression of excess, redundancy, or irrelevance.[1] This tendency is particularly obvious in works like Susan Minot's "Lust," Kimiko Hahn's "Afterbirth," and William Gass's "In the Heart of the Heart of the Country," which combine visible gaps with a quasi-encyclopedic form of profusion. The distinction between the fragmented texts studied in Chapter Three and the expansive ones we will examine here is thus somewhat artificially imposed. Nonetheless, the separation of the two categories allows us to focus on how the rhetoric of excess is produced through the exaggeration of conventional figures and strategies of expansion.

In the Western tradition, as the opening stanzas of Ovid's *Metamorphoses* illustrate, the act of creation implies bringing order, rescuing substances from the raw, confused mass of chaos to produce unity and clarity. The idea that art creates order persists; we find it in Frost's description of a poem as "a momentary stay against confusion."[2] Nevertheless, this memorable phrase poignantly expresses the poet's awareness of the brittleness of the rampart holding back disorder. Indeed, his poems allow a glimpse of the confusion pressing at their borders, and at times, they permit its incursion. Thus, the formal unity of a familiar poem like "Stopping By Woods On A Snowy Evening" is apparently marred by the repetition of the last two lines,[3] although, at the same time of course, the poem is made memorable by it. The mystery and tension built up in the course of the poem concentrate in the haunting refrain, "And miles to go before I sleep," that recurs like a meditation, a mantra, a prayer, or a spell, summoning or holding off some unknown force. The speaker stands poised on the border of the woods, between the civilized and the wild, on the familiar, mapped line of the road but drawn by the uncharted space of woods; nevertheless, the incantatory repetition suggests that in his mind he has already entered a more primeval, chaotic state. Instead of stilling or staying the poem by providing it with a sense of closure, the final couplet introduces both an erratic movement, like the skipping of a needle in the groove of a record, and a sense of stasis, as the poem turns back upon itself. The speaker's language becomes opaque, since the repeated words seem to mean either more or less than they state. If, as we have seen in the previous chapter, fragmentation permits the incursion of Othering, dilation can have a similar effect. Repetition, amplification, and digression can destabilize the text, forcing it to accommodate what seems not to belong.

Conventionally, the recursive text disrupts the forward movement of writing in order to exert more control over meaning or effect. One of the basic strategies of communication, repetition is normally a means of clarification, emphasis, or emotional appeal. Yet, as illustrated in the final couplet of "Stopping By Woods On A Snowy Evening," repetition can also trouble clarity by pushing ordinary language into the realm of enigma. Both types of recursion appear in Kate Braverman's "Small Craft Warnings,"[4] a short story in which the homodiegetic narrator reminisces about the final months she spends with her grandmother, Danielle. On the one hand, the narrator uses repetitive parallel forms to represent the foundations of her mental world, so that some passages are built on the reiteration of simple sentence openers: "I thought .... I must have thought .... I lacked .... I lurched .... I knew .... I knew.... They dreamed .... They wanted .... I believed .... I believed .... I had .... I was thirteen" (6). These balanced repetitions lend a sense of order to a life that is far from conventional or structured. Indeed, the thoughts and impressions that they introduce are often lyrical and unreal. On the other hand, these attempts to organize chaotic experience contrast with the grandmother's quirkier repetitions. The first of these concerns Danielle's obsession with scented candles—"It was her season of fragrances and textures, she often said that" (1). The second is the phrase that she repeats on their final day together, and to which the narrator returns several times: "In the morning we sailed on the red-flagged, small craft warning harbor. "Hard a-lee!" Danielle cried, again and again" (16). Serving no conventional discursive purpose, the grandmother's repeated phrases become riddles demanding interpretation.

The fascination for "fragrances and textures" and the sailing term become pathways for the narrator to explore the enigma of Danielle's character. Indeed, the two recursions become intertwined as the narrator revisits her memories of the winter visit: "She had housewarmer candles in heavy squat glass vases, and she would lean over them as they burned, breathing the vanilla smell deep into her body. I thought of exotic cargoes in the holds of ships, mangoes and Chinese vegetables in colors like glazed violet and cerulean. That's how she was taking the odor into her lungs, like she was a vessel containing it" (5). Remembering her grandmother as a vessel, the narrator associates her with the small craft in which they sail on their last day together, so that rather than demanding that extraneous associations be suppressed in the process of reading, the text activates multiple definitions and connotations of the word "vessel" simultaneously. A container for the sensuous experiences she craves, Danielle is not only rich and full, but also tainted and damaged by her openness: "My grandmother's voice was hoarse, rough edged, like she had opened her mouth to too much wind. It was a throat things had blown into, autumn leaves the red of maples in abrupt transit, leaves russet and auburn. And rocks, and the residues of olive and almond trees with their sweet and subtle scents" (6). Subtly, the idea of the vessel as a ship recurs here in the evocation of wind and exotically scented wood. Yet added to that, through the dead leaves and "residues," is the association with unclean flesh (the sexually experienced woman as a polluted vessel). Later, in a punning recursion of the word, the narrator states: "the vessels were collapsing. Her cargo would be trapped" (11). Though the word "vessels" denotes the weakened arteries of the aging woman, it also permits the return of the ship metaphor.

As the narrator recalls the words her grandmother shouts into the wind in her final courageous voyage, "Hard a-lee!" becomes "Heartily," connecting the old woman's receptiveness to experience with her imminent death. At first, the phrase portends mortality: "I thought she was saying "heartily," and somehow talking about her heart, how it was dissolving in her chest cavity, how it was beating erratically, how it was somehow fading like stamps on an old passport" (12). However, when the narrator returns to the same phrase later in the narrative, the connotations change, so that the grandmother's heart appears like a dangerous harbor: "I thought she was talking about her heart, how there were waves in it, channels, eddies, sandbars, places where you must post triangular warning signs" (16). In a final recursion, a new interpretation offers a loving tribute to the old woman's freedom from convention: "Certainly she was talking about her heart and how it belonged to the sea and the wind and the fluid elements, tattooed and unfading ..." (17). The text becomes freighted with a rich cargo of metaphors that, rather than bringing clarity, produce ambivalence, bringing opposites together to suggest disease and vitality, refuse and opulence, mortality and eternity.

On the one hand, as we have just shown, repetition can overload words with significations, introducing ever-burgeoning chains of associations. On the other hand, it can also evacuate meaning from words. This is the result produced in Gayl Jones's short story, "Your Poems Have Very Little Color In Them."[5] The polar opposite of Braverman, Jones writes without color, emptying her prose of images or adjectives, and then amplifying the resulting flatness of tone through repetition. In this short story that is little more than an account of a very tedious evening on a college campus, the narrator communicates in a style that, paradoxically, combines redundancy with extreme economy to simulate the triteness of social interaction. The first part of the text describes various exchanges mainly through indirect discourse and extreme concision: "The man in the corner with the beard isn't saying anything now. Once he was standing talking, once he even talked to me, but I didn't know very much to say to him" (18). The sentences have the repetitive simplicity of a reading primer, but rather than producing clarity, they communicate nothing at all about the reported conversations. Whether people talk or not in this story, they say very little. Narrative recursion only stresses the futility of interaction: "There are two kinds of people, those who don't talk and those who can't talk. .... There are some people who can't talk or don't talk or don't know what to say. These are the people you have to get to know. They are sometimes very nice people too" (18). This variation on the clichéd division of "people" into two groups parodies the content of social discourse, exposing its vacuity, yet in repeating the same phrases, making the hollow words echo, the narrator gives that emptiness weight and heft, making it oppressive, transforming words into obstacles to communication and silence into something meaningful.

Another kind of repetition, perhaps linked indirectly to Jones's title, occurs when the narrator describes her past habit (discontinued when her companions became bored) of "making up funny songs and telling funny stories to the girls in the dorm" (18). Her songs and stories offer the only hint of race in this story by an African-American writer, since they include one of the earliest and most common Delta Blues songs ("Make me a palette on your floor."). The narrator runs through her repertoire in a kind of minstrel act made up of rhyming nonsense verse and folk anecdotes. Independent of the meaning of the words, the songs' repetitions communicate a beat and a mood. In contrast to the oppressively empty recursions discussed earlier, the rhythmic verses animate the text, breaking the oppressive monotony. They recall the *ritournelles* (refrains or jingles) that Deleuze and Guattari describe in *Mille Plateaux* as ways of claiming territory or warding off chaos.[6] There is potentially a causal link between the analeptic reference to the silencing of this folk music and the narrator's present inability to find a voice. Still, neither form of discourse represented in the text has any informative function. Thus the short story unfolds in the area where language borders, on the one hand, nonsense and, on the other, silence, opening up a disquieting communicative void.

Associating recursion with music allows us to see these narratives in a new way. Refusing linear structure, they follow looping patterns, returning to restate familiar melodies, themes or rhythms. While Jones imitates spare blues refrains, Braverman's composition is more like a sonata. In "Small Craft Warnings" the narrator recounts variations on the past, following the spiraling pattern of memory. The recurring lexical chains appeal all the more strongly to the imagination in their failure to produce unitary patterns of sense.

Another common feature of language that can produce the effect of excess is metaphor. Of course, embellishment is one of the features that give art its special cultural status, and insofar as it exceeds the requirements of conveying information, all literary language could be deemed semantically redundant. In the rhetoric of excess found in Othering texts metaphor is elaborated well beyond its usual function of clarifying one domain through analogy with another.[7] Metaphor produces an Othering effect when it goes beyond its ornamental or expressive functions in order to indicate something that has no name in the system.

In the passages from "Small Craft Warnings" examined above, metaphor supplants description, speech or acts to become a means of defining character. The narrator begins the portrayal of her grandmother by quoting her mother's dismissal of her as "merely corrupt and sociopathic" (1). Though reductive, this characterization of the opium-smoking woman with a history of inappropriate lovers would probably find a consensus. Subsequently, though, the narrative demands a revision of this judgment through the elaborately developed and shifting metaphor associating Danielle with a vessel: a container for fire and fragrance (1), for refuse (6) or "sacred food" (5), but also a ship traveling to exotic harbors (5) and braving storms (11), and finally, a free and generous heart (17). In Braverman's writing, metaphor takes the place of other forms of expression and becomes a poetic form of thought that liberates her characters from conventional stereotypes or definitions. In fact, metaphor becomes a way to undefine character, allowing the narrator to claim for Danielle: "her own angle … her own spin" (2).

In a more radical attempt to name the unnamable, amplification through simile allows C.K. Williams to associate multiple referents to the invisible, intangible "something," that is the subject of his poem,

"Halves."[8] This poem combines many of the features of the rhetoric of Othering, using indexicals and repetitions to identify the ineffable "it" that the speaker is searching for:

> I am going to rip myself down the middle into two pieces
>   because there is something in me that is neither
>   the right half nor the left half nor between them.
>   It is what I see when I close my eyes, and what I see.

With the repeated negations (the "neither ... nor" of the lines quoted here, but also lines 5-6, "neither ceiling/ nor floor, not space, light ...," and lines 13-14, "neither before me/ nor after, not up, down ..."), the speaker dismisses the binary logic that divides up the world into neat patterns of opposed contraries. He is searching for a way to express what lies outside the area mapped out in the mind through language. After dismissing what "it" is not, he nevertheless insists, "it is quietly here...."

To find words to express the inexpressible, the speaker makes use of simile (almost as if true metaphor would make too forceful a claim to define the indefinable). If the piling up of negations proclaims the impossibility of revealing "it," the extravagant series of similes begin to suggest a way:

> It is like the dense, sensory petals in a breast
> that sway and touch back. It is like the mouth of a season,
>
>   the cool speculations bricks murmur, the shriek in orange,
>   and though it is neither true nor false, it tells me
>   that it is quietly here, and, like a creature, is in pain;
>   that when I ripen it will crack open the locks, it will love me.

Of course, these similes do not simply refer back to the mapped, known world. Instead they make original lexical connections that produce strange, dreamlike images projecting us beyond the system. Human body parts become sensuously animated like aquatic plants; concepts, objects, and colors are given voices, so that the familiar world becomes alive with infinite possibilities. Finally, the action of splitting is reclaimed; from a divisive binary operation it become an organic process of ripening and opening to otherness. The "I" fractures and disperses in order to make room for something else, so that in place of the "Halves," we can imagine the "Haves," those who are not divided by the choices imposed by the system.

In the Othering process, we are not confronted with the familiar literary device of extended metaphor, but with mutating metaphor. The idea expressed in the Greek root of the word for carrying over or beyond conveys a particular sense in the rhetoric of Othering, for metaphor becomes the vehicle that transports thought beyond the conventional limits of language, permitting potentially unlimited associations. Margaret Gibson's "Burning the Root" can serve as an illustration.[9] The poem deals with an erotic cliché from "a blue movie"—a couple making love in front of the fireplace. Metaphor allows, first and foremost, a movement away from the visual cliché, so that the burning cedar becomes, in the transmuting fire: "a splay of staghorn put to the torch.../ ... a relic of Georgia O'Keefe's." The association with the artist embellishes the scene, but it also permits the speaker to gain aesthetic detachment from what she is describing, as suggested by the last line of the poem's first stanza: "We distance ourselves from the cedar's simple wood ...". The stanza break associates this distance both with the subsequent description of the couple literally moving back from the fire's heat, and with the poem's departure from the literal through metaphor. This initial distancing opens up a space for transformation. The couple become "shape-changers," [10] not simply because they are engaged in the contortions of sexual intercourse, but because imagination permits them to see differently. The woman imagines her partner as a burning stag, again turning a cliché about male sexuality into a vibrant erotic image: "you burn there,/ fire licking your horn, your fine fur." In a trope that captures the interactivity and contagiousness of desire, the lover is burning and burnt by the erotic caress. So far, the poem still plays with the conventions of erotic verse. However, rather than linking the imagery together in a unified conceit which elaborates on a single concept, the rhetoric of excess that produces Othering both multiplies and dissociates metaphorical chains so that a vehicle can be coupled with a new tenor. The setting changes from a domestic interior to "a saracen plain, [where] a cedar root turned/ sacrificial ram on the spit ...." Such a transformation introduces a final dimension of metaphor in the Othering process: it brings volatility to the text, so that words and images begin to change places with one another. The lovers burn like the cedar, taking on the shapes glimpsed in the flaming logs. Afterward, the sleeping pair internalize the fire, keeping their "secrets/ smoking, banked down deep," until, in the final stanza the smoldering fire transmits to the couple an image from a pornographic movie, "the smoke a curl of contempt/ in the wind, not unlike the smoke of a cigarette/ held to a bound woman's nipple." Through their superabundance and instability, these mutating metaphors evoke the violence and mystery of sacrificial acts that have been trivialized by pornographic commercialization and overexposure.[11]

Charles Simic's "The Stream" offers a more extreme example of the way in which metaphorical divagation allows readers to venture beyond the confines of the representational system.[12] Like Gibson, Simic builds on familiar conventions of literature and clichés of language; nevertheless, in "The Stream" these points of departure have become almost unrecognizable. The title, together with the sinuous displacement of the subject from stanza to stanza, suggests that the eponymous stream is not simply a body of water, but also the stream of consciousness, the metaphor used by William James to describe the flow of inner experience, taken over as a term for a modernist literary technique.[13] The poem follows the random thoughts of an insomniac, whose "night long" meditation takes him through a strange, oneiric landscape to a body of water. Thought allows the speaker to project himself elsewhere: "Summoning me/ to be/ two places at once…" (152). Language itself dictates the trajectory, beginning with the poem's very strange opening stanzas:

> The ear threading
> the eye
>
> all night long
> the ear
> on a long errand
> for the eye

A punning association between the eye as organ of sight and the hole in a needle apparently suggests the verb "threading." The lines suggest how the ear works together with the eye, associating words with images to create imaginary landscapes. So the ear "on a long errand" serves as a scout or pathfinder, picking out the trails through language for the eye (and of course the I) to follow. These pathways lead "over no man's land," territory that is unoccupied because it is no more than a construct of the mind.

The transmutations in Simic's metaphorical journey are achieved because conventional connections between tenor and vehicle have been loosened. Normally, the mind journeys through language like a stream within its banks, guided, perhaps even constrained, by the metaphorical associations that have accrued in the system. In Simic's poem, though, the mind both pictures a rivulet of water and progresses in the flow of interior language, bringing the speaker to: "the brink—/ as it were/ of some deeper utterance" (153). Freed from the obligation to refer to the material world, words float through the poem like wonderful and menacing fish in the stream of thought: "luminous verb/ carnivorous verb" (153).

The polysemy of words and their placement within different lexical networks permit the poem to meander in surprising directions. "Stream" carries with it a lexical connection to "brink," and this liminal spatial position evokes in its turn a threshold in time: "at daybreak." In Simic's hands, the arbitrary semantic system, usually controlled by rigorous editorial policing to eliminate extraneous associations, is used to make words perform in new ways. Freed by the rhetoric of Othering their usual attachment to referents and habitual collocations, words and images mutate into new contexts, producing hitherto unimaginable ideas. The word "brink" allows a place to become a time, just as the "long" of "her long skirt" changes from a measurement of space to one of time: "trailing/ a bit longer" (154). Removed from their structural placement in the system and transformed through their association with other lexical networks, words gain the dynamic force to found a new poetic world situated "on the brink," or in "no man's land," a terrain that is neither established nor claimed, but always in flux, in the process of becoming.

Since words are bound to be repetitions of the already spoken, it is difficult to prevent them from reiterating the already thought; nonetheless, the incursions of excess that we have studied so far have the effect of derailing language from its predictable tracks. The texts thus resist the tendency that George Orwell berates in his famous essay, "Politics and the English Language," that condemns speakers for using: "phrases tacked together like the sections of a prefabricated henhouse."[14] In fact, the "abuses" that Orwell attributes to specific political tendencies derive just as much from the normal workings of the machinery of language. To imagine that we choose words "for the sake of their meaning,"[15] is, to a great extent, an illusion. Words also choose each other and choose us, assembling themselves in our speech into configurations that are already scripted in the linguistic system. Their predictability operates as much within texts as in individual sentences. Thus Orwell's essay deals with meaning and meaninglessness, social conditions and political orators, dead metaphors and worn out clichés. He does not digress into other subjects like animal husbandry, gardening, or travel. To do so would be to breach discursive decorum. Habitually, the introduction of given themes or topics generates certain expectations about their outcomes. Excursions into description, anecdote, or memory normally serve a purpose, even if it is only the pleasurable deferral of the conclusion; however, they are not expected to detract from the general orientation of the text. When pursued to excess—to the point where the text's center or goal no longer holds up—digression becomes an Othering tactic. Digressions become "lines of flight" understood as fields of divagation. They create new departures, deflecting the text from its expected goal, or they make it expand at its periphery, pushing it off-center.

Events in a narrative structure conventionally unfold toward a resolution or denouement. The threads of the story unravel to bring complication to an end in revelation and the return of order. John Yau's prose poem, "A Gargoyle in the Garden" works in the opposite direction. It has some of the outward features of a narrative, except that what at first appears to be a progressive structure turns out to be radically digressive. The text is composed of three prose paragraphs. It begins, like a conventional narrative, with a descriptive passage that apparently sets the scene and introduces characters: "Around noon the women began strolling on deck, their lace dresses stretching tightly from the fifth rib to the bruised thigh."[16] The setting is obviously a ship, as the words "deck" and later "hull," "ocean," and sails" confirm. If this text were to follow the conventions of narrative, we would expect that the speaker's initial attention to the women's torsos would lead to some kind of development; the lace seems to cover bodies that have been subjected to violence, so that we wonder about the cause.[17] The subsequent descriptive details—the sun, the odors, the sounds and colors—seem to mark a pause before the narrative moves on to the crucial events that lead to a denouement. The analepsis beginning the second paragraph adds to the suspense: "We had been waiting all night, tilted back and forth by the ocean's smooth blue muscles." At the same time, the poetic current in the text moves it in a radically different direction from conventional narrative.

The text proceeds to invert the usual values, and digression in the narrative becomes central, or rather, distinctions between the essential and the peripheral become blurred. The associative logic of metaphor takes over from the causal logic of narrative. The narrator progressively gives increased agency to the setting through personification:

> The ocean gently slapped its mirages against the sides of the hull. Orange sails dangled like curtains in an open window.
> We had been waiting all night, tilted back and forth by the ocean's smooth muscles. (26)

At the same time, the protagonists gradually lose the power to act. First they are infantilized by the action of the waves. The ship becomes: "A giant cradle rocking helplessly beneath the hapless stars." By the final paragraph, the narrator has been transformed into an inert object:

> And perhaps I was even unlucky to survive. For that is how I got to be a
> gargoyle in the garden. A monumental mass. A hideous lump waiting and
> watching. Pondering the next impossible step.

Usually an excrescence on an imposing edifice, the gargoyle occupies
center stage at the end of this oddly shaped prose poem. It would be easy
simply to dismiss the text as a whimsical piece of comedy. There is humor
in the final situation: the gargoyle seems to inhabit its unaccustomed place
in the garden to provide the title's combined assonance and alliteration;
moreover, the revelation that the narrator claims to be this grotesque
ornamental figure moves the text into the realm of nonsense. Nevertheless,
suggestions of violence and fairy-tale transformation tease the mind into
trying to make sense of its pseudo-narrative structure. Progressively
though, readers' interest in following the story to its denouement gives
way to fascination with the strangely mutating scenario.

In place of the climax or clarification that we would expect in a
narrative, the prose poem ends with a situation that is parodically blocked;
the narrator has turned to stone. He arrives at this impasse through an
abrupt and self consciously literary change in the setting:

> I still remember the hair, wet and taunting, floating to the surface like gray
> porcelain hearts; I still see the smiles hovering above us. Yet perhaps I
> peered through the curtains once too often, so that what I am really
> remembering is an opera I once heard in Florence.

The shipwreck has become a memory that may itself be fictional—a scene
from an opera. A figure of speech ("orange sails . . . like curtains") effects
the scene shift, allowing the narrator to move from the ship to the theatre
to the garden. Language carries out transformations that would be
impossible in reality. The speaker in the text performs wonders, but in so
doing, he consents to be a hollow conduit, devoid of substance, like a
gargoyle "waiting and watching" for rain. Conjuring with illusion, Yau
exposes the artifice of literature for readers' consideration.

As we have seen in "A Gargoyle in the Garden, digression works hand
in hand with convention in the Othering text, soliciting readers to make
sense of emergent form and formlessness. A double movement is at work,
with the unfolding of a central problem being accompanied by apparently
unnecessary divagations toward the periphery. We will see how, in Denis
Johnson's "The Rockefeller Collection of Primitive Art,"[18] Dan Chaon's
"Prosthesis"[19] and Russell Banks's "Searching for Survivors,"[20]
digressions undo distinctions between margin and center, or to use a
metaphor from the visual arts, between foreground and background. The

effect in these texts is rather like that of the ambiguous visual image devised by the Danish Gestalt psychologist, Edgar Rubin. In his famous figure white and dark space occupy equal proportions of the page, making it difficult for viewers to decide whether they are seeing a vase or two silhouetted profiles. Othering texts create a different kind of ambiguity because in reading, perception cannot be instantaneous. Still, the digressive text disturbs the pattern-forming process of interpretation, breaking pre-existing conceptual molds, and forcing us to see double.

Like John Yau, Johnson, Chaon, and Banks choose titles that privilege part of the work, placing the rest at the periphery, even though this may seem contrary to the organization of the text. Johnson's "The Rockefeller Collection of Primitive Art" begins with a description of the sound of the neighbors making love, and it returns to the couple in the last stanzas. Primitive art is mentioned in only a few lines of the 44-line poem; it may be positioned at the center of the text (lines 20-22), but the speaker's attention is apparently elsewhere most of the time. Readers may wonder whether the love-making is a distraction from the real subject or whether it is not, in fact, the poem's main concern. Dan Chaon's "Prosthesis" creates a comparable problem of emphasis between background and foreground. The short story begins with a description of the protagonist Suzanne, a forty-year-old married woman, helping a man with a prosthetic arm in the library (153-4). The description of this meeting leads, inexplicably, to the narrator's declaration: "It was said that her former lover had been badly disfigured in a fire" (154). Subsequently the narrative focuses on Suzanne's memories of the unnamed burn victim as well as on her interaction with her husband (also unnamed). The narrator returns only fleetingly (for two paragraphs) to the first man: "For several weeks, perhaps almost a month, she was in love with the man with the prosthetic arm. That is to say, she began to think of him regularly, a slow, romantic ache opening up inside her" (158). Although she fantasizes about "the curved metal" of his prosthesis, there is no reason given for her interest: "She was at a loss to explain it, the power of this image" (158). The story thus seems to emphasize what is peripheral, leaving readers no wiser than the protagonist about the prominence accorded the prosthesis. Russell Banks's "Searching for Survivors" seems similarly disproportionate. Most of the story deals with the narrator's memories of his adolescence, and at its center there is the account of an unsatisfactory reunion with an old friend; however, at the beginning and end, the narrator muses on the fate of the explorer, Henry Hudson. The title apparently refers to the long lost adventurer, because at the end, the narrator imagines driving a dogsled to Hudson Bay to look for "signs that Hudson had made it to shore" (5).

Once again, the reasons for the protagonist's obsession remain unelucidated, and the importance given to the long dead explorer appears exaggerated. Each of these digressive texts seems to circle a subject, unable or unwilling to pin it down. Apparently, something escapes them or remains beyond them, while the inessential fills the gaps.

Of course, in interpreting these texts, we are tempted to give them a center or to recenter them, to identify the main subject or to establish connections between different threads, thereby turning divagations into purposeful progressions. For example, we could take the title of "The Rockefeller Collection of Primitive Art" as diversionary tactic to cover up the speaker's overriding interest in the lovemaking going on beyond the walls. We might even question the claim to carnal knowledge, since it seems overstated: ""I'm only a spinster,/ I'm not a virgin. I have made love. I have known desire" (141). The reminiscence about "follow[ing] desire through the museums" (141) might suggest that the claim to knowledge is spurious, and the excursion through the collections, the museum restaurant and "out beyond Coney Island" might simply be a detour before arriving at the real object of fascination, the lovers next door: "I think of them always" (142). Similarly, in "Prosthesis" Suzanne's fascination with the young man with the prosthetic arm and the narrative recursions to him and to the former lover who had been disfigured in a fire could be seen as representing escapist flights from her marriage. Her marital difficulties are conveyed only fleetingly, in a shift of internal focalization to her husband: "He stood smiling as she disengaged her key from the door, hopeful and helpless in the stream of whatever had been happening to them lately. He did want to change things, or at least to slow what had begun to seem inevitable" (155). Suzanne's wandering thoughts could be taken as an indication of her unwillingness or inability to address her marital problems. Finally, in "Searching for Survivors," readers could build on the narrator's admission following his brief encounter with his boyhood friend: "for a second I thought I felt lonelier than I'd ever felt before" (4), and attribute his fascination for Henry Hudson to unresolved grief over the passage of time and loss of past attachments. Such psychologizing interpretations neatly dispose of the troubling incongruities in these texts by attributing them to the protagonists' maladjustments. They account for the digressions by evacuating the texts' elaborate strangeness. They draw on conventional structures of thought in order to explain away the unconventional, reconverting Othering tactics by drawing on strategies elaborated within the system.

In fact these divagations toward what seems to be peripheral or inessential lead us to recognize that some forms of knowing are unavailable through the system. Denis Johnson's poem "follow[s] desire" from the easily imaginable lovemaking next door, "through the museums," to an unexplainable dead-end (or an opening into mystery) in, among other places, the Rockefeller Collection of Primitive Art. Museums are initially places of knowledge and control, where one proceeds toward instruction. Visitors are classified and accounted for just like the objects in a museum, so that the speaker progresses "along the clicking ascent/ of numerals in the guards' hands." Arriving at the museum restaurant, "where the natural light was so unnatural/ as to make heavenly even our fingernails and each radish," she experiences a series of epiphanies: "I saw ...,/ I saw ...,/ and I heard .../ saw . . ." (141). This list of revelations is interrupted by a mark of ellipsis that suggests it could continue indefinitely, and a new stanza introduces a series of questions:

> Why are their mouths small tight circles,
> the figures of Africa, New Guinea, New Zealand,
> why are their mouths astonished kisses beneath drugged eyes,
> why is the eye of the cantaloupe expressionless
> but its skin rippling with terror,
> and out beyond Coney Island in the breathless waste
> of Atlantia,
> why does the water move when it is already there? (141-142)

At the center of the poem, then, is an avowal of puzzlement rather than understanding. The Rockefeller Collection of Primitive Art houses enigmas that are not to be resolved. They are paradoxical figures of lassitude and energy, impassivity and emotion, stasis and movement, which tax the speaker's conceptual powers to their limits. Finally the poem rejects illumination for the darkness that frees the imagination: "it is the dark that lets us it is the dark" (142). Yet, as the repetition of "dark" in this chiastic phrase suggests, the real objects of fascination are those that remain obscure: "I can imagine them then/ why can't I imagine this?" (142). The recurrence of a question mark in this final line recalls the poem's other questions, suggesting that the lovers ("them") are indeed peripheral to the poem and that its real concern is the mysterious "this" (like the "it" in Creeley's "Halves") beyond the reach of knowledge.

In "Prosthesis" the narrative focuses on events whose outcome is singularly inconsequential. However, it is this very inconclusiveness that makes them the object of the protagonist's attention. Suzanne is drawn to no longer viable possibilities for connection: "Something might have happened, then [in the library] "(159); the burned ex-lover "might have once made her pregnant" (156). On her desk she has a picture of her father who "no longer exists" holding her infant son who "has long disappeared into his own thoughts and feelings" (158). Like Johnson's poem, Chaon's short story focuses on questions for which there are no answers. Suzanne is "at a loss to explain" her fascination with the young man with the prosthesis. Looking at her husband, she wonders: "What if they'd never met?" (159). She asks whether if she had not jumped off a haystack with her high school lover: "would there have been a fire? Would there, instead, be a grown-up child, another husband, another life? How many people are forever different, how many people ceased to exist every time she turned one way rather than another?" (159). These questions reconfigure what had seemed to be narrative digressions as paths showing the way to the intangible or the irrecoverable. They give rise to a meditation on what lies outside the familiar grids of time and space according to which stories are plotted. The digressions lead to unknowable outcomes that are similar to those imagined in chaos theory in the example of the "Butterfly Effect." But rather than being reassuringly mastered by scientific discourse, the uncertain and unaccomplished past is presented in the short story's powerful conclusion as an electrifying and terrifying force: "she could feel the pulse of other choices, other lives, opening up beneath her. Her past crackled behind her like a terrible lightning, branches and branches, endless, and then nothing" (159). In these closing lines the questions raised in the text are answered obliquely through metaphors. Missed possibilities, encountering one another like tectonic plates or splitting the sky like an electric storm, end in a gaping void or a very pregnant "nothing" that opens onto Othering.

In "Searching For Survivors," the narrator's long, fanciful meditations on Henry Hudson also lead to the irrecoverable. He dwells on the unrealizable or the imaginary, pretending that it is "as if" he had accompanied the explorer himself on his last journey (1), and finally dreaming of driving a team of sled dogs toward Hudson bay, "into the timeless, silent whiteness" (5). Like Chaon's protagonist, Banks's narrator ruminates on what has disappeared. The image of Hudson and his boat vanishing into the ice-bound bay frames the text. First the narrator envisions his departure: "a black speck on the sheet of white-rimmed lead behind us" (1); then he imagines "Hudson and his three loyal sailors ... dragging the shallop filled with their dwindling supplies all the way across the endless, silent ice pack" (5). This final image opens out onto infinity, suggesting both a threat of oblivion and a realm of infinite possibility.

These digressive narratives move via memory or fantasy toward that which eludes vision and consciousness. They cross the borders between history and fiction, recollection and invention, in order to go beyond what is predictable or known. Their divagations violate narrative or poetic decorum in order to create the conditions for Othering.

The rhetoric of Othering that we identify in this chapter and the two preceding ones does not involve inventing a new language; instead writers employ recognizable grammatical features or rhetorical figures and distort or exaggerate them to make words work otherwise, to allow them to escape habitual modes of thought. Figures that generally work toward clarification or elaboration are used excessively so that they have the opposite effect of promoting indeterminacy or even evacuating sense. Conventional forms of elaboration inevitably reformulate notions that are already contained within the system. These writers use an unconventional rhetoric of excess in order to point toward that which has no name. Instead of moving toward revelation, they move toward obscurity, to the outer edges of language and thought. Meaning is never fixed in these texts; instead repetition, amplification, and digression set it in motion, setting off a process of infinite reformulation. Redundant, recursive patterns break with the linear, goal-oriented directionality of writing, introducing spiraling movement and music-like variations. These patterns create confusion about what is central and what is peripheral, undoing such distinctions. The rhetoric of excess overshoots the subject as topic, seeming to miss the mark in the conventional sense, but aiming at something else outside the conventional. Excess is neither an ornament nor an excrescence, but an admission of the insufficiency of words. Often deriding conventional formulae (as shown in the texts by Jones, Braverman, Gibson or Simic, for example), these texts suggest that language is inadequate or frustrating because it simply rehearses what has already been thought or said. Through the rhetoric of excess Othering texts reclaim words for the new purpose of indicating what lies beyond them.

Notes

[1] Frey reaches the same conclusion in *Interruptions*: "The text from which something is missing does not supply what would be required to understand it. So long as something remains unrelated, there is too little there. But one can say just as well, inversely, that the fragmentary text contains too much. The elements in it that cannot be related to anything and therefore are not meaningful are superfluous. It is this superfluous quantity that makes it impossible to conceive the text as a whole. So the deficiency in meaning is at the same time, if one looks at it differently, an excess of signs" (50).
[2] Robert Frost, "The Figure a Poem Makes" (1939), *Selected Poems of Robert Frost* (New York: Holt, Rinehart, and Winston, 1963) 2.

[3] The rhyme scheme is broken in the last stanza by the repetition of the line, "And miles to go before I sleep"; this produces the pattern aaba bbcb ccdc dddd.

[4] Kate Braverman, "Small Craft Warnings," *Small Craft Warnings* (Reno, Nevada: University of Nevada Press, 1992) 1-17.

[5] Gayl Jones, "Your Poems Have Very Little Color In Them," *White Rat* (New York: Random House, 1977; Lawrenceville, N..J.: Northeastern University Press, 1991) 17-21.

[6] *Mille plateaux* 368 and 382-383.

[7] Cognitive linguists see metaphor as a basic cognitive function; see, for example, George Lakoff and Mark Johnson, *Metaphors We Live By* (Chicago : Chicago University Press, 1980).

[8] C.K. Williams, "Halves," *Selected Poems* (New York: Farrar, Strauss and Giroux, 1994) 23.

[9] Margaret Gibson, "Burning the Root," *Long Walks in the Afternoon* (Baton Rouge: Louisiana State University Press, 1982): 30.

[10] This image recalls the traditional ballad, "The Two Magicians," in which the shape-shifting male pursues his elusive lady until he takes her maidenhead.

[11] Eroticism is sacrificial in the sense Bataille gives it; see Georges Bataille, *Eroticism*, translated by Mary Dalwood (London & New York: Marion Boyars, 1962 [1957]).

[12] Charles Simic, "The Stream," in *Selected Poems: 1963-1983* (New York: George Braziller, 1990),152-154.

[13] William James, *Principles of Psychology* (1890).

[14] George Orwell, "Politics and the English Language," *Collected Essays* (London : Secker & Warburg, 1961) 355-56.

[15] Orwell 353.

[16] John Yau, "A Gargoyle in the Garden," *Sometimes* (New York: Sheep Meadow Press, 1979) 26.

[17] Violence is suggested not only by the "bruised thigh," but also by the strange mention of the "fifth rib," which recalls the recurrent stabbings in 2 Samuel (2:23; 3:27; 20:10).

[18] Denis Johnson, "The Rockefeller Collection of Primitive Art," *The Throne of the Third Heaven of the Nations Millennium General Assembly: Poems, Collected and New* (New York : HarperCollins, 1995) 141-142.

[19] Dan Chaon, "Prosthesis," *Among the Missing* (New York: Ballantine, 2001) 153-159.

[20] Russell Banks, "Searching for Survivors," *Searching for Survivors* (New York: Fiction Collective, 1975) 1-5.

PART III

THE RHETORIC OF INTEGRATION

CHAPTER FIVE

FAILED ATTEMPTS AT WHOLENESS

The preceding chapters have examined texts that disrupt conventions in order to point beyond what can be expressed through the cultural system. Deliberately creating disjunctive discursive patterns, those texts refuse consistency through discrepancies, gaps or excesses. By implication, the contrary aesthetic impulse toward unity, wholeness, and harmony would seem to uphold the system and hence to lie beyond the scope of this inquiry. Nevertheless, a number of texts center on the quest for some form of totality or perfection only to illustrate that this very pursuit creates at the same time its opposite. Hans-Jost Frey expresses the dilemma clearly:

> The ideal of the whole endangers meaning, since it would like to enclose meaning out of fear of meaning's borders. ....The whole pretends to be immune against that which is outside of it. But by striving to exclude meaninglessness from itself, the whole exposes itself to it.[1]

This chapter will examine texts that pair the aspiration toward forms of wholeness with the complementary incursion of its contraries. The poems and short stories we have chosen illustrate how attempts to isolate absolutes, to shape icons of oneness, purity or permanence from the cultural magma, produce instead contamination, ambivalence, or alienation. Ineluctably, the search for forms of wholeness discloses the uncontainable, disruptive elements that are supposed to be suppressed, and hence leads to the discovery of the Othering function. The texts we will study in this chapter could be seen as attempts to impose order that inadvertently represent disorder, or, on the contrary, as works that emphasize the principles of form so as, paradoxically, to point beyond it.

The problem we want to consider here is posed exquisitely in Chase Twichell's poem "Japanese Weeping Cherry."[2] The opening lines represent a poet at work, wrestling with the problem of shaping a changeable material world into stable artistic form: "The bed seems a raft set adrift/ in the inadequate moonlight/ by which I write." The insecure raft and the feeble illumination of the notoriously variable moon are not presented as ideal conditions for poetic creation, yet from this inauspicious source, a beautifully crafted haiku emerges:

The weeping cherry
drowns in its blanching waters,
trailing shell-pink sprays
across the screens. (Lines 4-7 of the poem; our italics.)

In the formal perfection of the haiku, the writer seems to have achieved a victory over mutability, recreating the shifting scene in a sophisticated poetic form. Conventional structures produce the illusion of stasis; the three haiku-like lines that we have italicized freeze the tree at its loveliest moment, thereby seeming to halt the process of mutation. Simultaneously though, the haiku includes traces of impermanence, since the unifying water imagery presages the scene's disintegration. The trailing sprays suggest a falling movement, while the verb "drowns" foreshadows an imminent disappearance. Imposing stasis on an instant of natural beauty is a form of death rather than preservation; instead of coming to fruition, the blossoms "drown."

The second stanza of the poem develops the contradiction implicit in the haiku. If the writer's mastery of form approaches perfection, it does so only through distortion. To capture a perfect image, the poet has to exclude temporality:

Time is a foreignness
in the forms of things.
Asymmetrical and Japanese,
a tree enters a poem
and is fixed there,
an ignorant stroke of blossoms.

Time, the force that transmutes structures, is obviously alien, even hostile, to the artistic ideals of unity and permanence. When the writer stabilizes one form by changing it into another, achieving perfection through artistic mastery, she displaces or defers the inevitable corruption. Arresting the flux and continuity of the observed scene, the haiku falsifies it. With a stroke of the pen, the writer deprives the tree of a future, creating "an ignorant stroke of blossoms."[3] Thus the haiku denatures the tree rather than capturing its essence, as the concluding lines of the second stanza admit: "Anything can be corrupted/ for the sake of a new pureness."

Though the inset haiku in "Japanese Weeping Cherry" offers a temporary illusion of completeness, making the cherry tree seem momentarily self-contained, the surrounding text breaks the illusion. The haiku is embedded in a sentence that appends an extra four-syllable line to the classic seventeen-syllable form. Moreover, with this addition, the weeping cherry is not shown in splendid isolation but is viewed through the screens of the bedroom window. This could be a framing element, a geometrical form encasing the image and defining its limits, but the screens obscure or distort it. They overprint the emblem of the ideal with something secondary, a veil that troubles the image's clarity. The frame makes the object incomplete. Rather than revealing the permanent inner truth beyond the inessential,[4] formal beauty deforms the real complexity of things.

This falsifying artistic perfection does not belong to natural objects, which exist in a constant state of flux, but it is created in and for the eyes of the beholder, in a process that seeks to eliminate imperfection and to arrest time. The impulse toward perfection comes from Western society's devalorization of mutability, impurity, mixedness and impermanence. Yet rather than attempting to relegate these disturbing factors to its exterior, Twichell's poem includes what is normally inessential or supplementary. The larger structure framing the inset haiku draws attention to the way the outside not only defines the inside but infiltrates it and mixes with it: "one form/ infects another." Moreover, the attempt to fix something brings on its opposite: "The tree becomes/ corsages crumbling in a drawer." Paradoxically, the desire for stability only accentuates the ravages of time, and the rage for permanence tacitly recognizes the power of change. Indeed, the artistic enterprise is doomed to incompletion: "And there is never an end to this,/ except when consciousness ends,/ and it does not end here." The poem concludes in openness, admitting that rather than accomplishing her work, the writer always leaves something unsaid. The deictics "this" and "here" imply not only that the process of mutability cannot be arrested, but also that the poem is unfinished. Rather than a means of correcting the ravages of time, any attempt at completion is inevitably ephemeral, since it interrupts a dynamic process that only comes to an end, "when consciousness ends." The poem's last line marks an end to neither the speaker's nor the reader's mental interaction with the world, so that the process of change continues beyond the poem's reach.

Twichell's "Japanese Weeping Cherry" frames its inset haiku with a disavowal of the permanence artistic form can bring. It draws attention to the artistic mechanism of framing and also tries to suggest everything that the frame excludes. The poem's repudiation of the aesthetic of wholeness thus provides a good starting point for our consideration of Othering texts that seem to pursue it only to reveal its spuriousness. To constitute an icon of unity like the haiku's weeping cherry, the object or scene has to be isolated and stabilized, fixed in formal perfection through the strategy of excluding what is deemed inessential, impure or fluctuating. As Frey insists:

> Wholeness, coherence, unity, completeness, completion are seldom neutral terms: they are value judgments. What is ordered and made into a whole is regarded as meaningful, what is meaningful as valuable. [5]

To gain shape and consistency, the icon of perfection has to be placed within a frame that centers and contains it. Edges and borders have to be constructed, defining an inside and an outside. Ultimately, though, this constructed frame draws attention to the relatedness of center and periphery, which exist not in opposition to but in collaboration with one another, each creating and defining the other, so that they are not distinct but inseparable, overlapping, and interpenetrating.

Systemic thinking stakes out a center in relation to a border, defines fullness in relation to emptiness and the essential in relation to the inessential, thereby imposing false dichotomies on the real. At the same time, paradoxically, the system needs to imagine that these dichotomies could exist in isolation, as pure essences. In the Othering process, the dream of perfection brings on its inverse, so that concepts that are opposed in the system become inextricably entangled in the text.

Consider Lee Li-Young Lee's poem "From Blossoms,"[6] in which the speaker elevates the simple act of eating a peach to a kind of communion:

> O, to take what we love inside,
> to carry within us an orchard, to eat
> not only the skin, but the shade,
> not only the sugar, but the days, to hold
> the fruit in our hands, adore it, then bite into
> the round jubilance of peach.

Like a priest, the speaker venerates the beloved object before consuming it in a ritual that connects a diverse series—"not only . . . but . . ."—in apparently blissful unity. Simple food, readily endowed with sacramental associations, figures in the poem as an icon of plenitude. The peach incorporates everything around it into an all-encompassing totality. Divisions between inside and outside dissolve in this mystical Eucharist, so that in eating a single fruit, communicants "carry within [themselves] an orchard." Boundaries of time and space disappear too in the ingestion of "shade" and "days." Nevertheless, the illusory quality of the dream of plenitude is already expressed from the start in the wishful "O" and the forward projecting infinitive.

The poem's circular structure gives this icon of perfection an appropriate frame. "From Blossoms" begins with the inception of the fruit in spring: "From blossoms comes/ this brown paper bag of peaches." It moves to the moment of consumption in summer: "succulent peaches we devour." Then finally, in a repetition of the opening phrase, it returns to the source: "from blossom to blossom to/ impossible blossom, to sweet impossible blossom." In moving from blossom to peach to blossom, the speaker encircles the peach in a truncated cycle of life that (impossibly) omits winter and decay, lending the fruit (and the eater) a spurious form of immortality. This circular structure seems to offer a protective magical power that keeps destruction at bay. However, this magic is exposed as a distortion. Like the writer Twichell depicts in "Japanese Weeping Cherry," Li-Young Lee's speaker corrupts "for the sake of a new pureness." The celebration of the fullness and pleasure of "the round jubilance of peach" comes from considering only the processes of ripening and fulfillment and none of the things that follow. In willfully excluding death from the cycle, the speaker creates a "sweet, impossible" falsification.

Indeed, the obviously wishful dream of a return to the source is haunted by finitude. The very title "From Blossoms" implies a linear movement toward something that the poem occults, replacing it in the concluding stanza with the "impossible" dream of endless repetition. Still, right in the middle of the poem, the very thing the speaker seems intent on avoiding manifests itself insistently: "[From]   succulent/ peaches we devour, dusty skin and all,/ comes the familiar dust of summer, dust we eat." In their wholeness, the peaches include the dust that recalls finitude. Thus the poem allows for the contamination that the dream of perfection creates and tries to occult. The speaker performs a double role: he voices an aspiration toward perfection that would deny finitude, and, at the same time, he confesses the impossibility of the dream and names the polluting element that negates it.

This dual role is performed by the narrators of three short stories that, in different ways, exemplify the search for forms of wholeness. This duality results not so much from resignation to contradiction but from the discovery of the complexity of our desire for completion. In David Means's "The Gesture Hunter," Lesley Marmon Silko's "Storyteller," and Robert Ollen Butler's "Fairy Tale," the quest for a form of perfection or totality shapes the narrative; however, in each of these stories, the element that needs to be excluded is the vital motor of the story, impossible to eradicate because of its constitutive role. In each of the stories, the protagonist is caught in this paradox. Represented as less conscious of their own contradictions than Lee's speaker, the protagonists' confessions reveal the element of self-deceit in their totalizing impulses.

The autodiegetic narrator in David Means's short story, "The Gesture Hunter,"[7] describes the quest for the perfect gesture that has become his sole obsession. The gesture hunter, an elderly man whose only son has been killed in Vietnam, wants to add a third perfect gesture to the two that he preserves in his memory, elevated to the realm of the sacred through the terms that describe them: "Twice I've been consecrated by pure gestures" (145). These two gestures performed by his son, the first as a baby and the second as an adolescent, are represented in terms of absolutes; they are: "cleansed . . . holy . . . purified" (144). Moreover they are lovingly prolonged and repeated in the narration:

> the perfect gestures that, held still on the back of my eyelids, remain my salvation: my son's gesture in the stream, the heavy wash of water against our waders, and that other one in which he was in the tub, gleaming sheens of water over his smooth baby belly.... It seized me and sent me reeling, knowing full well that what I was seeing would never repeat itself and was certainly the most beautiful sight in the world. (150)

Here the narrator's eyes function like a camera, framing, freezing and preserving the vision to give it permanence. Through the metaphor of holding them still, he transforms the two moments into snapshots that can be shared with the reader and that somehow sustain the illusion of his son's continuance. To complete them (presumably by achieving some sort of mystical or magical triad), he spends his days searching for a third: "I needed the whole thing, united and graceful and, most of all, full of revelation, stark wonderful revelation" (141). These revered icons of perfection combine wholeness, unity, fullness, and purity; they also defer the recognition of mortality, termination, waste and incompleteness implicit in the death of a son. Nevertheless, the quest that founds the narrative impulse already suggests the impossibility of plenitude. If the gesture hunter needs another icon, his cherished signs of perfection are necessarily incomplete.

Moreover, the two gestures the narrator holds up as perfect are tainted with traces of pollution and transience. Far from being "pure," the act of disengaging the fishhook is contaminated with blood that the narrator emphasizes even in the effort to efface it: "smiling at the pain and flicking my fly back, swiping the blood from his wrist. Blood I couldn't see and will never see" (145).[8] The gesture is also strangely veiled in darkness: "barely visible, maybe not visible at all to me in the falling darkness"

(145). This odd denial invites questions about the narrator's obsession with the purity and authenticity of the gesture. The narration is put in doubt; what is represented as obvious becomes obscure; the icon that appeared whole comes to seem irremediably fractured. Moreover, the two gestures the narrator cherishes and attempts to endow with permanence are staged against backdrops that evoke Heraclitean changeability: one occurs in the middle of the river and the other amidst the gleaming water of the bathtub. Thus, futility seems to be built into the quest to preserve these fleeting moments.

When the narrator thinks he has found the third perfect gesture, he "delineate[s] " it not simply by describing it but by drawing lines around it, representing the architecture that frames it:

> To delineate the obvious, to consecrate that scene, the pure gesture, that before me appeared on the short narrow steps, three in all, leading to the front door of the funeral parlor, covered by the heavy shadows of the pine oak growing out front: They were there out front of Olsen's establishment. A man and woman embraced by grief. Embracing. The man in a sports coat and blue jeans with that stooped expression, slightly bent beneath some gravitational weight of his own grief; the woman in a long violet dress tightening then loosening against her hips as the breeze rippled the fabric—those hips I'll never forget, I suppose, jutting lightly against his own, as much a part of the embrace as anything. She bent and shifted with the great forces against her the way someone on the deck of a boat must adjust himself to a changing horizon—it was right there before me, the gyroscope of their pain holding the gesture, making it as pure as carved stone, petrified forever, the brass rails holding up the canopy overhead, green-and-white-striped. (148)

The three steps leading up to the scene lend a kind of inevitability to the third gesture, which is framed in the entrance to the funeral parlor. The doorway and canopy create an architectural niche to house the sculptural icon of grief. The narrator fixes on the image of the sorrowing couple to compensate for his own refusal to come to terms with impermanence. Still, the metaphor of the boat on the "changing horizon" recalls the signs of mutability found in the gesture hunter's earlier icons of perfection. The striking image of "the gyroscope of their pain" holds in tension the contradictory forces of inertia and movement.

Though seized upon as another perfect gesture, the vision of mourning seems to bring the narrator to the brink of some new understanding:

> Suddenly a blinding purplish brilliance lit the front of the parlor afire. I was past. It was behind me. That beloved, graven gesture—near perfect— was gone, faded off into some infinite point along the lines   of   my   life,

dissolved by time and by the human movement. I felt then acutely, and for
the first time in years, the sorrow of my loss. (148-49)

The blinding purple flash presages the disintegration of his strategy of
denial, and the oddly suggestive use of prepositions—"I was past. It was
behind me."—intimates the narrator's passage to a new phase.
Nevertheless, instead of beginning the long-delayed work of grieving, the
narrator makes the fatal decision to return for a second look, "I headed
around the block, hoping the gesture would still be there. It was the kind
of frail, stupid hope that can only betray" (149). In attempting to recapture
the instant, he definitively fractures the perfect triad he has tried to create.
The third gesture turns out to be a simulacrum. In returning, the narrator
sees the lights and cameras of a film crew and realizes that the mourners
are simply actors simulating grief.

Instead of recognizing the impurity of the fleeting moments that he had
tried to erect into absolutes, the narrator turns against the fabricators of the
gesture. He drives his car toward the camera, killing the director of the
film. Readers discover finally that the narration belongs to the
confessional genre in which an accused criminal recounts his story in
order to defend his acts. The narrator justifies his crime in a series of
rhetorical questions:

> Was I to be betrayed or to be a betrayer? Were there not obligations to the
> dead that had to be taken into consideration, punishments to be dolled out?
> Was it not a crime to grieve, falsely grieve, and in that false bereavement
> to create what is essentially a perfect human gesture? What else was I to
> do? (149)

These questions imitate the moral complexity of the traditional revenge
plot in which the avenger becomes a murderer like his adversary.
However, the adversary's only crime here is to create a mimesis of
mourning, to "falsely grieve." The murdered film director becomes a
scapegoat and the narrator's evocation of revenge tragedy serves as a
decoy, allowing him to persist in the illusion that something transient—"a
... human gesture"—can be "perfect." Beyond its play with the revenge
plot and confessional genre, "The Gesture Hunter" interrogates the
function of art, revealing the futility of its aim to immortalize transient
mortal beauty in formal perfection.

Leslie Marmon Silko's "Storyteller"[9] is also a narrative describing a
quest to restore wholeness, though it evokes Native American rather than
Euro American aesthetics. Like "The Gesture Hunter" the story is partly
modeled on the revenge plot, although in comparison to Means's narrator,

the Eskimo girl at the center of Silko's short story has a more
comprehensible reason for exacting revenge. Her grandmother reveals that
both her parents died of alcohol poisoning because the white storekeeper
sold them a product that was not fit for consumption. The narrative
unfolds in a fragmentary and retrospective manner, intertwining three
interconnected stories involving the three generations and three different
storytellers: first, the Eskimo girl's putative grandfather tells the tale of a
hunter pursued by a bear, a story drawn out over months; then the
grandmother tells her granddaughter how her parents were murdered; and
finally, the Eskimo girl begins to relate the story of how she exacts
revenge for her parent's death. The non-linear ordering of the three stories
underscores the importance of the revenge plot, since it begins
retrospectively with the imprisoned girl watching her window for signs of
the land being overtaken by ice, an apocalyptic event that she expects will
definitively expel the whites (identified as the Gussuks in the girl's
discourse): "The cold stopped them, and they were helpless against it"
(18). The interwoven stories converge on the girl's vision of total stasis,
observed through the window of her jail cell:

> Look at the sun. It wasn't moving; it was frozen, caught in the middle
> of the sky. Look at the sky, solid as the river with ice which had trapped
> the sun. It had not moved for a long time; in a few more hours it would be
> weak, and heavy frost would begin to appear on the edges and spread
> across the face of the sun like a mask. (18)

The narrator uses free indirect discourse here to signal that the Eskimo girl
interprets the solstice as a sign that the Gussuks' encroachments are
coming to an end. In her vision, the sun, sky and river are to merge with
one another, as time is arrested and the world reunified in a deadly totality.
    The art of storytelling appears to have the power to effect this
transformation and to stop the march of time. Aiming at perfect
correspondence between the time of the narration and the time of the
actions described, the storyteller seems to possess the magical power both
to delay events and to provoke them. Art seems able to create and unmake
the world. The old man's story begins with a prediction of doom:

> 'It is approaching. As it comes, ice will push across the sky.' His eyes were
> open wide and he stared at the low ceiling rafters for hours without
> blinking. She remembered all this clearly because he began the story that
> day, the story he told from that time on. It began with a giant bear which he
> described muscle by muscle, from the curve of the ivory claws to the
> whorls of hair at the top of the massive skull. And for eight days he did not

sleep, but talked continually of the giant bear whose color was blue glacier ice. (22)

The incredibly slow and detailed story seems to produce its own reenactments, as first the white storeman pursues the girl across the frozen river, and then the frost chases the sun in order to rout the Gussuks. The different narrative threads are thus unified by the motif of the hunt. In luring the white man out onto the ice in pursuit of her, the girl mimics the chase between the man and the polar bear that she has heard related in the old man's story.[10] Then she sees the sun as the prey of the ice in the final hunt:

> She looked out the window at the frozen white sky. The sun had finally broken loose from the ice but it moved like a wounded caribou running on strength which only dying animals find, leaping and running on bullet-shattered lungs. (32)

All the stories move toward stasis: the old man's finishes with his own death as well as that of the hunter in his tale; the girl's parents and the grandmother die; the white storeman is swallowed up by the ice; and implicitly, in the narrative's associative logic, the girl's storytelling purchases the sun's immobility at the cost of her life. When the art of storytelling achieves totality, it turns out to be deadly.

Indeed, the aspiration toward totality turns out to be both insidious and undesirable. First of all, the aim of blanking out the Other ominously replicates the racist ideology of the whites, who want to eradicate the Eskimo language and subjugate the tundra. The total whiteness of the ice promises to obliterate all distinctions between earth, water, and sky, thereby effacing the colors introduced into the landscape by the Gussuks, and associated with them: the "stringy yellow wadding" of their insulation (18), the blue of the storeman's eyes (29), and finally the red of the customer's hair, of the sweet wine he gives her, of the tin oil barrels left by the drillers, and, most of all, the "something red in the grass" (24) that the girl remembers on the morning after her parents' death. Paradoxically though, the color that the girl wants to efface plays a vital role in the story. The red in the white landscape stops her from being lost on the ice like her victim. She has chosen to cover her house with the red tin left behind by the oil drillers, and this reminder of their incursion is precisely what saves her when she loses her bearings on the river: "the boundaries had been swallowed by the freezing white. But then in the distance, she saw something red, and suddenly it was as she had remembered it all those years" (30). The red tin offers the girl a way back to the original story, confirming the justice of her revenge and allowing her to get her bearings on the destructive ice. Nevertheless, her interpretation of the red also replicates the circular, totalizing logic that confounds the different threads of the story, for the red tin nailed to her house is a new element in the narrative, reminiscent of but not identical to the red tin in her parents' story, and it is not clear that the storekeeper is the same man who murdered her parents.

Indeed the color red is a complex and multivalent sign in "Storyteller," representing different things in different contexts. Though a mark of the contamination that causes the death of the girl's parents, it also stands for the irreducible remainder that cannot be incorporated into any totality: "something not swallowed up by the heavy white belly of the sky or caught in the folds of the frozen earth. It was time" (28). Although the girl aims at bringing on total whiteness and thereby obliterating the Gussuks and wiping out history, her story begins (and also ends) with "something red" (32), suggesting the ultimate futility of her effort to escape time. Moreover, totality threatens to obliterate everything, destroying the girl and her people along with the whites. Significantly, the clothing made by the grandmother as a protection from the cold mixes white and red. While her wolfskin parka is "creamy colored and silver, almost white in some places," the girl's sealskin mukluks are lined with "bright red flannel" and tied with "braided red yarn tassels" (20). Thus the regressive and destructive urge for totality symbolized by whiteness is undercut by the recurrence of red, an ambivalent symbol of destruction and protection. So although the young Eskimo storyteller aspires to racial and artistic purity, Lesley Marmon Silko's "Storyteller" reveals the fundamental mixedness of existence. Red and white do not so much oppose as invoke each other indissolubly.

To preserve perfection or purity, the speaker in "From Peaches," the narrator in "The Gesture Hunter," and the Eskimo girl in "Storyteller" construct totalizing forms to mask the pressing evidence of confusion. The desire for totality induces a kind of blindness in those that seek it, for they refuse to acknowledge the contamination that the quest for purity produces. A final example of this paradox can be seen in Robert Olen Butler's "Fairy Tale," a story in which the first person narrator, Miss Noi, a Vietnamese bargirl who has immigrated to America, attempts to recast her chaotic life in the idealized form of a fairy tale. In this case, however, the autodiegetic narrator moves from a false idea of perfection that excludes her to a more mixed form, closer to the hybridizing forms that we will study in Chapter Six.

Butler's short story begins with the narrator's reflection on the genre of the fairy tale:

> I like the way fairy tales start in America. When I learn English for real, I buy books for children and I read, 'Once upon a time.' I recognize this word 'upon' from some GI who ... spends some time with me and he is a cowboy from the great state of Texas. He tells me he gets up on the back of a bull and he rides it. .... I think this is very nice, how you get up on the back of time and ride and you don't know where it will go or how it will try to throw you off. (45)[11]

The new initiate into English re-poeticizes the clichéd introduction to fairytales, transforming it into a metaphor for life's vicissitudes. The abrupt changes in her life, signaled in her narration by the expletive "boom,"[12] are like so many falls from "the back of time." As in "Storyteller" and to differing degrees in the other texts we have looked at, time is the contaminating element in the quest for perfection. The narrator thus selects the timeless fairy tale pattern to impose order on her experience.

Unfortunately, Miss Noi's story parodies the fairytale, for her escape from the bars of Saigon only leads her to a similar setting in New Orleans. Her immigration to America constitutes the first aborted attempt to mold life into a fairytale pattern: "Once upon a time ... a dumb Saigon bargirl" (46) is lured by an American's promise of marriage, only to be abandoned by him in Atlanta. Moreover, her love for her "prince" is based on an error in communication due to his incompetence in imitating the tonal system in Vietnamese:

> He wanted to say in my language, 'May Vietnam live for ten thousand years.' What he said, very clear, was, 'The sunburnt duck is lying down.' Now, if I think this man says that Vietnam should live for ten thousand years, I think he is a certain kind of man. But when he says that a sunburnt duck is lying down—boom, my heart melts. (46-47)

Nevertheless, from this aborted fairy story, the narrator finds a motif to create a new one. After years as a dancer on Bourbon Street, she meets Mr. Fontenot, a shy, long-necked auto mechanic who claims to love "everything" Vietnamese (55). When he describes the people in Saigon as "pretty as nutria" (56), she no longer "understand[s] a word he's saying" (56), even though she comprehends his sincerity. Finally, she accepts his offer of marriage accompanied by his symbolic gift of an apple—the fruit she had craved in Vietnam. At the end of the short story, Miss Noi fashions a coda for her story out of her lover's incomprehensible remark

about nutria and the other American's misunderstood declaration in
Vietnamese. The short fable describes: "a duck with a long neck" who
"flies to another part of the land and ... finds a little animal with a nice
coat and though that animal is different from him, still he lies down beside
her" (57). In this new fairy tale, the oddly assorted couple enjoys a happy-
ever-after ending that is meant to predict the narrator's married life in
Thibodaux, Louisiana.

This miniature love story, bizarrely hybridized with the animal fable,
lends shape and closure to Miss Noi's life. It recasts a life of exploitation
and loss in the fairy tale mold, transforming the protagonist from a
Vietnamese bargirl to a contented American housewife. Yet the comically
mixed, even cartoonish tale that ends Butler's short story suggests the
protagonists' rejection of absolutes. The happy-ever-after ending bespeaks
a compromise patched-up between two outcasts, rather than a wish
fulfillment dream of prince and princess.

The story's shift from the high ground of ideals to the middle ground
of concessions is represented symbolically by the love gift that binds the
couple together. In Vietnam the narrator had chosen an emblem of
America that she charges with positive associations:

> Only when [the GIs] love me very much I ask them to get me something.
> In the place where the GI eats, they have something I cannot get in Saigon.
> This thing is an apple. I only ask for apples. I buy mangoes and papayas
> and pineapples and other sweet things to eat in the market, but in South
> Vietnam, an apple is a special thing. I hold an apple and it fills my hand
> and it is very smooth and very hard and it is red like my favorite aó dài. So
> I bite it and it is very sweet, like sweet water from a mountain, and it is not
> stringy like a pineapple, and it is not mushy like a mango or papaya. (49)

In the narrator's description, which delays identifying the object to arouse
the reader's desire, the apple becomes something rare. Before being
named, it is characterized as a special love gift, difficult to obtain. The
narrator associates it with purity in the comparison to mountain water and
with plenitude in the way "it fills [her] hand." Selected because of its
perfection and singularity, the apple becomes the unique object of desire.
Yet time and familiarity make these desired objects lose their appeal. The
memory of the fruit in Vietnam has more force than her later impression in
America:

> In New Orleans I buy many apples. I eat them in America whenever I want
> to. But is that memory not better? (49)

Miss Noi has had too much experience:

there have been very many men, I guess. It's like eating too many apples.
You take a bite now and you can make yourself remember that apples are
sweet, but it is like the apple in your mouth is not even there. (53)

Yet when Mr. Fontenot brings her an apple and asks to marry her, she
takes it as a victory over time and promiscuity. At first a rare, highly
desirable object, then a sign of surfeit, at the end of the story, the apple
betokens conciliation: "she never eats an apple unless he thinks to give it
to her. Though this may not be very often, they taste very good to her"
(57). From an emblem of perfection to one of both excess and loss
(recalling the Biblical motif of the Fall), the apple finally becomes a
symbol that mediates these extremes.

In the three narratives we have examined, conventional plot motifs do
not properly accommodate the experiences represented. Othering devices
complexify conventional narrative patterns like the revenge plot or the
fairy tale, revealing them to be patently artificial devices. The sense of
wholeness or accomplishment they provide seems forced and ultimately
unconvincing, inviting readers to consider what the familiar narrative
frames confine to their borders in order to create a sense of completion.
Means's and Silko's stories show not only that purity and totality are
impossible, but also that the very effort to represent them invites
contamination. Butler's quirky casting of a Vietnamese call-girl's story in
the fairy tale mode draws attention to the inadequacy of pre-made
concepts in the representation of experience. The role of the Othering
process in these texts is to reveal the contradictions produced by efforts to
fit experience into a totalizing system.

Akin to but different from narrative patterning as a spurious means of
creating wholeness is the selective recourse to memory. The evocation of
an idealized past can compensate for present loss and restore a sense of
plenitude. Yet, like the efforts to isolate symbols of perfection, the act of
constructing a venerated site of memory summons the very forces that it
aims to exclude. In Marilyn Nelson's "The House on Moscow Street" and
Thylias Moss's "Remembering Kitchens," two African American poets
recreate powerful sites of meaning, revealing ambivalence or division in
place of wholeness.

In *The Homeplace*,[13] a volume of poems relating an African-American
quest to reconnect with the past, Marilyn Nelson depicts a house to frame
the memories of her ancestors. The first poem of the collection, "The
House on Moscow Street," begins by tracing the architecture of the house,
establishing its planes and lines:

It's the ragged source of memory,
a tarpaper-shingled bungalow
whose floors tilt toward the porch,
whose back yard ends abruptly
in a weedy ravine. (4)

This poetic reconstruction of the homeplace does more than recreate a family snapshot; it forms a container by tracing outlines and creating limits, establishing a beginning ("the ragged source") and an end ("ends abruptly"). Having restored the family home, the speaker then peoples it with ancestors fixed in characteristic poses. The house is the place: "where my great-grandfather, Pomp, smoked" and "where Annie, his wife, measured cornmeal" (4). This imaginative re-membering of the long dead culminates in another frame inside the house—a mirror that contains the people most honored in the poem:

My grandmother, her brother, and five sisters
watched their faces change slowly
in the oval mirror on the wall outside the door
into teachers' faces, golden with respect. (4-5)

The double frame of house and mirror stops the fraying at the "ragged source." The speaker stabilizes change by making the images of her ancestors into golden effigies.

Even so, not everyone can be contained in this way: "Geneva, the randy sister" escapes the gilded portrait; she is associated instead with more changeable substances: "daubing her quicksilver breasts/ with gifts of perfume" (5). Even more problematically, efforts to retrieve the past through re-presentation induce discoveries of absence. Paradoxically, the eponymous house on Moscow Street acquires its privileged status precisely because time has distanced it from the mind, demanding an effort of memory and imagination to return. It has become a *lieu de mémoire* whose importance stems from the disappearance from living recollection of that which it commemorates.[14] "The House on Moscow Street" is a monument rather than a home, comparable "to the grave of a known ancestor" (5). Although the returning pilgrim tries to imagine lost family members and to fix them in the poem, they finally evade her. She seeks ghosts who "though I call with all my voices, do […] not appear" (4). Thus, the joyous return to "the ragged source of memory" in "The House on Moscow Street" is haunted by death. The poem's concluding "song" reveals this ambivalence:

Oh, catfish and turnip greens,
hot water cornbread and grits.
Oh, musty, much-underlined Bibles:
generations lost to be found,
to be found. (5)

In a half-comic, half-reverent manner, these lines evoke a hymn or a prayer. They even echo the refrain of "Amazing Grace" but with an important difference. Whereas those lines proclaim, "I once was lost, but now I'm found," in the poem the lost generations remain "to be found." They hover ambivalently between the "musty" past and the indefinite future, eluding the speaker in the present. Thus the pleasure of finding the homeplace intact is tinged with regret, and the poem's effort to recover the past also draws attention to its loss.

The kitchens in Thylias Moss's poem, "Remembering Kitchens,"[15] are similar *lieux de mémoire*, consecrated by loss. The meals remembered from "exceptional" Sundays are hallowed with sacred foods. At the center of the table (and of the poem) is the bread, "sliced . . . into a file to rival the keeping/ of the Judgment notes," but there are also cakes like "portable/ communion altars," and hams studded with "pineapple slices/ so as to form tonsured clerical heads." Cooking is represented in the poem's opening line as a peaceful and creative activity contrary to war and destruction: "In the kitchen we compensate for missiles/ in the world by fluting edges of crust . . . ." Yet the consecrated space of the kitchen cannot exclude the forces of destruction that are supposed to be kept at bay. To create the hallowed feasts that the poem celebrates, the cooks have to endure the sizzling heat of the stove, comically (and ironically) figured as a soldier in uniform. Violence surges up right in the middle of the protected space of the kitchen. The meal arrives on the table only after a struggle with the forces of time and devastation, so that the family's repeated Sunday celebrations are always only temporary victories over entropy. Finally, there is something regressive in this return to maternal space, where the "family suckles grace" in an infantilizing communion.

Besides representing the aspiration toward fullness through the return to origins, these two poems admit its impossibility by paradoxically figuring the loss, absence, or destruction that their return to the past seeks to overcome. Indeed, for these African American writers, recognizing this contradiction is probably as necessary as trying to overcome it. Although members of disempowered racial or ethnic minority groups may feel more than others the need to overcome loss and to restore a form of wholeness through memory, the quest for perfection, would, as we found in "Storyteller" and "Fairy Tale," reproduce the exclusionary values of the powerful. Hence, division and ambivalence characterize the *lieux de mémoire* that Nelson and Moss construct as much as the longing for wholeness.

A. R. Ammons and Thomas McGrath explore the paradoxical logic of exclusion inherent in the quest for wholeness in poems that take up the transcendentalist dream of finding completion through connection with nature. Ammons's "Gravelly Run" and Thomas McGrath's "The Return" represent viewers whose mystical experience of wholeness recalls Emerson's famous vision. For Emerson the gaze is the medium allowing continuity between the self and everything external to it, as he states so definitively in "Nature":

> In the woods we return to reason and faith. There I feel that nothing can befall me in life,—no disgrace, no calamity (leaving me my eyes), which nature cannot repair. Standing on the bare ground,—my head bathed by the blithe air and uplifted into infinite space, -all mean egotism vanishes. I become a transparent eyeball; I am nothing; I see all; the currents of the Universal Being circulate   through me; I am part or parcel of God.[16]

In becoming "transparent" and opening the self to the world and to "the currents of Universal Being," the eye heals the split between spirit and matter. Exposed in this way, the self becomes a channel connecting the "bare ground" to "infinite space." Yet already, this ecstatic celebration of union with nature reveals a contradiction that the later poets will explore. The seeing "I" obtains a sense of connectedness to "all" through the loss of everything else. The body disappears, supplanted by the strangely counterproductive "transparent eyeball" and the self is reduced to "nothing." Dissenting heirs of the Transcendentalists, Ammons and McGrath represent visions that fail to provide completion. Above all, in contrast to Emerson's claim to experience unity in and with nature, these poems reveal how consciousness alienates the viewer from what he sees, leaving him on the periphery of a mystical adventure that communicates absence as much as presence.

Ammons's poem draws particular attention to the role of sight, with the apparently redundant remark following the description of Gravelly Run: "So I look and reflect."[17] This observation on the viewer's observation draws attention to its framing and controlling function. At the center of "Gravelly Run" is an anthropomorphic vision of the eponymous natural setting:

> the swamp's slow water comes
> down Gravelly Run fanning the long
> stone-held algal hair

and narrowing roils between
the shoulders of the highway bridge:

This peculiar landscape, with its long hair and shoulders, seems to figure
forth the body of the world. The speaker looks and reflects in a double
sense, not simply meditating on the landscape but representing it as a
humanized but strangely distorted mirror image. He perceives
transcendental correlations, but disturbingly, the "algal-hair" and the
"highway bridge" shoulders mix the natural and the man-made, the wild
and the urban. This pantheistic divinity resides in a green cathedral:

holly grows on the banks in the woods there,
and the cedars' gothic-clustered
      spires could make
green religion in winter bones....

In this most Emersonian of the poem's stanzas, the scene is imprinted with
quasi-sacred signs of "holly" and "gothic-clustered/ spires." The vision
almost has the power to elicit a transcendental affirmation of faith ("green
religion in winter bones").

Nevertheless, the very privilege of seeing separates the viewer from
the vision. In "Gravelly Run" the air itself forms a kind of window that
contains each element of the scene and prevents transcendental
correlation: "the air's glass/ jail seals each thing in its entity." Unlike
Emerson's transparent eyeball, the visually split "glass/ jail" prevents
circulation, isolating the speaker from the scene he observes, so that he
concludes by admitting the futility of his desire to connect with nature:
"surrendered self among/ unwelcoming forms: stranger,/ hoist your
burdens, get on down the road." In spite of his effort to connect, the
viewer remains a stranger to the scene he observes. In fact, his desire to fix
nature in forms, to "look *and* reflect," above all in the form of language
makes it "unwelcoming," since words separate him from the world: "the
sunlight has never/ heard of trees." The visionary's quest to find a form of
wholeness in nature leads instead to the discovery of the Othering process:
the world is distanced by the act of structuring it conceptually. Hence the
quest for connection and containment produces both the speaker's
alienation and nature's strangeness toward him.

In McGrath's "The Return," on the contrary, the speaker begins with
the admission of exclusion and then relates his attempt to connect with
nature through a mystical journey to its heart. In the opening stanza the
speaker declares his love for the constant changeability of the landscape's
various features. Yet, in its paradoxical union of opposites, the natural

world excludes him: "that green noise, dying/ alive and living its death, that inhuman circular singing/ may call me stranger . . . ."[18] Implicitly, the speaking subject, circumscribed in time, feels estranged from the eternal continuum of Nature's cycles of life and death. However, in a journey that resembles an initiation ritual, the speaker attempts to reclaim this lost harmony:

> Or the little doors of the bark open
> And I enter that other home outside the tent of my skin . . .
>
> On such days, on such midnights, I have gone, I will go,
> Past the human, past the animal, past the bird,
> To the old mothers who stand with their feet in the loamy dark
> And their green gold praises playing in the sun ...

This backward movement, like reverse ontogeny or a symbolic return to the womb, brings the speaker before "the old mothers." These women, whose feet touch the earth and whose songs reach the sun, represent ancient telluric powers capable of connecting sky and earth, light and dark, into a harmonious whole. Yet going back to this state of connectedness entails giving up consciousness: "(It is a long way back.)/ But at least, and if but for a moment, I have almost entered the stone./ Then fear and love call. I am cast out. Alien . . . ." The return to the telluric origin promises permanence and stability, symbolized by the image of entering the stone, but these are gained at the price of immobility, insensibility, and the loss of humanity. In any case, the return is impossible, for various signs of Othering rhetoric overprint its representation, like the excessive hesitations, "at least" "if but for a moment" and "almost."

It seems evident from our study of these texts that the quest for totality inevitably provokes and even adverts the return of disruptive forces. In "Japanese Weeping Cherry," a poet tries to fix a blossoming cherry tree in immutable form but cannot exclude the finitude that she seeks to overcome. Similarly, in "Fairy Tale" and "Storyteller," efforts to bring stability to the flux of experience only emphasize their mutability. In "From Blossoms," the desire to represent plenitude demonstrates incompletion, and in "The Gesture Hunter," the search for purity and authenticity uncovers contamination and simulation. The longing for presence emphasizes absence in Nelson's "The House on Moscow Street," and in Moss's "Remembering Kitchens" the desire to return to a peaceful feminine space conjures up the violence that is supposedly excluded. Finally, attempts at communion with Nature heighten feelings of alienation in Ammons and McGrath.

The reactions to failure in these quests for totality are varied. While some of the speakers continue to cherish their totalizing fantasies, others express their awareness of the impossibility of the quest represented. The short stories by Means and Silko center on storytellers who refuse to recognize their failure. To a degree, their stories imitate revenge tragedies, except that the protagonists never seem to understand the significance of their actions. Other writers stage a discovery of the illusory nature of wholeness and portray varying degrees of acceptance. McGrath's speaker returns from his failed quest with renewed understanding of himself. By contrast, Lee's poem voices the yearning surrounding the fantasy of perfection; at the same time, the word "impossible" in the poem's last line suggests how awareness of its unattainability can exacerbate the desire for plenitude. The poems by Moss, Nelson, and Ammons express both the longing for wholeness and the humor that accepts it as unachievable. From the beginning Butler's "Fairy Tale" suggests the unlikeliness of perfect resolutions; moreover, it ends with a humorous compromise that rewrites the fairy tale in a comic vein, emphasizing hybridity rather than perfection. Twichell's speaker is the most lucid about the impossibility of perfection: though the haiku constitutes an endeavor to capture the ephemeral, the poem framing it insists on the inevitable failure of the attempt. The result of these quests for totality and purity is finally the discovery of mixedness, in other words, the very compromise on which the writers in the next chapter found their artistic creation.

Unlike the hybridizing texts to be discussed in Chapter Six and the experimental forms in Chapter Seven, which clearly manifest their aspiration to emancipation from the system, these texts may resemble efforts to rescue some form of wholeness, shoring up the system against disruption. Nonetheless, in a kind of conspiracy with readers against the system, even as the works studied in this chapter try to exclude unwanted elements like mutability, decay, or destruction through selective remembering and representing, the excluded terms return to provide the depth and complexity necessary to art. Though it may be figured as "a foreignness/ in the forms of things," time is shown to be a necessary component of the literary text. Impurity and formlessness are also essential to literature, since exclusion only evacuates the tension necessary to both fiction and poetry. We discover in reading these texts that utter perfection or totality would mean the end of literature. Thus Means's gesture hunter murders the film director who has staged the third, "perfect gesture," and in Silko's short story, though it would produce the perfect tale, the advent of the total whiteness that would erase all traces of the Gussuks' contaminating presence would also cause the silencing of the Eskimo storyteller. By allowing contradictions to fissure their attempts at perfection, the works we have studied in this chapter invite readers to discover the impossibility of wholeness and the inevitability of mixedness.

Notes

[1] From "Ending Beginning," Frey 24.

[2] Chase Twichell, "Japanese Weeping Cherry," *The Odds* (Pittsburg: University of Pittsburg Press, 1986) 27.

[3] The odd sounding phrase suggests also "a stroke of luck," and therefore the arbitrariness of the writer's selection. At the same time, it reminds us of the passing of time, "the stroke of the hour," that form tries to resist.

[4] Jacques Derrida describes and critiques this universalizing, idealist conception of art: "One makes of art in general an object in which one claims to distinguish an inner meaning, the invariant, and a multiplicity of external variations through which, as through so many veils, one would try to see and to restore the full, originary meaning: one, naked." Jacques Derrida, *The Truth in Painting*, trans. by Geoff Bennington and Ian Mcleod (Chicago: University of Chicago Press, 1987) 22.

[5] From "Fear," Frey 40.

[6] Li-Young Lee, "From Blossoms," *Rose: Poems by Li-Young Lee* (Brockport, New York: Boa Editions, 1986) 21.

[7] David Means, "The Gesture Hunter," *Assorted Fire Events* (New York: Context Books, 2000) 139-151.

[8] One of the intertexts evoked in this story may be Heinrich von Kleist's essay, "On the Puppet Theatre," *An Abyss Deep Enough: Letters of Heinrich von Kleist with a Selection of Essays and Anecdotes*, ed. and trans. Phillip B. Miller (New York: E.P. Dutton, 1982) 211-217. The essay argues that the most perfect gestures are produced by marionettes, who, lacking consciousness, are "incapable of affectation" (213). It also gives the example of a young man of "marvelous grace," who tries without success to repeat a gesture and thereafter loses all his ease of movement (214-215). That gesture, recalling, "the famous statue called the Spinario—the youth removing a thorn from his foot" (215), is strikingly similar to the son's second gesture in "The Gesture Hunter."

[9] Leslie Marmon Silko, "Storyteller," *Storyteller* (New York: Arcade Publishing, 1981) 17- 32.

[10] When the state trooper comes to inquire about what has happened to the white storeman, "the old man suddenly sat up in his bed and began to talk excitedly. He kept saying, 'The story! The story! Eh-ya! The great bear! The hunter!'" (31).

[11] Robert Olen Butler, "Fairy Tale," *A Good Scent From a Strange Mountain: Stories* (New York: H. Holt, 1992) 45-57.

[12] E.g. "Then boom. I'm in America ..." (46); "So boom, I am gone from that man" (47).

[13] Marilyn Nelson Waniek, "The House on Moscow Street," *The Homeplace* (Baton Rouge: Louisiana State U.P., 1990) 4-5.

[14] See Pierre Nora's brilliant essay, "Between Memory and History: Les lieux de mémoire," in *History and Memory in African-American Culture*, eds. Geneviève Fabre and Robert O'Meally (Oxford: Oxford University Press, 1994) 284-300.

[15] Thylias Moss, "Remembering Kitchens," *Small Congregations: New and Selected Poems* (New York: Harper Collins, 1993) 49-50.

[16] Ralph Waldo Emerson, "Nature," *Emerson's Essays*, ed. Arthur Hobson Quinn (New York: Scribner's, 1920) 4.

[17] A. R. Ammons, "Gravelly Run," *The Selected Poems: Expanded Edition* (New York: W.W. Norton, 1986) 11.

[18] Thomas McGrath, "The Return," *Selected Poems: 1938-1988*, ed. Sam Hamill (Port Townsend, WA: Copper Canyon Press, 1988) 118.

CHAPTER SIX

HYBRIDIZING TEXTS

The texts examined in Chapter Five reveal how the artistic impulse to embrace aesthetic absolutes such as purity or wholeness summons up the very surplus it aims to exclude. In this chapter, we will explore texts that surrender to the opposite impulse, welcoming the mixedness and the disorientation that is central to Othering. If, in the face of the disordering pressures coming from outside the system, writers attempt to unify their texts by isolating their subject in time and space, the reverse is also true. The hybridizing impulse favors heterogeneity rather than singularity; it creates openings rather than closure; above all, it admits movement in space and transformation in time,[1] which, as we saw in the previous chapter, "is a foreignness/ in the forms of things."[2]

We have chosen to speak of hybridizing rather than hybridity or the hybrid because those latter nouns tend to reify a process into an object. As so often in speaking of the Othering function, we come up against the problem of trying to use available terms to speak of something that breaks away from the ideological system. We might have tried to avoid unwanted associations by borrowing an equivalent from another language—the Spanish word *mestizo/a*,[3] with similar connotations of both mixing and ameliorating, or the French, *métissage*,[4] with its echo of *tissage* or weaving. We might also have chosen the term "creolization," a concept expanded by Édouard Glissant beyond its lingual or identificatory associations to denote an "unceasing process of transformation,"[5] except that it is be linked primarily with the Caribbean and with linguistic transformation. Like the English word hybrid, theses terms have been adopted to describe non-homogeneous cultural forms—but the words are just as ideologically charged. Moreover, borrowing from other languages might erroneously suggest that hybridizing is synonymous with code-switching or bi-culturalism. Though we do not exclude these possibilities, we have chosen texts that by and large use other means of cultural and linguistic mixing.

We have also chosen to speak of motifs and texts more than forms, since, as we hope to show, the hybridizing impulse destabilizes conventional structures to create texts that upset the values associated with form.[6] Hostile to unity and purity, the hybridizing process brings heterogeneous elements into contact not so as to blend them into a new form of wholeness on the model of the melting pot, but to destabilize fixed forms. Movement energizes formerly distinct elements to produce new relationships, transforming static juxtapositions or apparently fixed hierarchies into dynamic relations. Instead of striving for harmony, hybridizing creates irregularity, disruption, violence and change. In this way, it creates the conditions for the transformation of the cultural values attached to traditional forms.

Motifs representing hybridity abound in contemporary American texts. An archetypal example taken from folk art is the quilt, as described, for example, in Alice Walker's "Everyday Use"[7]:

> The [quilts] had been pieced by Grandma Dee and then Big Dee and me had hung them on the quilt frames on the front porch and quilted them. One was in the Lone Star pattern. The other was Walk Around the Mountain. In both of them were scraps of dresses Grandma Dee had worn fifty and more years ago. Bits and pieces of Grandpa Jarrell's Paisley shirts. And one teeny faded blue piece, about the size of a penny matchbox, that was from Great Grandpa Ezra's uniform that he wore in the civil war. (56)

Made from whole items of clothing that have been cut up, the pieces of fabric are combined in ensembles that do not mask the heterogeneity of their components. Since their separate pieces remain identifiable and carry their particular history, the quilts function as family records. Yet while they symbolize the family's mixed African American heritage, their function in the text lacks the dynamic quality of the hybridizing motifs found in Othering texts. The quilts are family heirlooms that are passed on to the more deserving of the narrator's two daughters. The narrator chooses to give the quilts to Maggie, the younger daughter who shares her home and her values. Maggie has learned quilting and will be the continuator of a living tradition rather than the selective conservator of a dead art form. The elder daughter, Dee, accepts her African American past only selectively, refusing the name she has inherited from the quilt makers.[8] Since the narrator's choice resolves the conflict represented in the sisters' contrasting characters through the exclusion of the troublesome Dee, the narrative affirms a form of hybridity at the expense of Othering. The story falls into a regular pattern, like the quilts, and produces an impression of harmony and closure at the end when the mother and the elected daughter: "sat there just enjoying, until it was time to go in the house and go to bed" (59). The story moves in a circular pattern, defining and affirming the narrator's African American values.

To qualify as a form of Othering, the hybridizing motif should disrupt the familiar and disturb received notions about aesthetics, including ideals of form. We will now explore a series of these disruptive figures in order to show how they modify familiar structures and thereby loosen up established cultural values. On the one hand, the hybridizing process transforms familiar tropes; hence, we will examine how Diana Chang and Stuart Dybek adapt the mirror motif in their short stories "Falling Free" and "Pet Milk," before turning to a selection of poems to show how A.R. Ammons, Gloria Anzaldúa and Richard Wilbur modify the garden topos in their poems "The Quince Bush," "Cultures" and "The Lilacs." On the other hand, writers adopt or invent their own hybridizing motifs, as we will see in the representations of the eggplant in Shirley Geok-lin Lim's poem "Brinjal" and of the town in Steven Millhauser's "Beneath the Cellars of Our Town," as well as in a series of original motifs from Stuart Dybek's "Pet Milk."

Through the hybridizing process, the mirror, archetypally a figure for the replication of the same, becomes a way of rethinking difference. The Narcissus myth offers a classic example of the reflected image as a motif representing sterile duplication. In Medieval and Renaissance developments of the emblem, Vanity is shown admiring her own reflection. In both cases the mirror isolates and imprisons the individual in barren self-absorption. In Gothic literature, mirrors may confront the self with the double, or alter ego. In *Jane Eyre*, for example, the heroine catches sight of Bertha Mason reflected in a dark glass. Still, the image of the doubled self continues to carry a negative charge, and the double has to be eliminated. In the hybridizing development of the mirror motif, doubling becomes an opening onto expanded possibilities of existence.

In Diana Chang's "Falling Free,"[9] the narrator encounters an unfamiliar persona in her reflected image, but the mirror becomes an invitation to discover that new self. In Chang's story, the ailing seventy-nine year old narrator has chosen to remain in the United States while her husband has returned to China. Alone, she is free to reminisce, to talk to herself, and, as the title suggests, to fall. Indeed, among the possible meanings of the title, the narrative suggests two contradictory but equally applicable interpretations. The narrator is free to die, to "Let it go," in a "flight of the pale body into pitch blackness" (60); at the same time, she is free to "fall" sexually, to abandon the persona of the dutiful Chinese wife and to yield to an American friend who has loved her for decades. These contradictory choices are paradoxically linked, since in falling victim to illness and old age, the narrator is also liberated from convention at last. The dizzying possibilities of multiple existence crystallize in the moment when the narrator glimpses her own reflection:

> In a section of plate glass the length of a building, I saw a woman hurrying along. Her knees raised themselves to climb but the sidewalk was level. Her stepping was hurried, stiff, floating. I gasped; she, too. 'That's you!' I said to me. I—who used to move like a dress hung on a hanger loose in the wind.
> The woman's hair was as silver as anyone's here. That's why I didn't grasp who she was. So, finally, she resembled the rest, weathered silver like any Caucasian. Hers was a new gait, a new identity. At the corner she and I put hands out for support on rear fenders of cars. 'You're me,' I said to her. 'you're me,' she said back. What I saw mirrored before me was also everything behind me. (65-66)

This passage could be said to describe a common, though often momentarily disorientating, experience of unexpectedly catching sight of one's reflection. Rather than clearing up the resulting ambiguity, though, the narrator exacerbates it in a number of ways. Strangely, the self reflected in the mirror is not Chinese, but Caucasian, like "the rest," and thus both alien and familiar at the same time. Moreover, the text multiplies indexicals, which, as we have seen in Chapter Two, is a feature of Othering rhetoric. Rather than identifying herself right away as "me," as might be expected, she addresses herself in the second person—"That's you!" She then prolongs the impression of disorientation by adding: "I said to me," splitting herself into destinator and receiver. She further complexifies the notion of identity by continuing to speak of the apparition in the third person: "That's why I didn't grasp who she was." In a playful evocation of the Narcissus myth, an echo effect is added to the mirroring: "'You're me,' I said to her. 'you're me,' she said back." The repetition creates an aural equivalent of the vertiginous effect of a hall of mirrors.

Moreover, Chang's mirror does more than duplicate the self in space; it also multiplies her in time. The present, but as yet unacknowledged image of a woman stepping in the ungainly manner of an invalid is superposed on another "I," the absent but remembered self who floats free and oddly detached from her body in the simile "like a dress hung on a hanger loose in the wind." The text confounds adverbs of space and time so that what is "behind" becomes "before," and the past becomes the future: "What I saw mirrored before me was also everything behind me." The mirror presents readers with an enigma that the narrative, which both progresses and regresses in time, complexifies. The varied embodiments of the self are both contained and confused in the story like the before and behind in the mirror. The mirror motif is not used according to convention for self-replication or self-evaluation, but as a means of living several lives or experiencing different forms of existence at the same time, not being one-self, but several selves at once.

Dybek's "Pet Milk" also offers a hybridizing variation on the mirror motif when the narrator glimpses the reflection of his girlfriend, Kate, as they celebrate his twenty-second birthday in a restaurant.[10] Their evening together has a certain poignancy because the young couple's plans for the future diverge; the narrator wants to join the Peace Corps and Kate intends to apply to graduate school in Europe. Like Chang's, Dybek's mirror is not really a mirror. Instead the narrator sees a reflection in an object that is not designed for that purpose, signaling its Othering function[11]:

> I caught the reflection of her face in the glass-covered 'The Street Musicians of Prague' above our table. I always loved seeing her in mirrors and windows. ... But this time, seeing her reflection hovering ghostlike upon an imaginary Prague was like seeing a future from which she had vanished. I knew I'd never meet anyone more beautiful to me. (170-171)

This found mirror blurs the boundaries of time and space to produce an enigmatic and powerfully suggestive icon. In this hybridizing configuration, which superimposes Kate "ghostlike upon an imaginary Prague," the narrator foregoes the visual possession of the female in order to imagine its opposite—his relinquishment of a woman (and also a city).[12] The mirror motif is dual, projecting Kate's freedom and the fulfillment of her dreams in the future as well as the narrator's mourning for her absence. It reflects an image of the narrator's paradoxical situation "of missing someone I was still with" (169). Like the mirror in Chang's "Falling Free" this motif projects us beyond the boundaries of the story, opening up the narrative to readers' creative imagination.

Like the mirror motif, the garden is a topos firmly established in the Western literary tradition. Rooted in the biblical representation of Eden, the garden is both a place of origins and a site of values. It is the *locus amoenus,* representing prelapsarian innocence, harmony, and concord. In its hybridizing adaptations, the garden becomes the site of accidental juxtapositions uncontrolled by the gardener's ordering hand. In the Othering transformations that we will now examine, the traditional *locus amoenus* is both denatured and regenerated. In A.R. Ammons's "The Quince Bush,"[13] a parasitic vine creates an unplanned combination when:

> The flowering quince bush
> on the back hedge has been
> run through by a morning

glory vine ....

Gloria Anzaldúa creates an apparently more dystopic variation on the
motif in the poem "Cultures," which depicts the backyard trash heap
where the family discards the refuse of consumer culture: murky Coke
bottles jostle "rubber-nippled baby bottles" and "cans of Spam with
twisted umbilicals."[14] And in a final example of the hybridizing of the
garden motif, Richard Wilbur's "The Lilacs" represents a paradoxical
space evoking contrasting seasons simultaneously. Like the superposed
and dispersed images in mirrors studied earlier, these heterogeneous
gardens valorize multiplicity and complexity rather than unity and purity.

     As an Othering function, hybridizing brings together in original
combinations things that are normally kept apart within the cultural
system. A.R. Ammons's "The Quince Bush" is a case in point; the garden
it depicts is open to the disorderly and disruptive forces that are normally
excluded from the *locus amoenus*. Though the title of the poem seems to
signal the centrality of the quince bush, in fact, it is only mentioned in the
opening line. It is subsequently upstaged, made into a "has been," by the
usurping morning glory vine that mobilizes attention for several stanzas,
as if it were the star in a spectacle in which the quince bush was only a
supporting actor: "and this morning three blooms/ are open as if for all
light,/ sound, and motion...." Then, the morning glory is itself displaced as
the speaker's attention moves "elsewhere" to consider young men, a child,
an old man, a caterpillar, and finally "wailing walls," before returning to
the morning glory vine. Even then, something else usurps the center: "a
day pours through a morning glory/ dayblossom's adequate, poised,/
available center." Like the quince bush that "has been/ run through," the
morning glory vine has been penetrated in its turn. Entities no longer exist
in isolation, but transform into one another. Like the bush holding up the
vine, Ammons's poem "The Quince Bush" becomes the structure that
holds together the speaker's roaming thoughts in provocative patterns.
Like the blossom transfused by daylight, the poem becomes a porous
container open to a multitude of disparate images which are transformed in
contact with one another.

     The poem's heterogeneous juxtapositions of images encourage readers
to venture out of familiar conceptual structures in order to imagine new
relationships. Ammons's representation of the garden breaks out of normal
boundaries. His flowers:

          ...reach for
     stellar reds and core violets:
     they listen as if for racket's

inner silence,

and focus as if to starve, all motion:
patterns of escaped sea
they tip the defeated, hostile,
oceanic wind:

Much more than a response to unexpected beauty, this description ventures far beyond safe, familiar categories like personification or metaphor, mixing and multiplying them beyond the limits of what can be visualized. Far from producing a static landscape portrait of a garden, the poem evokes a pulsing, mutating, restless field of energy. Moving from the sublime "reach" of their color, upward to the stars, inward to the "core," and outward to "patterns of escaped sea," the morning glory blooms also pass through a Zen-like moment of stillness, listening for the unimaginable silence in noise. The poem positions its subject on impossible frontiers between incompatible states of being, for when the blossoms "focus as if to starve, all motion," they could be at the extreme of either stillness or mobility. Perplexing clusters of imagery like these introduce Othering into the garden.

Each of the poems revisiting the topos of the *locus amoenus* revises the idea of the garden as that which excludes. Though death is absent from paradise, it coexists with life in these poems. Death and birth are not binary opposites but comparable traumatic moments of passage, transformative events that both end and give life. The garden in Wilbur's "The Lilacs" resembles a battlefield, with the bushes emerging "Like walking wounded/ from the dead of winter."[15] The poem does not confine mortality to its habitual season; instead, springtime awakening is brutal and traumatic:

Out of present pain
                    and from past terror
Their bullet-shaped buds
                    came quick and bursting … . (118)

Death and sexuality converge in this charged poetic language. Destruction and growth are not opposites but part of an unselective natural world. Indeed, heterogeneity seems essential to growth, as Gloria Anzaldúa suggests in "Cultures":

when it rots
trash replenishes the soil
my mother would say

but nothing would grow in
my small plots except
thistle sage and nettle.

Though the speaker protests that her yard produces "nothing" except spiky, prickly, stinging plants, these weeds are signs of irreducible vitality. If, on the one hand, the plots are compared to "graves," on the other hand, "the earth's dark veins" contain abundant reserves of life:

my sweat dripping on the swelling mounds

into the hole I'd rake up and pitch
rubber-nippled baby bottles
cans of Spam with twisted umbilicals
I'd overturn the cultures
spawning in Coke bottles
murky and motleyed . . . .

Values mix and mutate in this description: the earth, with its hole and swelling mounds seems at once masculine and feminine; the speaker's relation to it is both violent and nurturing; the mounds both abort and generate life.

In these hybridizing treatments of the garden, the transitions from birth to maturity to death are not represented as natural cycles or circles, but as unpredictable and disjunctive mutations. This is the effect of Richard Wilbur's unconventional representation of the changing states of the lilac bushes in his poem. In Spring the bushes "waken" not into new life, as might be expected, but: "To rot and rootbreak,/ to ripped branches...." This description seems to mix up the seasons, superimposing on the springtime scene the destruction and decay associated with fall and winter. Time moves backward to the past: "as the memory swept them/ Of night and numbness...." When the bushes finally blossom, it happens "suddenly" in abrupt mutations from "ripped branches" to "bullet-shaped buds" to "big blooms." The words amplify the violence of the transition through the plosive consonant "b." Then, seemingly the past is forgotten, and the lilacs keep silent about:

. . . their mortal message,
                                        unless one should measure
The depth and dumbness
                                        of death's kingdom
By the pure power
                    of this perfume (119).

In these lines the heady scent of lilacs, conventionally enjoyed as one of the delights of Spring, both masks and evokes mortality. The "perfume" seems far away from "death's kingdom," but only because its proximity has been forgotten. The idea of the year as a series of distinct seasons that separate birth from death relies only on our ability to suppress memories of continuity and coexistence. Wilbur's lilacs force us to remember the complexity of life in time.

These poetic revisitings of the *locus amoenus* hybridize the familiar motif partly through what they include in their gardens, and partly through their means of representation. Conventional devices like metaphor and personification permit unlikely combinations in textual space. Thus hybridizing is, to a certain extent, synonymous with literariness. The Othering function comes into play when texts go beyond literary norms to include such a mixture of contraries that textual space becomes unfamiliar, an adventure into the unknown. This is the invitation extended in Shirley Geok-lin Lim's poem "Brinjal."[16] Though the poem focuses exclusively on describing an object—the eggplant or aubergine—it does so through such rich metaphorical language that it creates a new hybridizing motif bringing together numerous contradictory associations in a single dizzying exclamation:

> Fragrant brinjal, purple hazed or
> sheen of amethyst; ovaloid female,
> pendulous; as shoe polish slicked;
> unevenly round, glowing moon's rump
> smelling of colors; in farm's wet
> morning—ordure of night soil; impenetrable
> skin like first sex; shiny as spit,
> as slippery; rubbery feel
> jousting the palm: you remind
> anything in nature is woman's
> and man's (overflowing potency,
> sultanate of suggestions by river flats),
> tickles fancy, excites memory's
> warm ooze—these water-smooth firm-toothed
> veggies, names jingling like slave anklets
> in rattan baskets heaped, abused
> by kitchen women, slapped into newspaper wrappers
> in the market this morning, fresh talents!

Naming the fruit only in the poem's title, "Brinjal," and then by its least familiar name, the poem's language estranges the familiar. Besides evoking such diverse substances as amethyst and shoe polish to describe its color, the speaker endows the fruit with a strangely mutating composite body made of internal and external, as well as male and female, organs. Ovaloid and pendulous at the same time, it evokes the breast or the womb ("ovaloid female"), the penis ("rubbery feel/ jousting the palm,") or the vagina ("slicked," "shiny as spit,/ as slippery,"), as well as buttocks ("moon's rump"), the mouth ("spit") and the anus ("ordure of night soil"). Finally, "smelling of colors," it provokes a kind of synaesthesia, a mixing of all sensations. In fact, the poem de-objectivizes the object by submitting it to a dizzying series of metamorphoses. Erotic imagery invites readers to implicate themselves in the adventure, to draw on "memory's/ warm ooze," to open themselves to "suggestions" and "fancy." The poem aims not to reproduce a recognizable image or even to pose a riddle, but to move through language into new possibilities.

Hence, Lim's hybridizing description necessarily stretches the conventions of poetic form. Its eighteen lines form a single sentence in which, though punctuation separates phrases from one another, a significant number of the lines run on, and the enjambments open up suggestive ambiguity, for example, "impenetrable/," "farm's wet/," and "excites memory's/." Moreover, numerous caesurae split the poem irregularly. The effect created is simultaneously one of syncopation and flow. The hybridizing process thus moves from content to form, though of course it calls into question the idea of form (associated ideologically with integrity, purity, unity, and correctness), as well as the idea that content could be separated from it.

As Lin's poem shows, new hybridizing motifs open up innovative possibilities, in terms of both cultural and literary values. Turning once again to Stuart Dybek's "Pet Milk" we discover in the narrative a number of hybridizing motifs that, unlike the quilt in Walker's story, have little significance in terms of plot.[17] Examined in the light of traditional critical criteria, they would appear to deform the narrative by their apparent irrelevance.[18] From the Othering perspective, though, they can be said to renew narrative through the hybridizing process. The opening paragraph introduces the motif that gives the story its title: "Pet milk isn't *real* milk. The color's off to start with. There's almost something of the past about it, like old ivory" (167). As opposed to "*real* milk," implicitly a guarantee of freshness and purity, the narrator associates Pet milk with alien substances and elapsed time. Like Proust's madeleine, it provokes reminiscences, evoking the narrator's grandmother; oddly, however, the grandmother plays a negligible role in the narrative. "Pet Milk" seems to feature as the title more for its oxymoronic juxtaposition of unlike words. What makes it particularly memorable is the way it mixes with other substances:

> ... I sat by her table watching the Pet milk swirl and cloud in the steaming
> coffee, and noticing, outside her window, the sky doing the same thing
> above the railroad yard across the street.
> And I remember, much later, seeing the same swirling sky in tiny liqueur
> glasses containing a drink called King Alphonse: the crème de cacao rising
> like smoke in repeated explosions, blooming in kaleidoscopic clouds
> through the layer of heavy cream. (168)

These liquids are not compounds uniting elements into a homogeneous
substance, but mixtures in which the different components diverge as well
as join. The effect is "kaleidoscopic" rather than synthetic; the colors
contrast and blend in movements as changeable as weather. Dybek's
images of contrasting liquids combining in "Pet Milk" better serves as an
image of the hybridizing process than the more static emblem of the quilt
that we examined initially. Though the cloth in Walker's quilts is torn or
cut, the pieces are recomposed and fixed in harmonious patterns. By
contrast, the liquid in the King Alphonse cocktail is in continual
movement: "rising like smoke in repeated explosions, blooming in
kaleidoscopic clouds ...." It combines violence and growth in a
paradoxical but vital mixture.

This mutable motif could serve as an image of the narration in Dybek's
short story, which passes from one image or episode to another by a
process of association that links disparate things together. Thus the
narrator moves from the Pet milk in his grandmother's coffee to the
yellow radio on her kitchen table, a second hybridizing motif:

> There was a yellow plastic radio on her kitchen table, usually tuned to the
> polka station, though sometimes she'd miss it by half a notch and get the
> Greek station instead, or the Spanish, or the Ukrainian. In Chicago where
> we lived, all the incompatible states of Europe were pressed down at the
> staticky right end of the dial. (167-68)

With utter disregard for geographical separations, the radio groups "the
incompatible" together and transmits the unpredictable. The apparent lack
of function of the objects so carefully detailed in these introductory
descriptive passages troubles readers' expectations. The direction of the
story becomes unpredictable, as these disorienting motifs estrange a
familiar American landscape.[19] Dybek's Chicago becomes a favorable
terrain for Othering experiences.

In hybridizing texts, as in the motifs, what matters is the escape from
fixity and predictability. "Pet Milk" blurs the boundaries of time and
space, moving backward and forward through a series of vignettes linked
through the logic of association. Though the short story ends with a train

ride, the express train does not reach its destination. Instead the narrative ends with the vision glimpsed from the train window as the narrator makes love to Kate in the empty conductor's compartment:

> A high school kid in shirt sleeves ... caught sight of us, and in the instant before he disappeared, he grinned and started to wave. Then he was gone, and I turned from the window, back to Kate, forgetting everything—the passing stations, the glowing late sky, even the sense of missing her—but that arrested wave stayed with me. It was as if I were standing on that platform, with my schoolbooks and a smoke, on one of those endlessly accumulated afternoons after school when I stood almost outside of time simply waiting for a train, and I thought how much I'd have loved seeing someone like us streaming by. (173)

Readers may recognize this as another hybridizing variation on the mirror motif. The movement of the train relativizes time, allowing the narrator the vision of himself "almost outside of time." In a montage that recalls all the text's other hybridizing motifs, he has the sense both of seeing a past self through the window and of being the inexperienced younger boy delighted with the image of his own future.

Steven Millhauser's "Beneath the Cellars of Our Town"[20] could be seen as the exact opposite of Dybek's "Pet Milk" in its exploitation of an original hybridizing motif as means of othering form. Millhauser's narrative, like Dybek's, develops the hybridizing motif at the expense of conventional plot, but whereas in "Pet Milk" hybridizing motifs multiply and mutate, in "Beneath the Cellars of Our Town" the hybridzing motif quite simply *is* the narrative. Even more than Dybek's, Millhauser's text can with difficulty be called a short story, since the text consists of the narrator's extended description of a New England town that superimposes two contrasting landscapes, one above ground and one below. Far from being a conventional hierarchical structure, this geographical anomaly hybridizes space, allowing the townspeople to undertake Othering excursions in both directions. Millhauser's title teasingly evokes the archetypal New England town represented in Thornton Wilder's *Our Town*. Indeed, above ground the town presents all the standard American landmarks, but these familiar sites contain openings to a world below:

> We descend through openings that lie scattered throughout the township, not only in the north woods but also in parking lots behind stores on Main Street, in the slopes of the railroad embankment, in the picnic grounds overlooking the creek, in the Revolutionary War graveyard, in weed-grown vacant lots and backyard gardens, at the edges of schoolyards, at the back of the long shed in the lumberyard, behind the green dumpster at the back

of the carwash, beside yellow fire hydrants and dark blue mailboxes on
maple-lined streets rippling with sun and shade. (212-13)

Initially Millhauser's text resembles an essay or treatise on the labyrinth of
passageways below the town, presenting different theories and arguments
about its formation and social significance. Yet unlike a conventional
essayist, Millhauser's narrator refuses to draw any conclusions, preferring
to foster ambiguity.

The stairways connecting surface and depth invite the discovery of
difference, even though its nature cannot be predicted or even adequately
defined: "...we assert the absolute separateness of the lower realm, its
radical difference, even if we can't agree, even if we scarcely understand,
why that difference matters" (220).   Moving in this sentence from
confident assertion to a baffled admission of incomprehension, the
narrator echoes conventional scientific language and then undermines its
objectivity. The difficulty of making any definite pronouncement on the
topic and the impossibility of drawing a clear distinction between the two
realms is crucial, for this is what opens the town to the Othering
experience.

Above and below the town described in Millhauser's "Beneath the
Cellars of Our Town," the landscape continually mutates. The upper town
boasts all the latest signs of modern life, but the cityscape is also
continually   modified   by   unpredictable   outcroppings   of   new,
"impermanent" openings onto the terrain beneath (213). Below ground the
landscape is also constantly mutating:

> The pattern of twisting and interconnecting paths, on several levels, is far
> too complex for anyone to master, and in addition the pattern is always
> changing, for old passageways become suddenly or gradually impassable,
> and new wall-openings and small connecting corridors are continually
> being formed by the fall of rock fragments or the gradual loosening of rock
> along fault lines—a process regularly enhanced by the workers with their
> busy picks. (215)

These continual alterations of the landscape place the town dwellers in a
constant state of perplexity. No exploration of the passageways can ever
be repeated. The underground labyrinth in Millhauser's "Beneath the
Cellars of Our Town" disorients those who venture down, completely
inverting values: "it seems to us that only there, under the ground, do we
experience the true exhilaration of height: the town itself, imagined from
below" (222). Beneath the town, space is paradoxical. The passageways
are contradictory in breadth and length: "even the broadest give an

impression of narrowness" (212); "Others argue that the passageways, though limited in space, are in effect endless" (221).

Hybridizing motifs jumble conventional points of reference, throwing into confusion orderly categories of thought. We have already seen how the mirror motif in Chang's "Falling Free" confounds "behind" and "before," blurring boundaries between time and space. In hybridizing texts, adverbs of space or time such as up and down or before and after, often assigned absolute value in common language, become reversible.

In the hybridizing process, mobility is vital and, at the same time, erratic and unpredictable. Not surprisingly, these texts feature various modes of connection or passages between one place and another— stairways, streets, railway lines, passageways, even telephones— permitting exchange and variation. The stairways connecting the upper and lower levels of the town in Millhauser's story are openings onto dual possibilities, allowing residents to "immers[e] [them] selves in two different atmospheres" (228). Stairways do not present either/or propositions; they permit both "descent and ascent." These various modes of connection make other directions not only available but also desirable, making movement an end in itself rather than a means to an end.

Mobility ensures that subjects avoid being placed in the system, hence the recurrence in hybridizing texts of the motif of crossing borders or frontiers, whether real or metaphorical. Not surprisingly, the motif is especially noticeable in works by writers of immigrant origin, or those from racial or ethnic minorities. The characters in Sandra Cisneros's fiction cross back and forth from Mexico to the United States, movement that involves dislocation, but also the enjoyment of new liberties. In "One Holy Night" the narrator's family history is shaped by a pattern of criss-crossing the border in order to elude the stigma attached to deviant behavior:

> I could hear Abuelita and Uncle Lalo talking in low voices as if they were praying the rosary, how they were going to send me to Mexico to San Dionisio de Tlaltepango, where I have cousins and where I was conceived and would've been born had my grandma not thought it wise to send my mother here to the United States so that neighbors in San Dionisio de Tlaltepango wouldn't ask why her belly was suddenly big. (33)[21]

Motivated by the desire to elude the neighbors' gossip, this back and forth movement at the same time reinforces and evades social laws and controls. Although freedom exists on neither side of the Mexican American frontier, border-crossings loosen up social strictures. These meanderings also make available the multiple and even contradictory value systems evoked in the short story's mixed cultural references. Indeed, the name of San Dionisio de Tlaltepango, the place of the narrator's conception and future birthplace of her baby, is shaped out of cultural migration. It juxtaposes three different cults: Spanish Catholicism, the Greek cult of Dionysos, and the indigenous Mayan heritage. The short story's many references to Christian and pre-Christian religions juxtapose contradictory moral codes, between which the narrator threads her way. Not surprisingly, she describes her discovery of sex as taking "the crooked walk" (28), choosing a metaphor of movement for this rite of passage.

Identity is mutable in Cisneros's fiction. The narrator's lover in "One Holy Night" is an elusive, protean figure, whose various names attest to his resistance to being placed: "nobody seemed to know where he came from" (29). In the narrator's company he assumes the mythic persona of Chaq Uxmal Paloquín, from the Yucatan, "of an ancient line of Mayan kings" (27). More generally, on the American side of the border, he goes by the oxymoronic name of Boy Baby, a title which, though a sign of his reduced status, suits his elusive personality: "So he seemed boy and baby and man all at once, and the way he looked at me, how do I explain?" (28). The letters coming from his Carmelite sister on the Mexican side of the border deny his "Mayan blood" (33), identifying him as "Señor C. Cruz" (32), and as "Chato" (33). Finally, the newspaper clippings describing his arrest as a serial murderer halt his mobility, showing him in the hands of the police: "looking very much like stone" (34). Fixed in the newspaper's "black-and-white" representation (34), the narrator's lover is officially defined, but, his face is reduced to dots, no longer recognizable.

In hybridizing texts, acquiring identity does not entail the shedding of former selves, but rather the enjoyment of expanded possibilities of existence. This difference in attitude is the source of conflict between the narrator and her daughter in Walker's "Everyday Use." Once she leaves home Dee, the brilliant, college-educated daughter, sheds her given name, inherited from her Southern family, and adopts an African identity, Wangero Lee-wanika Kemanjo" (53). On her return home, her mother first shortens this to "Wangero" (53), before finally assigning her the hybridizing designation, "Dee (Wangero)" (55), recognizing her claim to a mixed heritage.[22] Indeed, portrayals of hybridized American subjects rarely depict a new breed; instead, as we have already shown in the analysis of the mirror trope, they deal in dual or multiple subjectivities. Rather than abandoning their old identities like snakes shedding their skins, hybridized subjects add new selves that coexist in unstable relation with the old.

For the autodiegetic narrator in Diana Chang's "Falling Free," an immigrant from China to the United States, identity is a fluctuating international mixture:

> All of us are Chinese some of the time, I say. But I'm not certain what I mean. Other times, I'm a Calvinist, familiar with dimity and yokes. My favorite summer dress is Danish, my gold ring Greek, my face cream French, my daydreams I can't place. For someone so unsure of who I am, from time to time I have such definite statements to make. (61)

In listing these heterogeneous affiliations the narrator refuses the unity implicit in the term identity.[23] The passage begins with a universal declaration that seems paradoxically to assert individuality: "I have such definite statements to make." Yet the pronouncement about Chinese identity, "All of us are Chinese some of the time," mocks the idea of an essential ethnic self, not simply because it includes all humanity (a characteristically Western form of rhetoric), but also because it adopts a typically American idiom, ironically echoing the saying attributed to Abraham Lincoln. Moreover, it is immediately undercut by equivocation: ("I'm not certain what I mean."), ensuring that the self remains shifting and indefinable, even to itself.

Constant mutation eliminates any notions of beginning or end. Hence, rather than being founding or terminal events, birth and death become moments of passage. In "Falling Free" the narrator describes her grandson's birth as a kind of border crossing:

> I remember the day he arrived in American—purplish-red and kicking out of Mimi at Doctors Hospital, the mayor oblivious a couple of blocks away of still another 'Oriental' who'd slipped over a border. (69)

The boy is portrayed as an alien—"purplish-red"—who enters, though the odd choice of the adjective "American" rather than the noun "America," an unfamiliar linguistic and cultural system. Death is not seen as an end, but another transformation: "I'll leave through the skylight, God sucking me upward through his straw. …. For once, I'll be his aspiration, momentarily in the light and years of galaxies" (64). This humorous image of passing inverts and destabilizes conventional representations of acceding to a permanent, transcendent state. Rather than aspiring to God, the ailing narrator wants to be "his aspiration" in a momentary reversal of hierarchies. Contrary to the expectations raised by the text's reflections on death, the narrative ends in a new beginning. In contact at last with the American admirer she has always resisted, the narrator is ready to accept love once more: "I can blossom, I can attract bees" (75). A new interpretation of the title becomes possible; "Falling Free" suggests the narrator's birth into a new freedom.

The metamorphoses in these hybridizing texts differ from those found in Ovid's *Metamorphoses*, where transformation, often induced as a means of punishment, or, on the contrary, a mode of escape from danger, is usually permanent. In the hybridizing process, there is no final goal, no ultimate resting point, and certainly no accomplishment of a stable hybrid entity. In Othering texts, hybridizing brings difference together in irresolvable confrontations, for resolution would simply produce a return to the values of the system. Thus, in "One Holy Night" the conflict between Christian and non-Christian values is never decided, and the young narrator's representation of her situation remains ambiguously double. In her sexual initiation she comes across partly as the innocent dupe of a dangerous psychopath and partly as the lucid and willing participant in her admittance into an experience that the dominant Christian culture condemns.

Cisneros's story disturbs because of its unresolved clash of values. Even as she defies the adults' rules, the narrator voices her agreement with their values, for example, when she accepts the bad news about her lover because: "The youngest [sister] , a Carmelite, writes me all this and prays for my soul, which is why I know it's all true" (33). Still, sacrilegiously, her narrative rewrites the nativity story, pairing a Chicana eighth-grader and a pedophile murderer as a new Mary and Joseph. Like the nativity, the "holy night" of their union mixes the sublime and the squalid:

> You must not tell anyone what I am going to do, he said. And what I remember next is how the moon, the pale moon with its one yellow eye, the moon of Tikal, and Tulum, and Chichén, stared through the pink plastic curtains. (30)

The narrator's voice is also mixed; sometimes lofty and biblical, sometimes poetical, and sometimes naïve, mundane or even trite, the different styles clash and combine in a strange polyphony.

The hybridizing process does not ensure harmonious transformations; indeed, the places where contradictory values come into contact are zones of violence as well as productivity. Gloria Anzaldúa describes the borderlands as:

> *una herida abierta* where the Third world grates against the first and bleeds. And before a scab forms it hemorrhages again, the lifeblood of two worlds merging to form a third country—a border culture.[24]

The divided society described in Anzaldúa's poem "Cultures," where the split is as much between genders as cultures, is ambiguously both sterile and fruitful. In "One Holy Night" Cisneros explores, through a more extended narrative, the fertile and murderous contact of contraries. In striking contrast to the Catholic tradition, where the Immaculate Conception is figured in images that convey purity and integrity, like the passing of light through glass, the narrator experiences her defloration as both assault and parturition. "Then something inside me bit me, and I gave out a cry as if the other, the one I wouldn't be anymore, leapt out" (30). Her initiation into sexual knowledge splits her in two and also brings her into the world of time, giving birth to a before and after. She awaits the birth of her child impatiently, but she also perceives it as an alien other, ready to do her violence:

> I count the months for the baby to be born, and it's like a ring of water inside me reaching out and out until one day it will tear from me with its own teeth.
> Already I can feel the animal inside me stirring in his own uneven sleep. (34)

This hybridizing representation of pregnancy juxtaposes the gentleness of ripples of water and the savageness of a sharp-toothed animal. It does not mask the ambiguity of the child's dependent, parasitic relation to its mother.[25]

Although violent imagery may be particularly prevalent in hybridizing texts by America's racial and ethnic minorities, it is by no means confined to them. Any deviation from expected trajectories produces both liberation and anxiety. Hence, divagation is represented as a form of violence in Millhauser's "Beneath the Cellars of Our Town." The tangled passageways of the underground labyrinth drop downward abruptly, rupturing continuity with a paradoxically pleasurable shock:

> then it ought to be clear why we never experience monotony in our passageways, but on the contrary a sensation of pleasurable uncertainty, of surprise and adventure. When all is said and done, what we feel, when we go down among our passageways is a sensation of expansion—as if some inner constriction were suddenly bursting. (223-24)

The discontinuity of the passages produces a violent form of release, like something "bursting." Moreover, emerging from underground produces a shock that is just as intense. Rather than the comforting restoration of the familiar described in the usual accounts of adventure, the returning town dwellers experience a second assault in emerging from the labyrinth, as, "for an instant, the lost world enters us like a sword ..." (228). Notable in these contrasting images of "bursting" as an interior sensation produced by the outside and the outside "enter[ing] ... like a sword" is the reversibility characteristic of the hybridizing process.

In these Othering texts, violence should not be seen in the usual systemic terms as a negative quality. On the contrary, it is inseparable from and necessary to life, as Cisneros's evocation of sexuality suggests. Ammons's "The Quince Bush" offers more mysterious contrasts, introducing into the meditation on the garden images that might emanate from contemporary conflicts:

> Elsewhere young men scratch and fire:
> a troubled child shudders to a freeze:
> an old man bursts finally and
> rattles down
>
> clacking slats: the caterpillar pierced
> by a wasp egg blooms inside
> with the tender worm: wailing
> walls float
>
> luminous with the charge of grief . . . .

The place where "young men scratch and fire," might be an image of matches striking outside the garden, or of sexual awakening, but the lines also suggest war, terror, and death. At first the violence seems to be placed "Elsewhere." We might imagine young fighters firing their weapons, while perhaps in the same conflict, perhaps in other circumstances, a child freezes and an old man collapses. Yet violence and death occur "inside" in the garden too. In a lethal parasitic relationship that recalls Blake's "The Sick Rose," a "tender worm" consumes a caterpillar "pierced by a wasp egg." Then the two seemingly contradictory zones converge, as the poem concentrates beauty and sorrow in the hallucinatory mirage-like image of "wailing walls float[ing] / luminous with the charge of grief: ..." The wall no longer divides one space from another, but "floats" in between. New life "blooms" within the dying caterpillar; the flowering quince "has been/ run through by a morning/ glory vine..."; and finally, "a day pours through a morning glory/ dayblossom's adequate, poised,/ available center." Penetration is ambiguously destructive and productive, painful and glorious.

From the stimulating contradiction of paradox to the combative, even deadly struggle of parasitism, hybridizing texts do not simply juxtapose heterogeneous elements, they place them in dynamic relation to one another. Insofar as they set in motion a process without any foreseeable end, hybridizing forms differ fundamentally from the hybrid. The hybrid brings different elements together in order to attain a result that is stabilized in a reproducible phenomenon. The hybridizing process, on the contrary, avoids either absorbing difference in unity or ossifying it into conventional patterns of either harmony or opposition. In Othering texts, there can be no resolution, because that would imply recuperation by the system. Instead of evoking hybridizing forms, then, we might speak of de-forms, since these texts both destructure traditional motifs and themselves resist fixity. In a culture in which choice is represented as an essential freedom and responsibility, hybridizing texts take the liberty of not having to choose one thing and reject another, but instead imagining a world where heterogeneous and even conflicting possibilities coexist in relation to one another. The dynamic movement of hybridizing texts ensures that difference exists not as fixed oppositions, nor as alternatives, but as multiple and ambivalent possibilities. Most important, the hybridizing combination of destruction and generation produces a disruptive force, creating openings onto what is imagined to exist beyond the system.

Notes

[1] Francois Laplantine notes the limitations of spatial metaphors as ways of thinking about hybridity in his discussion of "vers" [towards] in Francois Laplantine and Alexis Nouss, *Métissages de Arcimboldo à Zombi* (Paris: Pauvert, 2001) 581-584. "Si la pensée du métissage est bien une pensée de la médiation qui se joue dans les intermédiaires, les intervalles et les interstices à partir des croisements et des échanges, elle ne saurait se réduire au et, à l'entre et à l'entre-deux, qui sont des catégories spatiales. C'est contrairement au mélange et à la mixité, une pensée de la tension, c'est-à-dire une pensée résolument temporelle, qui évolue à travers les langues, les genres, les cultures, les continents, les époques, les histoires et les histoires de vie" (581). (If the concept of *métissage* is indeed one of mediation that comes into play in the in-betweens, the intervals and the interstices occurring in intersections and exchanges, it cannot be reduced to and, or between, and in-between, which are spatial categories. Contrary to the concepts of mixture and mixedness, it is a concept of tension, that is to say a deliberately temporal concept, which develops across languages, genres, cultures, continents, ages, histories and life histories [Our translation.].)
[2] The phrase is from Chase Twichell's "Japanese Weeping Cherry," discussed in Chapter Five.
[3] The term is used by Gloria Anzaldúa, in her groundbreaking work, *Borderlands / La Frontera: The New Mestiza* (San Francisco: Aunt Lute Books, 1987).
[4] Laplantine and Nouss use the term, which gives them *"Métis sages"* [clever hybrids] in their punning title.

[5] Édouard Glissant, *Caribbean Discourse: Selected Essays*, trans. J. Michael Dash (Charlottesville: University Press of Virginia, 1989) 142. Glissant, Anzaldúa, and Laplantine and Nouss have all been extremely helpful in our consideration of the hybridizing impulse.

[6] Besides being linked with the essentialist aesthetic (and often moral) qualities discussed in Chapter Five, such as closure, unity, or purity, the word "form" is, not surprisingly, associated with social values and practices such as decorum and rules and regulations.

[7] Alice Walker, "Everyday Use," *In Love and Trouble* (New York: Harvest, 1967) 47-59.

[8] "I couldn't bear it any longer, being named after the people who oppress me" (53). Another example of her selectivity is seen when she claims the dasher and the top of the butter churn (55), leaving the churn itself, which is thus rendered useless.

[9] Diana Chang, "Falling Free," in *Charlie Chan is Dead: An Anthology of Contemporary Asian American Fiction*, ed. Jessica Hagedorn (New York: Penguin, 1993) 60-75.

[10] Stuart Dybek, "Pet Milk," *The Coast of Chicago* (New York: Picador, 2003) 167-73.

[11] This hybridizing motif thus anticipates the Othering nodes that will be explored in Chapter Nine, "Objects of Disorientation."

[12] In literature on the city (for example, Dos Passos's *Manhattan Transfer*) the city is often associated with a desirable woman who stands for all that city dwellers dream of possessing.

[13] A.R. Ammons, "The Quince Bush," *The Selected Poems: Expanded Edition* (New York: W.W. Norton, 1986) 68.

[14] Gloria Anzaldúa, "Cultures," in *Borderlands*, 120.

[15] Richard Wilbur, "The Lilacs," *New and Collected Poems* (New York: Harvest, 1988) 118.

[16] Shirley Geok-lin Lim, "Brinjal," *Monsoon History: Selected Poems* (London: Skoob, 1994) 111.

[17] We base this observation on the Chekhovian premise that an object brought to the reader's attention is destined serve a function; Chekhov gives the example of the gun introduced in Act I that can be expected to go off in Act III.

[18] Because of their apparently digressive nature, these motifs recall the rhetoric of excess discussed in Chapter Four.

[19] Though these hybridizing motifs delineate objects, since they have no function in the plot, they are not of the same order as those discussed in Chapter Nine, "Objects of Disorientation." They resemble them, though, in that they are very ordinary things which become the focus of inordinate fascination.

[20] Steven Millhauser, "Beneath the Cellars of Our Town," *The Knife Thrower and Other Stories* (New York: Crown, 1998) 211-28.

[21] Sandra Cisneros, "One Holy Night," *Woman Hollering Creek and Other Stories* (New York: Random House, 1991) 27-35.

[22] There is obvious irony in the contradiction between Dee's refusal of her grandmother's name and her desire to possess the quilts. In this, Walker's story prefers a form of didacticism to the more stimulating paradoxes of Othering.

[23] The *American Heritage Dictionary* gives the following etymology: "French identité, from Old French identite, from Late Latin identits, from Latin idem, *the same* (influenced by Late Latin essentits, *being,*, and identidem, *repeatedly*), from id, *it*; see i- in Indo-European roots."

[24] Anzaldúa, p. 3.

[25] Cisneros' representation of pregnancy in this short story evokes the tangled images produced in the same context of maternity that will be studied in connection with objects of disorientation in Chapter Nine.

CHAPTER SEVEN

EXPERIMENTAL FORMS

This chapter could be considered as the counterpart of Chapter Five, its orientation turned upside down, so to say. In the texts studied there, the search for formal perfection provokes the return of Othering forces tending to destabilize them. The imposition of a conceptual frame on the formlessness of reality brings to light the speciousness of the division between unformed reality and man-made coherence. The formlessness of reality calls for coherence but that very coherence always cites its chaotic origin. Both aspects of representation should be considered as two facets of the same reality. It is only by a willful perhaps inevitable omission that form is given undue precedence. When either of the facets is minorized the whole representational project is disrupted. The Othering principle is the textual trace of that disruption. In Chapter Five, idealized forms were shown to provoke the return of contrary impulses; in contrast, the present chapter examines texts that give destabilizing forces a free rein. Although they eschew attempts at achieving harmony or coherence through conventional means, the problem of form remains crucial. Texts that are ostensibly in flagrant defiance of traditional forms have to break new ground and invent their own structures. Three strategies are predictable: some texts evince deviant forms by reversing conventional patterns; others create original forms by piecing together the fragmented elements of traditional forms; still others completely reject all pretension at formal definition. All these Othering forms place readers in a precarious position: rather than mapping out conventional structures, they rely on their readers' ability to find new paths leading beyond received aesthetic formats.

Yet, Othering forms are not hidden flaws in or aberrations from the system but its obligatory counterpart. Othering structures are not completely chaotic; they simply seek innovative strategies to produce meaning. Our constant preoccupation throughout this study is to denounce the preconceived idea of a cultural system blocking all other possibilities of thinking around or against it. We believe, on the contrary, that whenever we resort to systematic thought we activate, at the same time, the aspiration to follow and to escape its principles. Attempts at perfection inevitably draw attention to the imperfections that are being eliminated. The converse proposition is also true: whenever the Othering (dis)orientation is given full scope, as in the texts considered in this chapter, form remains an absolute necessity. Yet, this obligation cannot be undertaken as a deliberate move comparable to the ordering gesture described in Wallace Stevens's poem "Anecdote of the Jar."[1] When the jar is introduced into the "slovenly wilderness," it remains an alien feature in a scene that derives unity from its presence. The question is different when the "slovenly" Othering principle dominates, when the urn is broken, and the text's orientation is placed outside the norms of the system. In that extreme situation a guiding principle remains; although tradition is disqualified, form is no less essential. As the imposition of the jar in Stevens's poem aptly shows, the artistic artifact makes "The wilderness r[i]se up to it," as if to civilize it and give it definition, but paradoxically, though "no longer wild" from the perspective of the jar, the wilderness has gained a space and a form while preserving its original slovenly nature.

This paradoxical situation can perhaps be clarified if we reexamine the concept of form. The Othering orientation does not challenge the recourse to structuring principles in poetry or fiction; nor does it promote an amorphous conception of texts. Meaningfulness cannot be associated with either empty or chaotic forms. Aesthetic creation, in whatever field, is always the product of a balance between form and formlessness, neither side of this duality being given precedence over the other. The writers that we are going to consider in this chapter turn away from the ingrained expectations that constitute the basis on which readers fashion their interpretations. These preconceptions are all the more importunate as they appear to be definitionally attached to the concept of form. Operating at a pre-conscious level, they are not usually submitted to critical analysis. This is precisely what we have to do now in order to understand the difficulties facing the creators that we are about to discuss, and to appreciate the solutions they have adopted to solve them.

Underlying all the texts under consideration is the desire to unyoke form from its association with a certain number of conventions. The first of these conventions is, to put it simply, that texts necessarily begin somewhere, in an implied or explicit source, and they are oriented toward a denouement. The second of these premises follows from the first: almost automatically continuity is projected between origin and ending; ideally, everything in the text, discontinuities included, should contribute to the connection between these extremities. The third premise is even more deep-rooted: a text, whatever its form, has to have a center, a purpose, or a theme. The fourth principle is so deeply imprinted on readers' minds that

it seems constitutive of their positions as readers: whoever reads expects to
be detached from the real world and transported into a fictitious universe.
In various ways, our chosen texts call into question these implicit
assumptions. Not only is the difference between fact and fiction often
effaced but also such familiar notions as before and after, origin and
ending, or pertinence and deviance. Yet none of these categories is
abolished; they are distanced but always cited while submitted to Othering
revision.

In order to return to a more useful conception of structure we would
like to disqualify the word "form," since beside the above-mentioned
preconceptions, it conveys a dichotomy between container and content. If,
on the contrary, we adopt a definition of structure as "function," we can
combine the traditional concept of form with the Othering experiments
that we are about to describe. "Form" and all the notions attached to that
word are indissociable from texts' fundamental communicative function.
This corresponds to the informational function that regulates the transfer
of a certain message from an originator to a destinator. The orientation of
informational texts is centrifugal; they proceed from a focus and convey
content to an anticipated receptor. The texts that we are analyzing are
rather centripetal; they revisit an experience that they want to preserve and
translate into words. Consequently, readers no longer occupy the positions
of receptors of information; rather, they are confronted with an
imaginative experience that they are invited to reenact and to a large extent
recreate. The text itself is no longer a medium; it becomes a gesture, an
invitation to participate, a script to improvise a reading. Writers relinquish
some of their authority: they no longer attempt to capture their readers'
attention; instead, they elicit a response and possibly an act of communion.
The formal structure of the texts ceases to be a means to an end; it
becomes an end in itself, a summons to readers' creative explorations.

In order to further document this unfamiliar situation, we have chosen
to examine A.R. Ammons's "Center."[2]

A bird fills up the
streamside bush
with wasteful song,
capsizes waterfall,
mill run, and
superhighway
to
song's improvident
center
lost in the green
bush green

answering bush:
wind varies:
the noon sun casts
mesh refractions
on the stream's amber
bottom
and nothing at all gets,
nothing gets
caught at all.

A cursory reading of the poem might yield a paraphrase representing a fairly banal situation: a bird's "wasteful song" appears to be unduly diverting attention from the complexity of a scene in which it figures as an interloper. Yet this superficial summary in no way encapsulates the poem. Because of the song's saliency it seems to occupy the center of the riverside scene, but it turns out that "center" is just a word humorously placed halfway down the poem and "lost in the green." All around that "wasteful," "improvident," spurious focus, the features of the scene have "capsized" in a state of disarray. Words assemble in curious combinations of regular and discordant rhythms: "lost in the green/ bush green/ answering bush." The expected association between "green" and "bush" is dislocated in order to suggest new associations, new forms of meaning nested in language such as "bush green" and "answering bush." In fact, beyond the poem's middle, humorously marked by the word "center," the poem evokes a dispersion of the midday light that brings about its puzzling conclusion: "and nothing at all gets/ nothing gets/ caught at all." We recognize the same staccato rhythm as in the preceding passage and the same cumulative accretion of repeated segments. But this time, the line breaks induce a string of disparate suggestions: "nothing at all gets" could somehow, through the polysemous word "get," be paraphrased as "nothing makes sense." Then, if we resist the impulse to find a univocal meaning that would block our perception of an Othering interpretation, in the following line, which repeats the phrase without "at all," it seems, on the contrary, that "nothing[ness] prevails." Finally, following the same wayward logic, the last line, which reiterates "at all" in the final, emphatic position, could signify that nothing is finally trapped in totality. There is no final meaning in this poem but rather a performative force of persuasion based on rhythm and syncopation. The poem does not so much state as make possible the meaning it attempts to convey. It should be experienced as an invitation to displace the straightforward "nothing gets caught at all," and imagine the alternative combinations that the poem suggests. Form as gesture does not express a content; it shapes a cognitive process.

The texts presented here are not always as radical. They reveal the Othering process in various forms and degrees. Most texts are only superficially affected by this orientation. Nonetheless, they should not be considered as less daring or less illustrative of the way Othering can impact conventional forms. This is the case with Grace Paley's story, "A Conversation with My Father,"[3] which uses distancing to defuse the information transfer function traditionally associated with texts. The narrative is no longer concerned with telling a story, but simply with relating a conversation between father and daughter. As a matter of fact, as in Ammons's poem, the text has no center, only a certain indeterminacy in orientation. The conversation is about the writing of stories, and on that point the father's and daughter's opinions diverge. In the space between the story as related by the narrator and the story as it should be told according to her father's tastes, Paley invites us to discover a pathway. The daughter, also the autodiegetic narrator, is a writer who despises plots that follow "the absolute line between two points" (162). She thus asserts her unconventional priorities, while her father favors more traditional narratives. Desiring to oblige her terminally ill father, the narrator proposes two versions of the same story about the relationship between a mother and her junkie son. There is an obvious mirror effect of the text-within-text structure that prevents a straightforward unfolding of the storyline. Perplexing peripheral insights replace direction of interest and fortuitous parallelisms, thematic orientation.

The narrator's fairly straightforward first version of the story falls to pieces at the father's insistence upon more serious justification and character building. In additions such as: "However, she never cooked anything but chili, and that no more than once a week" (165), the obliging daughter introduces a humorous slant. Another effect of distancing stems from the way the mock-serious story mirrors the framing relationship except that it inverses the characters' genders. The same pathetic attempt to communicate between generations opens a gap that storytelling is supposed to fill. The gap between the father and daughter is compounded by their total inattention to context: the father who insists on a tragic ending is himself terminally ill, while his daughter seems more compassionate to her characters than to her own father. The misunderstanding is nearly total, so that the short story ends in a stalemate. Readers are left dangling, their attention at the same time provoked and disappointed by its conclusion. Yet, since their expectations are denied, their participation is needed. At the point when readers have to fill in for the defecting narrator, the Othering perspective takes over. Father and daughter are incapable of constructing a story together, which is indeed what the story-within-the story is mimicking. But to what purpose other than in both cases denouncing the assumption underpinning the storytelling relationship which predicates a minimal complicity between the storyteller and his listeners?

This narrative dead-end produces the typical Othering situation that we also discover in Carver's story, "The Calm."[4] Four characters are gathered in a barber's salon. The narrator is having his hair trimmed, while the other two are waiting their turn. The center of interest in the narrative seems to lie in a story told by one of the waiting customers about a very frustrating deer hunting party in which, because of the speaker's son's blundering behavior, a wounded deer is abandoned in the forest. After that rather insignificant anecdote, the customers fall out with each other as if, in spite of the ostensible bone of contention (in good hunting practice, the deer should never have been left behind in the forest), a quarrel had been brewing between them. Indeed, it seems as if the men's frayed tempers were only looking for a pretext to flare up. They eventually leave the barber's shop, without a release of the accumulated tension, so that the barber turns on the narrator: "'Well, do you want me to finish barbering this hair or not?' the barber said to me as if I was the cause of everything" (198). Nevertheless, inexplicably after this outburst of animosity, a feeling of calm descends upon the narrator. This development is blatantly illogical, and the story's conclusion only reinforces the enigmatic atmosphere. The barber gently touches the narrator's scalp:

> He ran his fingers through my hair. He did it slowly, as if thinking about something else. He ran his fingers through my hair. He did it tenderly, as a lover would. (198)

The narrator repeats the phrase describing the barber's gesture, assigning it two contradictory motivations. This turns out to be the moment the narrator finalizes his decision to abandon his wife: "in the barber's chair that morning, I had made up my mind to go" (198). It would be easy to consider these rhetorical hesitations and logical gaps as ironical and support that judgment by drawing conclusions about men's callousness. Yet, the final lines of the story imply the contrary: "I was thinking today about the calm I felt when I closed my eyes and let the barber's fingers move through my hair, the sweetness of those fingers, the hair already starting to grow" (198). Men's humanity is not so much in question as the illusion of consistency that the storytelling format induces in us. We want our stories to be plausible even at the cost of falsifying human nature. We cannot put up with illogicality and are blind to the banal but powerful undercurrent of existence: "the hair already starting to grow" (198). Life-changing decisions can be made for no apparent reasons, and life continues.

Dan Chaon's story "Falling Backwards"[5] carries the defusing of narrative forms even further. The story's most intriguing characteristic is that is has two conclusions, one surprisingly at the beginning and one, as expected, at the end. The start of the narrative is the ostensible conclusion of a story that progresses regressively, while the ending can be seen as the origin and real conclusion of all the previous events.[6] Paradoxically, both the ending of the text and the final event in the chronological sequence of events are strangely inconclusive.[7] As a consequence, the narrative gives the impression of a bizarrely disconnected string of arbitrary events presented in reverse order and building up to a foregone conclusion. Let us consider the two "endings" and the main narrative separately just as the writer invites us to do.

The first sentence in the narrative introduces an object oddly presented to readers as an important piece of evidence that could explain everything: "This is a braid of human hair" (216). Discovered in a family chest by Colleen, the female protagonist, the blond braid evinces the traces of both thoughtfulness: "Someone has secured each end with a rubber band, so the braid itself is still tight" (216), and brutal negligence: "The edges at the thickest end of the braid are ragged and uneven, as if it has been sawed off by a dull blade" (217). Colleen has been carrying the braid for years in her professional travels around the world. Her interpretation—"She supposes that this is ironic" (218)—is a possible justification. Once again, as in Carver's "Calm," irony serves as a decoy to deflect the reader's attention. The character's reflections are proposed as further diversion: "...it has become a kind of talisman, not necessarily good luck, but comforting" (218). The readers' attention is focused on an enigma that will be left unexplained. None of the events that ensue contribute to clarifying the initial presentation of the braid, except that we learn that the heroine's hair is also blond and that her father loved to stroke it (228).

In the course of the narrative, we learn that the father lavished affection on his daughter while neglecting his wife. No reasons are given to explain why the couple has fallen out, nor about other key events in the story, such as why the heroine gets divorced from her husband or why she has become estranged from her only son. The narrative's retrospective arrangement seems to imply that it all occurred because of the events related in the story's final segment, which happens to be its chronological beginning, yet no logical causes are adduced. Continuity is upset together with the illusion of origin and destination and the associated prospect of rational development. In the final scene, father and daughter are shown falling backward into a safety net suspended beneath a bridge under construction. Although, like the braid, this event is represented as replete with significance, its meaning remains unclear: "She does not understand the look in his eyes when he clasps her hand. She doesn't think she will ever understand it, though for years and years she will dream of it, though it might be the last thing she sees before she dies" (232). The two "conclusive" incidents framing the main body of the story seem somehow to mirror each other. We are tempted to interpret them as having a Freudian justification, suggesting that the young woman, because of her exclusive relation with her father, has been "castrated," deprived of her feminine attributes figured in the violently torn-off braid of hair that she carries with her as a talisman. Still, this tentative reading might also be just another decoy, like the other stratagems that we have indicated. Like the specious contiguity between the story of the deer hunt and the narrator's final decision in "The Calm," the Electra complex in "Falling Backwards" could just as easily provide a plausible explanation for the repeated misfires in human relationships that the story accumulates. For the most part, this succession of scenes staging failures in human communication at various moments in the protagonist's life (reminiscent of the series of pointless outbursts of anger in "The Calm") are left unexplained. Like the father and daughter whose backward tumble replicates the backward movement of the narrative, readers are forced to "plunge backwards into the air" (232). Far from fixing experience in logical form, as traditional patterns would encourage us to do, the narrative's chronological waywardness replicates the confusion that lies at the core of human existence.

Beginning with its paradoxical title, Russell Banks's "My Mother's Memoirs, My Father's Lie, and Other True Stories"[8] accumulates the signs indicating narrative distancing. Since his parents' stories systematically prove to be erroneous, the narrator's story cannot be conventional; it merely compiles the lies that his parents tell together with his own disclaimers. If the stories are overtly untruthful, so, indirectly, is the narrator's own story. This is clear from its first line: "My mother tells lies about her past, and I don't believe them, I interpret them" (30). Stories are a substitute for communication that is implicitly bound to be mendacious. The narrator suggests that people tell stories in order to be loved, so that they should not be read for their informational content but "interpreted" in terms of their function as social link. Yet, as a direct disclaimer of that project, the narrative closes on a final anecdote that is left unelucidated.

The episode is trivial, even pointless. The old woman tells the tale of a distressed young man sitting in a restaurant. She approaches him but fails to proffer the assistance that he seems to invite:

> You know the type. But something pathetic about his eyes made me want to talk to him. But honestly, Earl, I couldn't. I just couldn't. He was so dirty and all. (38)

The mother and son's reactions are intriguing: "What's it about?" the son asks. The mother replies, "About? Why, I don't know. Nothing, I guess" (38). This final story leaves both mother and son perplexed, but, paradoxically, for the first time, they share a moment of tenderness. The narrator abandons his position as interpreter: "I put my arms round her" (38). They have never been closer to each other. For once, in spite or because of its pointlessness, storytelling has accomplished its love-inducing function. But for readers that final anecdote might be false like all the others or true for the first time and for that very reason devoid of meaning. The irony is double: if the incident is real, a pointless encounter has brought mother and son nearer; if it is false, and so intended to convey something about their relationship, then they have both failed to interpret the situation's implications—the young man's resemblance to the narrator and the mother's incapacity to offer love. It follows that their newfound intimacy is superficial. The inserted story fails both as a relation of events and as a relation between people.

The final paragraph gives another twist to the paradox. The conclusion stages an unexpected reversal of perspectives, as the narrator becomes a third person seen through his mother's eyes: "Her blue eyes filled, her son was leaving again, gone for another six months or a year, and who would she tell her stories to while he was gone? Who would listen?" (39). At this point readers, placed in an uncomfortable aporetic situation, recall the narrator's question: "What's it about?" (38). What kind of faith or attention can we devote to a narrator who no longer controls his story? Aren't his stories as mendacious as his mother's? What point does he want to make? How are we, as readers, to interpret his interpretations? Do stories require an interpretation or just sustained attention? This is the kind of perplexity that Adorno extrapolates as being the vocation of all art forms: "Every act of making in art is a singular effort to say what the artifact itself is not and what it does not know."[9]

Through various distancing devices all the texts that we have analyzed so far reject traditional scenarios. Although discarded, these patterns are nevertheless cited. The Othering process, intense and disruptive as it is, is imprinted as a watermark upon recognizable templates. It can only be interpreted by reference to the very conventions that it indirectly contributes to invalidating.

The texts to which we now turn our attention attempt to define alternative structures in open contradistinction to conventional formats. In them the Othering factor traces original patterns through textuality. These texts have nothing to do with either information transfer or thematic building. Rather than conduits they are pathways conceived to guide readers through the various steps leading to the recreation of a vision, an experience or a state that lie beyond the confines of our cultural system. We have divided the texts into two groups: those that maintain the notion of form as an objective, and those that completely dispense with it. We designate them respectively as "alternative forms" and "formless forms."

Paradoxically, among all the alternative forms imaginable, those that are least adapted to expressing the Othering orientation are those relying on unconventional spatial layout. Although their insistence on the material aspect of language is conspicuously deviant, it is also invariably predictable. After cummings's verbal and typographical mannerisms and the Surrealists' experimentations, visual poems have been the least often practiced in contemporary poetry. By contrast, Mary Ruefle's "The Intended"[10] and Stanley Plumly's poem "Dove,"[11] while conventional in appearance, each in its own way proposes very original forms that explore the potentialities of language's syntactic and semantic creativity. Both poems discard the linear structure associated with information transfer to create webs of persuasion guiding readers through original textual constructions. The expected outcome is an experience in Othering, an individual peregrination through the poem's sometimes labyrinthine, always open-ended patterns.

Ruefle's "The Intended" is disconcerting to readers trained to look for guiding principles that offer a direction for interpretation. The poem's orientation deliberately remains erratic and ungraspable:

> One wants so many things . . .
> One wants simply, said the lady,
> To sit on the bank and throw stones
> while another wishes he were standing
> in the Victoria and Albert Museum
> looking at Hiroshige's "Waterfall":
> one would like to be able to paint
> like that, and Hiroshige wishes
> he could create himself out of the
> Yoro sea spray in Mino province
> where a girl under the Yoro waterfall wants
> to die, not quite sure who her person is,

but that the water falls like a sheet of tin
and another day's thrown in the sieve:
one can barely see the cherry blossoms
pinned up in little buns like the white hair
of an old woman who was intended for this hour,
the hour intended to sit simply on the bank
at the end of a long life, throwing stones,
each one hitting the water with the *tick* of
a hairpin falling in front of a mirror.

In this poem, all the available logical threads that we habitually grasp at prove untrustworthy: the title is ambiguous—is "Intended" verbal or substantive, active or passive? The sustained water symbolism is erratic, covering such diverse references as river, sea and even mirror. The logical frames regulating the evocation of Hiroshige's painting are also blurred. They confuse more than help our efforts to decipher the text: look-alike characters appear in and out of the painting, the river seems to be flowing and cascading, Hiroshige's desire to "create himself/ out of the Yoro sea spray" seems disconnected from his "Waterfall" painting. Our desire for order and clarification is baffled, but it is that very frustration that determines our readiness to apprehend a more fluid construction. No longer a transfer of our empirical knowledge of the world, the poem's structure proceeds from our always more or less suppressed perception of the ambivalence of language. If we accept the title's designation as simultaneously what is sought-after and what is fated to happen, project and destiny, then we can perceive a twofold structure dividing the poem into two sections of 10 lines hinging on the 11th that marks the turn from project to destiny. That 11th line is itself cleft at the line break between positive desiring and negative resignation: "a girl under the Yoro waterfall wants/ to die."

Nevertheless, even that very clear division of the poem can be misleading. Just like the ambiguity in the title that does not so much indicate the cleftness of desire as its constant reversibility and instability, the poem's partition cannot be considered as a simple mirror structure in which what is desirable in the first part is revealed to be fatefully enforced in the second. In fact, that structure, compelling as it is, does not so much oppose as mesh together the various vignettes that the poem contains. We are not only faced with an opposition but with a duality that links contradictory values. In that perspective the possibility of correlations are multiple: the lady throwing stones in the first part might very well be the old lady throwing stones in the second; the painter aspiring to create himself as sea spray evokes the girl wanting to die; the sea spray correlates with the cherry blossoms, and their resemblance to "little buns" connects them with the old woman's hair; the stones suggest the hairpins falling in front of the mirror; the falling cherry blossoms suggestive of defloration evoke a woman undoing her hair in preparation for a love scene. The poem weaves a number of similar webs that cut across but do not efface its logical structure. This is the typical Othering form—a structure that secretes in its expansion the conditions of its undoing, or as Adorno cogently states: "The articulation, by which the artwork achieves its form, also always coincides in a certain sense with the defeat of form."[12]

Plumly's poem "Dove" adopts a similar ambivalent strategy. Far from a simple transmission of information, the project it suggests to his readers is that of imagining vision not as instant perception but as proceeding in a succession of overlapping waves. The poem performs in language the program outlined in its first lines: "Shapes as a series of edges, each edge/ a wave exhausted yet extended just/ enough until the shoulder is complete" (40). This is the argument of the poem: shapes designate the expansion of matter that defines an object, and at the same time a complex of lines demarcating that object from what it is not; they create both recognizable forms induced by perception and a succession of correlated variations resisting stability. Thus the text's ostensible subject, "Dove," is only abstractly designated in its title—as "Dove" not "doves," "a" or "the dove"—and never again explicitly mentioned in the poem. Because of the poem's expansion by means of paratactic clauses, the "shoulder" in the third line becomes "elegant or useful," but also a "like a calla/ lily or cello or a mountain road"; the "leaf" in the fourth line becomes more specifically defined as "a big, flat-handed, star-pointed oak" at once closer to itself and to other different things; the "chair," in the same line, mutates into a "rocker," and the following words: "elder, utterly still," place an old person in the rocking chair, and, at the same time suggest that the chair is made of elder wood, thereby linking it to the leaf and to the old man. Instead of being fixated in words, things mutate into one another to suggest the multiple aspects and analogs of a dove's wing while avoiding their conceptualization. In the next movement—the second grammatical sentence in the poem—the same "edges" that contribute to the definition of shapes become the site of their dispersion. Shapes paradoxically define the limits beyond which they lose their distinctiveness as shapes and acquire indeterminacy like the "waves of the river rising/ from the river." It is at this point and precisely through a halo of indistinctness that we get our first glimpse of a dove, as if a shoulder had to be sketched and erased to become:

bend of the wing , the white wing bars, white
edges that at any distance become
integral to the losses of objects
wasting into the air like grain above
the harvest

Only the slightest suspicion of a link connects that vague outline of a bird about to disappear in the glare of the sun to the various "shapes" and "edges" evoked in the poem's opening sentence. As we have already said, the text proposes a number of possible pathways that can be explored in various ways: what produces Othering is the reader's act of connecting the various verbal suggestions in the poem, not the search for a new representation of a dove. The poem places itself at the juncture between representation and suggestiveness, form and non-form, between what the words denote and what they conjure up in our personal experience.

The formless forms that we want to observe in conclusion may appear at first sight traditional and even commonplace in appearance. With the exception of Elizabeth Bishop's "O Breath," which we treat as an extreme case of the Othering form, the two prose texts we have selected do not seem to present any particular difficulty. Their formlessness does not reside in any complication of language. As a matter of fact, David Foster Wallace's "Everything is Green"[13] and R.M. Berry's "The Function of Art at the Present Time"[14] are fairly straightforward texts. Yet, they certainly push the Othering orientation to its extreme development. None of the features that, at the start of this chapter, we considered as definitional of form seem to be present. In Berry's text, the guiding voice of authority that we expect in narratives is replaced by an insistent but uncommitted camera eye that discovers the unfiltered elements of a scene at the same time as they are described. In fact, the street scene that is the focus of "The Function of Art at the Present Time" reads like a list of stage directions for a movie set. In Wallace's text, on the contrary, the camera eye is placed inside the consciousness of an autodiegetic "I" who relates a dialogue with his girl friend, Mayfly, alternating reported speech ("She says", "I say"), as if he was at the same time an actor and observer in the scene. Moreover, in both texts, no perceptible focus of interest organizes the two scenes. More exactly, in Berry's text, we progress through a succession of centers of intensity and perplexity: notations like "In a scene extravagant with color the green leaps out" (199) or "Their look organizes everything" (200) alternate with, "Nobody looks, but that could be fear" (199) or "It seems important to say that this man [...] is exactly the same size as everyone else and does nothing distinctive" (200). The text seems for no apparent reason to be periodically firing up and petering out in keeping with the observer's erratic attention. Wallace's story juxtaposes two unrelated centers that coexist without interacting: the man's voice repeats obsessively, "I know I am older and you are not" (229-230), while the young woman repeats, "Everything is green" (230). Similarly, the couple's lines of sight never meet. While he looks at her, she looks out of the window, and even when he follows her gaze he does not see what she sees. Whatever seems about to happen in the two stories fails to materialize. They seem to remain at the initial stage of a narration that was never intended to take place.

The temptation is great to project upon these texts conventional narrative patterns in order to make them conform to the common mold. Yet, because of their absence of center and apparent banality, they achieve a radical destabilization of traditional models. Instead of being centered and focused, they become strangely porous and permeable, they open the text to the rest of the world. As opposed to a conventional text's concentration, they never form a self-contained microcosm; their penetrability invokes what is outside them. These texts consequently open a network of possibilities, offering various itineraries that readers create and explore. As opposed to the poems we studied earlier, these pathways are not induced by formal patterns, by our expectation of logicality, but by an absence of definition. The two scenes presented in the two prose texts are both recognizable in the sense that we can match them in our experience and impenetrable because we cannot meaningfully place them. In these mirror-like texts, the smallest details might be thrown into prominence or allowed to disappear. As in Hyperrealist artworks, our expectation of a meaningful reconstruction of reality is baffled when we confront an apparently unprocessed yet fictitious version of reality.

Both texts, in their own ways, produce the same impression of realism while accentuating the overall impression of fictitiousness. In "Everything Is Green" the narrator claims to take in everything with his gaze: "I look at her window and I can feel that she knows I know about it" (229). This knowledge, we can assume from the intertextual hint in Mayfly's name, is his conviction of her adultery.[15] Resolution of their problem is impossible. Instead, their gazes shift, so that when the narrator at last looks at Mayfly, inexplicably, his firmness evaporates: "She is looking inside, from where she is sitting, and I look at her, and there is something in me that can not close up, in that looking" (230). Closure, as well as judgment, has become impossible in this double reorientation that involves both her "looking inside" and his looking "at her." The reasons given are hopelessly inadequate: "Mayfly has a body. And she is my morning" (230). Finally, the narrator simply associates readers with his reaction: "Say her name"

(230). Although the name may seem to offer clues to interpreting the story (Is he afraid she may fly? Is she destined to be as short-lived as a mayfly?), like the January/May intertext, these are mere decoys. What counts is the exposure involved in calling the other by name.

In the conclusion of "The Function of Art at the Present Time," the long description of the street scene ends with the evocation of a brick wall showing a mural in which the preceding scene is replicated as in a kind of *mise en abyme*. Yet it appears that the mural is strangely warped, "The surface is turned at an oblique angle so the end with the mime . . . is larger than life, and the end with the cat converges to a grayish miasma, virtual nothing" (200). Rather than a mirror image, the mural exhibits a distorted version of the preceding scene. An inscription in one corner of the mural, "tantalizingly legible" (200)—perhaps the artist's signature—reveals that it is a painting in a museum. Is the painting's *trompe l'oeil* effect so compelling that we have taken the representation for real? Yet the painted mural is represented as slightly distorted, affected by minute differences. In that case, has our imagination instinctively corrected the artist's distortions in order to make it better fit our preconceptions? What is reality: the artist's impression or the product of our imagination? Is it the "function of art at the present time" to confuse our certitudes about illusion and reality or to confront us with our responsibility for inventing the real? Whatever the answer to these questions, they are probably no longer pertinent in the present context, what finally counts here, as in Wallace's story, is our ability to accept the disorientation involved in the Othering perspective; we have to cease thinking of ourselves as simple recipients or interpreters of stories to become personally exposed to them.

The last of the formless forms, Bishop's "O Breath,"[16] combines the two orientations that we have observed at work in Othering forms. It is at the same time an act of emancipation from the traditional forms that Bishop practiced assiduously in other poems, and it is an irrepressible expansion of the Othering urge through the frames and norms of poetry. "O Breath" is the last in a sequence of poems that has so far almost escaped the attention of the critics. The texts are thought to be unrepresentative of Bishop's poetry. They are enigmatic and obscure while her best loved poems are descriptive and graphic; they are highly charged emotionally while the traditional Bishop touch is inflected by reticence. Nevertheless, they represent a center of tumultuous energy that lies at the core of her more harmonious poems. If this center of energy comes to us in fragmentary form, it is not so much under the pressure of self-censorship as because the poem is too close to its vital sources of inspiration to find an easy outlet in language. The Othering urge has completely taken over the poem's construction.

Visually, the poem appears strangely split down the middle and fraying at the edges:

Beneath that loved   and celebrated breast,
silent, bored really   blindly veined,
grieves, maybe   lives and lets
live, passes   bets,
something moving   but invisibly,
and with what clamor   why restrained
I cannot fathom   even a ripple.
(See the thin flying   of nine black hairs
four around one   five the other nipple,
flying almost intolerably   on your own breath.)
equivocal, but what we have in common's   bound to be there,
whatever we must own   equivalents for,
something that maybe I   could bargain with
and make a separate peace   beneath
within   if never with.

One of the few critics who have written about the poem suggests that the gaps represent the respiratory blocks that Bishop experienced throughout her life because of her asthma.[17] It seems more probable that these gaps and open edges are the expression of the contradictions of the amorous situation in which the speaker is placed—the unbridgeable distance between the lover and the object of her love. Strangely, though Bishop is usually expert at organizing her poetry, she appears to have relinquished her usual artistry to produce an Othering form. The lines in "O Breath" seldom run on and are rarely organized in rhythmic segments; they are halting and disarticulated, as if the material could not fit into a metrical format. Even the syntax becomes erratic: the first seven-line-long sentence that covers nearly half of the poem fails to produce a stable referent. It joins together, in a very confused way, the breast of the person lying next to the speaker, the person herself and finally just "something" that seems intensely attractive and incomprehensible. We recognize the multiple centers and the shimmering reflections found in the Othering texts already discussed. The loved one is in turn an unpredictable subject, an object of desire and an unfathomable mystery. The gaps in the lines figure the lover's perplexity, the intensity of her desire, and the halting struggle of the speaking voice when confronted with the object of desire. Far from being placed in a position of panoptic vision as in Berry or Wallace, we are placed at the heart of a site of maximum opacity.

The middle section is bracketed off from the rest of the poem as if placed outside the limits of expression. "See" at the beginning of this parenthetical sentence is meant as an apology for the intensity of expression but also as an invitation for readers to participate vicariously. In this passage, we come upon the most intense but also the most bizarre representation of the love quest. The minute description of the androgynous nine hairs unevenly distributed around the beloved's nipples—"four around one   five the other nipple"—is unimaginable and unbearably placed beyond expression. In their unaesthetic irregularity the hairs represent a projection of lover's parasitic desire but also paradoxically an act of appropriation of her lover's body. The hairs mar the beloved's breast and yet are provocatively blessed with the caress of her breath. Rather than being conventionally demarcated, object and subject blend in one obsessive motif: nine hairs, black on white, impurity on absolute beauty, adventitious growth on a perfect form—a strange but not improbable association. The gaps in these parenthetical lines serve a different purpose: they simulate the catch in the breath that the lover experiences because of her fascination. The insupportable movement of the hairs exacerbates this malaise: they are described as "flying," then "flying almost intolerably," which expresses the contradiction of desire involving appropriation and servitude. In the baroque distribution of five plus four hairs on the lover's nipples, we discover the creation of an Othering object.[18] The observer fixes her attention on these irregularities not simply because they express her perception but because they place her in an ambivalent position as both predator and victim.

In the last segment of the poem, the speaker concedes that if love cannot be experienced as either total appropriation or reciprocal exchange, then it is an unknown "something" that must be envisaged without personal commitment. Paradoxically, after the agitation of passion comes a sedate contract, a disconcerting *modus vivendi*. The treaty conceded between the two lovers does not achieve reconciliation, only "a separate peace   beneath/ within   if never with." This very formal pacification comes as a very shocking denial, even a parody of the intensity of desire expressed in the preceding lines. Yet the emotion persists in the dislocation of the poem's structure—the poem is as fragmented in its wildest extravagance as in its firm resolutions. Apparently, contrary to Bishop's usual artistic mastery, no form or meter can contain the unruly force of desire. It can only find an outlet in fragmentariness and through the gaps of language.[19]

Are we reaching a limit in the Othering process where extreme deviance finds itself deprived of coherent expression, or alternatively, are we witnessing a very sophisticated simulation of authenticity? The question is bound to remain moot, yet it is safe to say that we are we are witnessing new forays in linguistic expressivity that have to be placed next to the subversive, deviant or trick forms that we have analyzed before.

Although we are far from having covered the whole range of possible alternative forms, we have tried to explore the limits inside which they can be situated. Some of the stories or poems that we have analyzed are involuted to the point of being obscure, while texts like "Dove" or "The Intended" verge on formal eccentricity; others like "The Function of Art at the Present Time" or "Everything is Green" refuse formal distinctiveness while the pressure of expression in a poem like "O Breath" barely attains intelligibility. Yet, even these extreme cases refer back to the system while trying to ignore it. None of these texts abandon representation, even less evade artistic responsibility; they only attempt to put the norms of society at a distance and in perspective. They help us look at them as if we were placed outside the system for the freedom that can be revealed by toying with its conventions. They achieve this goal with two opposite strategies: either they background the system by placing it at a distance or they propose alternative forms. Whatever the option, they distinctly turn away from the traditional formats of conventional art. They all propose pathways with alternative routes rather than accomplished forms. What characterizes these texts is their vulnerability, since they deliberately place themselves outside reading grids. They put the conventional categories of textuality in total disarray, accumulating gaps, illogicalities and distortions, juggling a multiplicity of perspectives, alternating moments of clarity and confusion. They venture off the beaten track to offer new horizons of experience.

Notes

[1] Wallace Stevens, "Anecdote of the Jar," *Collected Poems* (Boston: Alfred Knopf, 1954) 76.
[2] A.R. Ammons, "Center," *The Selected Poems*, Expanded Edition (New York: Norton, 1986) 52.
[3] Grace Paley, ""A Conversation with My Father," *Enormous Changes At The Last Minute* (New York: Farrar, Strauss & Giroux, 1960) 159-167.
[4] Raymond Carver, "The Calm," *Where I'm calling From: The Selected Stories* (London: The Harvill Press, 1998)194-198.
[5] Dan Chaon, "Falling Backwards," *Among the Missing* (New York: Ballantine Books, 2001) 216-32.

[6] It is helpful to keep in mind the narratological distinction between the order of the narrative—i.e. the arrangement of episodes in the text—and the order of the story—i.e. the chronological order of events.

[7] The sections of the story are headed by an indication of the main character's age, moving backward in seven year increments: (49, 42, 35 28, 21, 14, 7).

[8] Russell Banks, "My Mother's Memoirs, My Father's Lie, and Other True Stories," *Success Stories*, (New York: Harper & Row, 1986) 30-39.

[9] Theodor W. Adorno, *Aesthetic Theory*, trans. Robert Hullot-Kentor (New York: Continuum, 1997) 173.

[10] Mary Ruefle, "The Intended," *Life Without Speaking* (Tuscaloosa: U. of Alabama, 1987) 28.

[11] Stanley Plumly," Dove," *Now That My Father Lies Down Beside Me, New and Selected Poems, 1970-2000* (New York: HarperCollins, 2000) 40.

[12] Adorno 192.

[13] David Foster Wallace, "Everything Is Green," *Girl With Curious Hair* (New York: Avron Books, 1989) 229-30.

[14] R. M. Berry, Berry's "The Function of Art at the Present Time," *Dictionary of Modern Anguish: Fictions* (Normal, Illinois.: FC2, 2000),199-200.

[15] Wallace evokes the January and May story most famously treated by Chaucer in "The Merchant's Tale." But whereas in Chaucer's fabliau, January's certainty of betrayal is cancelled by May's clever lie, here the older man has to contend with an enigmatic phrase that simply confirms the difference in their perspectives. Moreover, Wallace's narrative begins after the action has implicitly already taken place; the story is effectively over.

[16] Elizabeth Bishop, "O Breath," *The Complete Poems: 1927-1979* (New York: Farrar, Strauss and Giroux, 1983) 79. The sequence it occurs in is called simply "Four Poems" (76-79).

[17] See Marilyn May Lombardi, *The Body and the Song: Elizabeth Bishop's Poetics* (Carbondale: Southern Illinois University Press, 1995) 15-43.

[18] See Chapter Nine, "Objects of Disorientation."

[19] Some of the observations in this reading of the poem appear in a different light in an article on translating poetry. See Jacky Martin, "La traduction éclatée: pourquoi et comment ne pas traduire la poésie," *Traduire* ou *Vouloir garder un peu de la poussière d'or...*, *Palimpsestes*, Hors Série (Paris, Presses de la Sorbonne Nouvelle, 2006) 77-88.

PART IV

OTHERING NODES

CHAPTER EIGHT

SITES OF EXPOSURE

In the preceding chapters the Othering excursion was first defined as a set of rhetorical tactics aimed at combining the pressures of constructive forces within the cultural system with antagonistic forces outside the system. Part II describes the destabilization brought about by various tactics which open new perspectives by disrupting conventional patterns. Part III reverses this orientation by examining the various constructions that showcase the conflict between the two opposite forces. Globally the approach followed so far has been rhetorical: the linguistic and textual strategies that we have identified encourage readers to make sense of the hiatus between disqualified formats and alternative orientations. This final part deals with what we call, for want of a better word, Othering nodes.[1] We argued in Chapter One that in the rhetorical webs created by Othering tactics, these nodes figure as remarkable intersections. They can be identified through two contrasting features: their lack of contextual relevance, like the braid of hair in Dan Chaon's "Falling Backwards," discussed in Chapter Seven, or their implausibility, like the dual world above and below ground in Millhauser's "Beneath the Cellars of Our Towns," studied in Chapter Six, and, paradoxically, by their intense power of suggestion. The rhetoric associated with the nodes is of a different nature; instead of a rhetoric of disruption, we discover a rhetoric of suggestion. As opposed to Othering tactics, which shape readers' interpretations by overprinting deviant patterns upon conventional ones, Othering nodes correspond to dead ends or deadlocks in interpretation that readers have to confront by using their own experience. While Othering rhetoric relies on recognizable properties of texts, Othering nodes mark points of rupture or lines of discontinuity at which meaning cannot be constructed through traditional means. These oddities signal fields of intensity where meaning disperses rather than concentrates. Nodes encapsulate the text's enigma that has to be faced in order to approach the distinctive contribution that cannot be conveyed using traditional formats.[2] Beyond the normal act of interpretation, reading demands a particular sensitivity to the enigmatic stimulation of nodes, an act of generating rather than elucidating meaning on the margins of the cultural system. That form of meaning is not predictable, stable and reproducible; it arises from a unique encounter between the Othering text and its reader. It is an alternative form of significance that entails the reader's readiness to respond to the text's suggestions.

Our observation of this performative process is complicated by the fact that the three nodes that we will discuss in this final section correspond almost term for term with conventional categories of textual analysis. They could easily be ignored or assimilated to existing categories. What we call "sites" could very well be considered as settings, our "objects" could be equated with symbolic motifs, and our "mediators" bear a likeness to fictional characters. Nonetheless, these nodes are of a radically different nature from the conventional categories they resemble. As opposed to conventional categories that can be considered as textually observable, nodes are both objective and virtual markers relaying images of our relation to the cultural system. Their potential for semantic suggestion operates in inverse ratio to our reliance on the system: it will be poor, even non-existent, if our attachment is strong and on the contrary strong if we have already experienced Othering. Rather than proposing concentrations of meaning like thematic motifs, nodes are concentrations of energy pushing readers to invent their own personal itinerary through the artwork.

Consequently, since the Othering nodes considered here inflect readers' experience in the process of confronting texts, they should not be expected to predetermine interpretation. On the contrary, they contribute to loosening up the norms of interpretation and enhancing the texts' potentialities. The reader's final position that we call a "stance"[3] can be described as a field of possibilities rather than an explanation. These possibilities are not indefinite since they have to be corroborated by the text. In that sense the nodes are performative; they determine a field of dispersion in which meaning can be produced. Within these limits no single reading can be preferred over another, yet each has to be in agreement with the text's tactics and nodes. It follows that Othering-engendered meaning is not prescriptive; it is multivalent and generative. In that respect, the Othering stance at the same time produces emancipation from convention and the opening of the cultural system.

We have isolated three nodes that we analyze in succession for the sake of clarity, although they can and most of the time do function in synchrony: sites of exposure (Chapter Eight), objects of disorientation (Chapter Nine) and mediators of escape (Chapter Ten). None of the three nodes is more susceptible to be misunderstood than the "sites of exposure" that we explore in the texts selected for this chapter, because these sites simply do not exist. We know by now that Othering does not refer to any definable space—whether real, imaginary or ideal—but coincides with an excursion outside the cultural system. It points to a space outside the common space, to an unknown that can only be accessed through the known, that is in fact demarcated by the limits of the known or knowable world. If broadly speaking, literature could be said to be about creating, exploring or rediscovering the various spaces opened up by culture, Othering sites are borderline positions that redefine the territories that conventionally contain human experience.

On first inspection the spatial organization in W.D. Wetherell's "What Peter Saw"[4] does not seem to fit this description. The family's position in the short story is highly conventional. Their summer home on Cape Cod appears, to the young adolescent protagonist, harmoniously "linked . . . with all the other places in the country" (164), although it harbors a strictly compartmentalized family group. The world of the parents and the world of young Peter remain juxtaposed until the moment when distant relations, the Gerards, accompanied by a young couple, Danny and Doreen Doe, cause the two spaces to intersect. The peace of the family circle is suddenly broken by the intrusion of the newlyweds in search of a private space to enjoy each other's presence in preparation for the husband's imminent departure; concurrently, Peter's private universe of physical dares and newly awakened sexual curiosity is suddenly shaken by the young couple's amorous quest. The story builds up to a humorous double anticlimax that returns both groups of characters to their initial divided positions: in the conclusion, the adults' connivance in the young couple's amorous interlude is shown to be pointless, while the young boy's anticipation of arcane sexual secrets is baffled. When he spies upon the couple from outside the bedroom window, what he sees defeats expectation. The coming-of-age plot ends in an aborted initiation that confirms the separation of social spaces, justifying the adults' demure abstention as well as Peter's youthful illusions. We are poles apart from the Othering excursion that questions the system's norms.

However, through the narrator's retrospective glance at young Peter's experience, we get what might be considered as the premises of an Othering experience. Left alone to clarify his thoughts after his unromantic vision, the young protagonist glances at a swan swimming in and out of a moonbeam on the pond below the house. Because of that ephemeral apparition, he realizes simultaneously that, "All summer long his knowing had butted itself against the secret, unreadable blankness of things...", and shortly after, "that behind distant islands and distant girls' camps and lowered flags and adult silences was nothing he could isolate and give answers to, nothing concrete, but only these intertwined bewildering strands of beauty and sadness and mystery combined" (184-5). Although the story sustains this meditative development, it nevertheless appears as an unnecessary supplement. The boy's vision may be ephemeral, but it counts as an Othering moment. It comes after a failure of the system as a means of access to the knowable, a perception of "the unreadable blankness of things" (184), that introduces the young boy to the complexity of values and sentiments. The swan is not the final memory that the adult narrator recounts; it is rather the young lover's attitudes, with their perplexing mixture of naiveté and strangeness, pathos and grace: "Doreen with her chewing gum reaching down to tie with inexpressible tenderness the laces of her husband's boots" (185). What Peter saw outside his bedroom window is exactly the reverse of the ethereal sight he glimpsed in the moonlight. Peter's experience of exposure is that the two visions will never match.

Something similar happens in Richard Wilbur's poem "A Hole in the Floor."[5] In this almost prototypical site of exposure, the Othering experience is not appended to the main argument; it is the center of the poem. Indeed, the relation between narration and the Othering experience is reversed: Wetherell's story ends with a final poetic coda, whereas Wilbur's poem relies on the resources of narration to construct a carefully organized, progressively discovered site of exposure. Although throughout this chapter we will explore the various facets of the word, for the time being, we will concentrate on two related aspects contained in the term "exposure," which combines the notions of increased visibility, and of vulnerability. As the poem reveals, exposure should be understood as a two-way process of transformation: once the carpenter has drilled a hole into the parlor floor, the parlor becomes a dichotomous space connecting, in a manner similar to Millhauser's world, a now transformed room with a mysterious underground extension. From a tri-dimensional structure, the parlor is transformed into a totally new, glittering, flat surface. Because of the carpenter's work, "A clean-cut sawdust sparkles/ On the grey shaggy laths..." (189), and further down "They are silvery-gold, the color/ Of Hesperian apple-parings." (189). Far from being damaged, the perforated floor becomes resplendent, evocative of Herculean quests, but surprisingly, its splendor is caused by its deterioration. This reversal marks the beginning of the Othering process. This golden effulgence radiates, in part, from a dark place below in which paradoxes abound. It is a place where:

A pure street, faintly littered
With bits and strokes of light,
Enters the long darkness
where its parallels will meet.

The radiator-pipe rises
Like a shuttered kiosk, standing
Where the only news is night. (189)

Here, as in the poems by Williams and Creeley that we will study later in this chapter, we find an extreme complexity of lines, figures and patterns that characterizes the sites of exposure. This newly opened, non-Euclidian space tallies with none of the designations that come to mind in what the speaker calls "the visible world" (189); suggestions like "Some treasure, or tiny garden?/ Or that untrodden place,/ The house's very soul" (190) that he entertains momentarily do not apply. That space remains a mystery until the moment when the crucial relation between above and below is metaphorically revealed in the poem's last stanza: "Not these but the buried strangeness/ Which nourishes the known" (190). The below-floor is the indispensable appendage to the upper space of normality. The "known" world and the basement's "buried strangeness" curiously interact; one "nourishes" the other. The undercurrent of air that issues from the hole fans the flame of the house-lamp, making the room above "wilder" and "dangerous." Far from being damaged by the carpenter's hole, the living quarters have acquired a new integrity, becoming, in the poem's final line, "the whole dangerous room" (190). Opening sites of exposure restores the most ordinary places to their natural strangeness, as if the categories used to describe them were like holes in reality. These spaces regain a flamboyance and a mystery that daily occupancy occults. The hole in the floor is both a fault in reality and an escape route for the imagination.

Whether it is represented as a crack or a fissure, a wall or a division, a ledge or an edge, a limit or a margin, a site of exposure is always a liminal space separating two antithetical but correlated universes. Yet, we should avoid pursuing the spatial analogy for fear of missing an essential element in the sites of exposure. They do not so much concern a pattern of exploration as a series of experiences associated with the act of discovery. The first of these experiences concerns the period preceding the Othering excursion; the second, the feelings of the person infringing the limits of the known; and the third, the various modalities of existence (s)he has to confront. This is the sequence of experiences that we intend to elucidate.

Of the three existential modalities that characterize the Othering excursion, the least developed concerns the circumstances leading up to the discovery of Othering site. Frequently, the subjects appear to be involved in a quest or exploration, but it rapidly surfaces that they are only superficially concerned or that this activity is only a cover-up for what turns out to be a form of expectant passivity. A case in point is the character in Louise Gluck's poem "Matins." Apparently, she is weeding her garden, but in reality she has placed herself in a position of humility and receptivity: "You want to know how I spend my time?/ I walk the front lawn, pretending/ To be weeding" (25).[6] She is waiting for a sign, "for some evidence" until she realizes, beyond the object of her quest, the force of her expectant situation: "Or was the point always/ to continue without a sign?" (25). At the Othering site, subjects are always poised in a state of abstraction or expectation. Something is going to happen to them, but they hardly know what. What is certain is that it cannot be anticipated.

Consequently, most of the time, the subjects' situations or occupation are of little importance. The weeding or the hole in the floor in the preceding texts are conducive situations that bring about the boundary-crossing associated with sites of exposure, but they are only remarkable for the changes they induce in the characters. Thus, rather than actually acting, the subjects in Othering situations are faced with strange occurrences or objects—a painting ("Contingencies"[7]), a drawing ("Cathedral"[8]), music ("October 23, 1983,"[9] "Sonny's Blues"[10]). In the majority of cases, they are not active participants; things just happen to them and are described as "incidents" ("Incident" is the title of Pollak's poem[11]), "intervals," or "pauses" (These are what the waking woman perceives in Levertov's poem "Night on Hatchet Cove."[12]). Finally, the experience that awaits them appears to be visited upon them, but paradoxically, because of its magnitude, it eclipses all the other events of their daily lives.

More rarely, subjects deal with intercessors,[13] chance encounters that help them reach the sites of exposure, yet in spite of the pressure to which they are submitted, they barely interact with them. A case in point is the story entitled "Tall Tales From the Mekong Delta,"[14] in which a Vietnam veteran's attempts to seduce the unnamed female protagonist in the story only contribute to giving substance to her visions of "blueness."[15] In the texts we have chosen, many of the intercessors associated with the sites are sleeping partners like the poet's husband in Levertov's "Night on Hatchet Cove", or inconspicuous "extras" such as the pianist in Jordan's poem, or the unknown personage in Strand's "Another Place." The two brothers in Baldwin's "Sonny's Blues," or the first person narrator and the blind man in Carver's "Cathedral" are more complex. An authentic relationship appears to be established between the protagonist and the intercessor, but that relationship counts for less than the attention they devote to a site of exposure. As matter of fact, it is the convergence of their glances that physically creates the site within which the characters' existences are going to be redefined. Thus in the conclusion of "Sonny's Blues," even if the resisting narrator participates in his brother's musical world, his attention is deflected to the "cup of trembling" (124) placed above his brother's head. The ambiguity of the biblical reference[16] referring to an object of affliction and terror, enigmatically glowing and shaking, transforms the whole scene into a site of expiation and rebirth.

Similarly in "Cathedral", when the blind man holds the narrator's hand to draw a cathedral, his participation can only be accessory since he cannot see. Yet, he seems paradoxically in charge of the situation: "We're drawing a cathedral. Me and him are working on it" (307), he explains to the narrator's wife; moreover, his hand appears to be guiding the seeing person: "His fingers rode my fingers as my hand went over the paper" (307). As a matter of fact, the two men appear to be transported into another world. The narrator has relinquished normal vision so that he is able to pierce through the carapace of prejudice, a form of seeing blindness, that has prevented him from being exposed to the wider perspective of existence as experienced from inside. Hence the disarming simplicity of the conclusion: "It's really something" (307), which expresses the narrator's impression that he has reached another quality of space: "My eyes were still closed. I was in my house. I knew that. But I didn't feel like I was inside anything" (307). In fact, the narrator and his surroundings can no longer be "situated" in keeping with each other. They persist in their normal coordinates but they also figure in another dimension that depends on the two characters' collaborating to bring it into existence—a duality of perspectives which is typical of sites of exposure.

The sensation of total disorientation that presides at the end of Carver's story traditionally characterizes the atmosphere of dreams. But reaching a site of exposure has nothing to do with the oneiric situation that leaves the dreamer perplexed and calls for interpretation. On the contrary, the Othering protagonists have the impression that in spite of their disorientation they have discovered something. Although they cannot name it they sense that their whole life depends upon it. The conclusion of "Cathedral" is deceptively simple: " 'It's really something,' I said" (307). This "something" is unnamable not only because it cannot be identified, but also because it refers to the indivisible totality that voluntary blindness has induced. Other texts place their protagonists in similar positions. The mysterious woman in Boruch's "Grief"[17] "is hauling silence/into the house," and in the end, "She stands forever in the middle of the thing." The unspecified "thing" designates the central but indefinable site of exposure in which she appears. Similarly, the speaker in Strand's "Another Place"[18] attempts and fails three times to designate the place to which he is coming, so that it is just "another place," "nothing," and it is finally simply "this." A similar failure of identification figures in Creeley's poem "The Edge"[19] in which the deictic "this," designating a space at the edge of existence, is left dangling at the end of the line between two stanzas. C. K. Williams's reiterated "this" in the conclusion of his poem "The Gap"[20] is also indicative of both the impact of the Othering site and of its ineffability: "...but this, too; so often, this, too."[21] Even though Merwin's "For the Anniversary of My Death,"[22] is inconclusive, doubt only affects the verbal expression, not the impression of being faced with an outstanding occurrence worthy of being revered: "And bowing not knowing to what."

Paradoxically, the combination of total presence and unspeakableness that characterizes the sites of exposure can be manifested in widely different environments. Most of the time they occur in secluded or hidden spaces, in obscure or nighttime scenes, in moments of calm or even total silence, but they can also be encountered in the midst of crowds or packed audiences (Baldwin), at the height of a musical experience (Jordan), or even in the throes of emotional disorder (Merwin, Pollak). None of these types of environments are important in themselves; their significance lies in the nature of the perception they allow of at last "being in the world." This is the feeling that we want to explore now.

This feeling is certainly induced by the nature of the sites of exposure, but as we already saw, they are not physical places in the sense that one could come to or even stay in them. Creeley's poem, "The Edge" gives us an idea of what a site is or rather feels like through the speaker's very failure to describe it; one could even say that his attempts at depicting it "create" a negative image of the site. The title presents it as an "edge," at the same time a limit between known and unknown and the cutting side of a blade, a liminal and a pivotal place. The whole poem hinges on a constantly defeated attempt to identify that "edge." It figures successively as a "here and now," an "end," "the weather's edge," "this," "beyond me" or as an "intersection," most of these designations being left suspended at the end of a line. The site defeats description, and it is as if words had to be emptied of their substance before they can come close to naming the experience. The snow that falls at the end of the poem matches the entropy that invades the text. The concluding lines sum up the poem's questing perplexity: "This must be the edge/ of being before the thought of it/ blurs it, can only try to recall it." The ineffable space at the edge is placed beyond language, even before thinking. The strange disappearance of the subject in the last proposition, "can only try to recall it," is revealing of the nature of experience at the sites of exposure: first, the subject is so exposed that his existence threatens to disintegrate; next, the singular experience seems to be happening on its own without human intervention; and last, the particular form of encounter is so unspeakable that it is inaccessible through language: it is just an "it."

The sites of exposure are not only beyond the reach of words; they also evince a drastic negation of traditional cultural markers. Creeley's "The Edge" describes "an intersection/ crossing of one and many,/ having all having nothing" (268). In the poem "Night On Hatchet Cove," reminiscent of the mystical experience of *The Cloud of Unknowing,* Levertov speaks of an empty space of inverted values:

>   let
> night cut the question with profound
> unanswer, sustained
> echo of our unknowing (15)

In "Another Place" Strand speaks of an empty world containing a very substantial "nothing":

> this is another place
> what light there is
> spreads like a net
> over nothing (116)

By contrast, C.K Williams in "The Gap" endows the site with a more epic dimension:

> So often and with such cruel fascination I have dreamed the implacable
>   void that contains dream.
> The space there, the silence, the scrawl of trajectories tracked, traced,
>   and let go;
> the speck of matter in non-matter; sphere, swing, the puff of agglutinate
>   loose-woven tissue;
> the endless pull of absence on self, the sad molecule of the self in its
>   chunk of duration; ... (235)

The sites are indeterminate, entropic and locked in contradictions. Either they represent something important but unintelligible, like Ammons's

"Nothing that gets,"[23] that can only be approached through the use of indeterminate words like "this" or "it" or "nothing" or "void", or because they elicit contradictory statements like "having all, having nothing" (Creeley) or "the speck of matter in non-matter," (C.K. Williams). The obvious reason for this absence of definition is that the sites are not places to see; they are, like Carver's cathedral, spaces only accessible to the inner eye. They have to be interiorized not as something tangible, but as an experience in being next to or being part of something that remains beyond comprehension. In that situation, the distinction between object and subject constitutive of the observer's position tends to disappear. A wealth of interactions normally occulted by that binary distinction takes over. This is the reason why we refer to the four Othering experiences that we are going to describe not by using substantives but by choosing process words: "seeing," "moving," "merging," and "surviving."

Paradoxically, the first process associated with the sites of exposure is "seeing," which is normally related to the discovery and exploration of space. Perhaps vision is the first faculty that needs to be reformed because it is the foundation of our construction of the world. Hence the experiences in seeing at the sites of exposure can only be attained by effacing the usual means of capturing reality; not surprisingly, then, two of our chosen texts deal with experiences in unseeing. "Cathedral," as we pointed out, associates the loss of sight with the discovery of the inner coherence of the world. In "Incident," Felix Pollak is even more systematic in his quest of that paradoxical sightless vision. He relates three easily recognizable experiences in non-seeing: the first refers to the experience of being blinded by a dazzling light; the second evokes a game of blind man's buff; and the last, the memory of tunnels suddenly plunging the travelers in darkness. But these familiar occurrences are abandoned because after the temporary loss of a major sense organ they underline the return to normality. Coming out of the tunnel, the speaker remembers exclaiming: ""We're back to normal, now everything will be safe again, and dull!" (19). These ordinary episodes prepare us for the final unspeakable Othering "incident":

I stand on the street, and there's no time to lose,
this is the moment to join the group that is crossing
the street. Wherefrom the sudden insane thought,
as I wait for the bus: *Is the skin of my face growing*
over my eyes? I resist the impulse to look into
the mirror of a store window. I know there would be
no reply. (19)

The speaker has become a sentient body without eyes. His "insane" question about whether his skin has grown over his eyes suggests not only that he has lost his normal eyesight, but also that he is also past caring and perhaps rejuvenated, because his whole body has become receptive to the impressions of the world around him. Kate Braverman in "Tall Tales From the Mekong Delta"[24] evokes a similar experience:

> She could remember being a child. It was a child's game in a child's afternoon, before time or distances were factors. When you were told you couldn't move or couldn't see. And for those moments you are paralyzed or blind. You freeze in place. You don't move. You feel that you've been there for years. It doesn't occur to you that you can break the rules. The world is a collection of absolutes and spells. You know you have a power. You are entranced. The world is a soft blue. (51)

This particularly vivid experience of the re-enchantment of the world through temporary blindness and bodily stasis helps us understand a more extreme experience described by Lucille Clifton in "perhaps":

> i am going blind.
> my eyes are exploding,
> seeing more than is there
> until they burst into nothing"[25]

All these experiences are problematic: the loss of vision entails the loss of the world and the self, but the ensuing experience, disastrous or ecstatic, is irretrievable in language. Deprived of normal vision the subjects become exposed, at once vulnerable and visible, lost to the world and strangely permeable to its influences. In all these experiences, even in the most extreme cases, vision is not occulted; it is on the contrary generalized, pushed to its limits or extended to the whole body. The accidental or voluntary obstruction of normal sight gives access to global vision.

The same contradiction affects "moving," the second modality experienced at the sites of exposure. In the same way as the "seeing" subject loses its sighted status in order to merge with the world, the sites also affect the subject's fundamental capacity to move in space. The basic principles of movement are abolished; the Othering subject is at the same time the originator and the object of movement, a moving body and the medium in which it moves. Replacing the notion of transit, we have to deal with situations involving flux, merging and transformation, as for example, in the river metaphor underlying Stephen Dobyns's poem "Refusing the Necessary," which in its opening and concluding lines evokes states of total confusion and suspension in a moving stream:

"Becoming the river, we are the river," and "Between the surface/ and bottom, we may hang forever."[26] In the conclusion of "Tall Tales from the Mekong Delta," the heroine is plunged in a maelstrom of sensations that compact objects and places in blueness:

> She opened her mouth but no sound came out. Instead, blue things flew in, pieces of glass or tin, or necklaces of blue diamonds, perhaps. The air was the blue of the pool when there are shadows, when clouds cross the turquoise surface, when you suspect something contagious is leaking, something camouflaged and disrupted. There is only this infected blue enormity elongating defiantly. The blue that knows you and where you live and it's never going to forget. (60)

The objects (glass, tin, diamonds) that we recognize as belonging to the narrative material of the story remind us of the early stages in the progressive invasion of the young woman's consciousness by blueness like the "shadows on the far side of the pool" (103), and of the erosion that affects appearances and progressively engulfs her personality. Yet these perturbing signs of her existence's general liquefaction now coalesce into a substance (a "blue enormity") in which she is totally exposed, at the same time trapped and revealed, in a manner that she has perhaps never experienced before. Like the inverted vision of the "seeing" modality, "moving" is paradoxically invalidating and reformative; it is a form of regeneration though dispersion in space.

A similar transformation happens to Sonny, the jazz musician in Baldwin's short story, when the mood finally comes upon him:

> He [*the lead musician*] was having a dialogue with Sonny. He wanted Sonny to leave the shoreline and strike out for the deep water. He was Sonny's witness that the deep water and drowning were not the same thing. (121).

Because this powerful current is initiated, allowing submersion without total perdition, Sonny's obdurate brother is able to perceive his own life retrospectively in a state of unbroken flux:

> I saw the moonlit road where my father died. And it brought something else back to me, and carried me past it, I saw my little girl again and felt Isabel's tears again, and I felt my own tears begin to rise. (124)

A similar experience of movement in immobility is described at the end of Clifton's poem "perhaps":

> or perhaps

in the palace of time
our lives are a circular stair
and I am turning (150)

The I's free-floating movement in space contrasts with the rest of the world's purposeful trajectories; whereas most people perform the circular upward movement of climbing a staircase, she is "turning," just moving in place or perhaps mutating. Whatever the social or psychological benefits attached to the "moving" modality, they are accessory compared to the enriched perception that the texts promote. Instead of discovering the world in terms of hard-and-fast norms, the same artificial values are shown in a new light. Exposed, they become at the same time highly visible and immaterial, flagrant and fragile. Yet, at the height of this blissful perception of life in a state of flux, both Braverman's heroine, who senses that "The night stayed outside" (60), and the narrator in "Sonny's Blues" are aware that their experience is transitory:

that this was only a moment, that the world waited outside, as hungry as a tiger, and that trouble stretched above us, longer than the sky. (Baldwin 124).

The ambivalence inherent in the sites of exposure is again reinforced in the third modality, "merging." Although not expressly developed in all the texts, it should be seen as the prime mover at work behind the reversal of normal assumptions described in the preceding modalities. In poems like Elizabeth Bishop's "At the Fishhouses"[27] and June Jordan's "October 23, 1983," the sites of exposure revealed in these poems—the moving seawater on the boulders in Bishop's poem or the waves of music in Jordan's—are metaphors for the elemental beat that pulses through appearances and activates the sites of exposure. Indeed, in these poems the ambivalence that we have described in the first modality and the movement of flux in the second combine as the outside and inside manifestation of the same principle. It is as if what we normally consider as the constituents of our world were actuated from the inside by a powerful undertow that at the same time perturbs and unifies the global economy of appearances. In order to approximate that movement in words, the Othering text strips the world to its essentials, opens cracks, fissures or holes in reality, places us on the edge, forces us to abandon our sense of sight to be carried away in a general flux in which the division between self and world does not obtain. It is as if the previous modalities were just the exterior manifestation of an underlying force that generates the world of appearances.

In Jordan's poem the perception of that force is instantaneously suggested by the piano music:

> The way she played the piano
>   the one listening was the one taken
>   the one taken was the one
>   into the water/
>   watching the foam
>   find the beautiful boulders (70)

Immersion in music occurs immediately in this poem, while the observer remains detached in Bishop's poem. There the final discovery is meticulously prepared. In a kind of obligatory rite of passage, the reader's attention is progressively guided from the fishhouses' rooftops, down the various pathways leading to the pier, and finally to the water's edge where the vision takes place—a vision in Bishop as opposed to an immersion in Jordan. In both poems, the discovery reveals the interplay between two opposite elements strangely similar in both poems: the "grey stones" and the "cold deep dark seawater" in Bishop's poem recall the "boulders" and the "foam" in Jordan's. Although the elemental nature of these two contrasting motifs is essential, it is their collision that captures the attention. Stones and water rub and crash into one another as if attempting an impossible fusion. Jordan's poem explicitly contrasts words suggesting an idea of disjunction such as "distilled," "isolate" or "syncopate" with those that denote coalescence such as "fused" or "tuning." The poem even envisages in passing the possibility of "constellations" as fluid constructions organizing isolated stars until the idea of a possible "gathering" emerges:

> collecting the easily dark
> liquid
> look
> of the beautiful boulders
>
> in that gathering
>   that water (71)

This conclusion has already been suggested to the reader by previously mentioned synonyms like "meeting" and "collecting." These words' obvious attractiveness, as opposed to those designating fusion, is that they presuppose a principle and a will presiding over the reunion of opposite elements.

That conjunction between opposites is equally perceptible in Bishop's poem. Yet, in "At the Fishhouses" the focus of attention is not a gentle "gathering" of listeners brought together by music with the "beautiful boulders" (Jordan 71), but a stark vision of clashing elemental forces:

> The water seems suspended
> Above the rounded gray and blue-gray stones.
> I have seen it over and over, the same sea, the same,
> slightly, indifferently swinging above the stones,
> icily free above the stones,
> above the stones and then the world. (65)

Although as in Jordan's poem, the general impression is one of mobility and resilience, the timeless oscillation of the waves upon the boulders does not suggest an experience but an abstract form of knowledge. In Bishop's conclusion, as compared to Jordan's liquid impression, everything is "flowing and drawn," and immediately after "flowing, and flown." The use of a comma after "flowing" suggests that flux is inevitably associated with extinction—one leads to the other. The two poems reveal the two extremes of the process of mutability and transformation attached to the sites of exposure. Jordan's poem points toward its transformational side while Bishop's discloses its destructive potential. In that incessant process of mutability, the signs of culture are not abolished; they are defused and distanced. They are reshuffled in constantly changing combinations and these combinations are validated, not because of their truth-value, but because of their ability to remain in a state of flux. By unsettling the organizing principles of culture, the sites of exposure reveal the general commutability of signs.

Being "exposed" in sites of liminality obviously places the subject in situations of stress, anguish and danger. The passage from the reassuring confines of culture to the destabilizing universe of Othering is dramatized in Hayden's poem "The Diver."[28] As the diver plunges beneath the surface of the water, he yearns to:

> ... have
> done with self and
> every dinning
> vain complexity. (4)

He is lured by the intriguing sights around him:

> the livid gesturings,
> eldricht hide and

seek of laughing
faces. (4)

and the "rapturous / whisperings" (4), but he is also progressively put off
by them. After a moment of fascination, he senses danger in:

the
canceling arms that
suddenly surrounded
me, fled the numbing
kisses that I craved. (4)

Actuated by a reflex reaction, he finally undertakes "the measured rise" (4)
and abandons the site. After the illusion of an unfettered world, the
difficulty associated with a site of exposure like Hayden's diver's consists
in determining how the subject can stay at the junction between two
worlds while avoiding being permanently fixed in one or the other.
"Surviving" is the last modality associated with the sites of exposure.

This situation is given ample development in C. K. Williams's poem
"The Gap." The lyrical invocation, "So often ... ," that recurs like a
leitmotiv through the poem testifies to the subject's periodic return to a
site that he describes as "the implacable void that contains dream" (235).
The ambiguity of the word "contains"—implying both inclusion and
restriction—indicates that this escape is not like the nightmarish
underwater world that Hayden's "Diver" explores, but some unknown
region of the self, "the endless pull of absence on self" (235), or of the
mind, "a gulf that might be inherent in mind" (235). As we pointed out
earlier, the sites of exposure are fields of discovery that open areas in
which the mind can not only expand but also overpass its limits,
sometimes at its own peril. After reading Wilbur's poem about the hole in
the floor that gives access to the underpinnings of the house, we receive
confirmation that the "beyond" to which the mind aspires is not an escape
into fantasy but the necessary complement of, or perhaps an antidote to,
our existence in a world of norms and system. Just as Wilbur's speaker
discovers that the unlit basement encloses "the buried strangeness/ Which
nourishes the known" (190), Williams's persona discovers the necessary
continuity that connects the rational to the irrational:

                                        . . . it comes uncalled for
            but it comes, always,
      rising perhaps out of the fearful demands consciousness makes for linkage,
            coherence, congruence,
      connection to something beyond, even if dread. (235)

That "something beyond" might even be an integral part of our mind, a part that we occult when consciousness prevails.

The difficulty that the "I" faces in Williams's poem consists in controlling these periodic trips over the border between system and non-system, and ultimately in avoiding entrapment on one or the other side. Fraught with anguish as the poem is, it nevertheless produces an important answer to that difficult predicament. In its sinuous course through the various options, the poem defines a possible position of stability. As "trace" of the spirit's meanderings, the poem itself opens a halfway site that the poet reveals to his readers. This is probably how the never elucidated title, "The Gap," should be understood; the poem is a middle term, opening a gap (similar to Creeley's "edge"?) between two antagonistic worlds so that the conclusion can be seen as a sign of reassurance: "So often, by something like faith, I'm brought back in the dream; but/ this, too; so often this, too" (236). The first occurrence of the word "this" probably refers back to the anguish encountered in the world "beyond," but the second "this" marks the certainty accrued in the writing of the poem. The two are similar, although the addition of "too" as an afterthought leaves room for doubt.

An analogous situation is revealed in W.S. Merwin's poem "For the Anniversary of My Death." The very strangeness of that title—its semantic impossibility—points to the fact that death is not really the object of the speaker's meditation but the recurrence of the thought of mortality brought about by the return of the imagined date of his death. Death would certainly be a release, since it would put an end to the constant passage from reassurance to misery that the speaker experiences each time he arrives at the anniversary of his death. That unknown date transforms his existence into a site of exposure constantly divided between life and life-in-death or life after death. His actual death will be the consolation of a "tireless traveler/ Like the beam of a lightless star" (58), the final loss of light that comes after the alternation of light and darkness that plagues existence. Just like Williams's persona, but in a more despondent mode, Merwin's speaker finds himself astride two worlds: "in life as in a strange garment" (58). The poem's ending should be perceived as an act of acceptance, a surrendering, not to mortality, but to the mutability of existence, to the nagging alternation between life and death, the coexistence between the "wren's song" and the "falling." When the speaker says in conclusion that he is "bowing not knowing to what," the bowing that coincides performatively with the composition of the poem matches Williams's "this." Both poems build upon their own tangible existence as a possible refuge.

The sites of exposure that we have been visiting through various texts contribute to defining the complexity and the productivity of the Othering nodes. The sites of exposure constitute the first stage in the definition of the Othering excursion. They define at one and the same time a space, a relationship and a process. The two other nodes that we explore in the next two chapters presuppose that a site has previously been opened between the cultural system and what lies beyond; the recurring images of a "hole" or "wall" or "edge" or "gap" testify to the perception of that space as a middle ground between two territories. That in-between area is not a neutral or transitional space but a complex site of liminality in which the subject-object relationship is redefined. The world is no longer "offered" to the eye to be observed and named because the mind's categories no longer apply. The eye has to become blind to reality and the body has to regain its fluidity in order to become amalgamated and coextensive with the "out there" (in Pollak's poem the skin is growing over the subject's eyes as if the body was mutating and in Jordan's poem the body appears to be liquefied). In that state of flux but also of disintegration, the Othering self experiences a feeling of exposure that comprises in equal parts elation and dread, reassurance and threat. The sites of exposure stage the fluidity of the categories, norms and concepts of our existence, sometimes experienced as floating and interacting with one another, as in Braverman's "blueness." Finally, the poems or stories that we considered are not simply textual constructions but zones of exposure in which the characters and, vicariously, the readers are both threatened and regenerated. This paradoxical situation gives them a particular saliency. They no longer deliver a message or resolve a situation. Through the circumstances that they relate, they reveal the traces of past experiences, and sometimes retrace the steps leading up to a perception or an event that can be reconstructed by readers. The avowal of confusion at the end of Merwin's poem, the ostensive deictic "this" in Williams's poem, as well as Bishop's or Jordan's visions of flux and mutability create the prerequisites for imaginative explorations. As opposed to the rhetorical devices calling for intellectual response that we observed in Parts II and III, the nodes describe potential experiences that call for sympathetic reenactment.

Notes

[1] By node we wanted to designate something like the protuberances or outgrowths in plants that mar their harmonious growth yet concentrate vital energy.

[2] See our discussion of enigma in Chapter Seven, as well the treatment in Adorno's *Aesthetic Theory,* to which we refer.

[3] By using the word "stance" we do not refer to an individual's personal opinion but to the reader's involvement in the text as co-constructor of its significance.

[4] W. D. Wetherell, "What Peter Saw," *Hyannis Boat and Other Stories* (Boston: Little Brown, 1989) 163-185. The story's title obviously pays homage to *What Maisie Saw*, Henry James's sustained experiment in limiting the center of consciousness in narrative.

[5] Richard Wilbur, "A Hole in the Floor," *New and Collected Poems* (New York: Harcourt Brace, 1989) 189-90.

[6] Louise Glück, . "Matins," *The Wild Iris* (New York: HarperCollins, 1992) 25.

[7] Stephen Dobyns, "Contingencies," *Velocities, New and Selected Poems 1066-1992* (New York: Penguin, 1994) 38-39.

[8] Raymond Carver, "Cathedral," *Where I'm From, The Selected Stories* (London: The Harvill Press, 1998) 292-307.

[9] June Jordan, "October 23, 1983," *Living Room: New Poems* (New York: Thunder's Mouth Press, 1985) 70.

[10] James Baldwin, "Sonny's Blues," *Going to Meet the Man* (London: Corgi Books, 1965) 87-124.

[11] Felix Pollak, "Incident," *Tunnel Visions* (Peoria, Ill.: Spoon River Poetry Press, 1984) 18-19.

[12] Denise Levertov, "Night on Hatchet Cove," *Poems 1960-1967* (New York: A New Directions Book, 1983) 15.

[13] We will deal in more detail with the intercessors in Chapter Ten.

[14] Kate Braverman, *Squandering the Blue* (New York: Fawcett Columbine, 1989) 35-60.

[15] The meaning of "blueness" will be explored later in this chapter.

[16] Zechariah 12:2, 3.

[17] Marianne Boruch, "Grief," *View From the Gazebo* (Middletown, CT: Wesleyan UP, 1985) 19.

[18] Mark Strand, "Another Place," *Selected Poems* (New York: Alfred Knopf, 1993) 116.

[19] Robert Creeley, "The Edge," *Selected Poems* (New York: Marion Boyars, 1991) 268-69.

[20] C. K. Williams, "The Gap,*"* *Selected Poems* (New York: Farrar, Strauss and Giroux, 1994) 235-236.

[21] We form the hypothesis further down that these two occurrences of "this" might not have the same referent.

[22] William Merwin, "For the Anniversary of My Death," *The Lice* (New York: Atheneum, 1967) 58.

[23] A.R. Ammons, "Center," analyzed in Chapter Seven.

[24] Kate Braverman, "Tall Tales From The Mekong Delta," *Squandering the Blue* (New York: Ballantine, 1989) 35-60.

[25] Lucille Clifton, "perhaps," *New Bones, Contemporary Black American Writers in America*, Eds. K.E. Quashie, J. Lausch & K.D. Miller (Upper Saddle River, N.J.: Prentice-Hall, 2001) 150.

[26] Stephen Dobyns, "Refusing the Necessary," *Velocities: New and Selected Poems 1966-1992* (New York: Viking Penguin, 1994) 49.

[27] Elizabeth Bishop, "At the Fishhouses," *The Complete Poems: 1927-1979* (London: Chatto & Windus, 1991) 64-66.

[28] Robert Hayden, "The Diver," *Collected Poems*, ed. F. Glaysher (New York: Liveright Publishing Co., 1985) 3-4.

CHAPTER NINE

OBJECTS OF DISORIENTATION

There are obvious connections between the sites of exposure and the objects of disorientation that now come under consideration. The sites mark the first degree of projection outside the cultural system when, instead of freely diffusing through the texts, the figures of discordance (Part II) or integration (Part III) that we observed in the rhetorical section of our study concentrate in enigmatic nodes where the system can be observed from both inside and outside. But these outposts on the edge of the knowable world are often fantastic fabrications that involve isolated characters. The objects of disorientation are more wide-ranging. They are often selected from among commonplace objects in our surroundings, but they are described or positioned in such a way that they provoke intense perturbations in and between the people around them. In this sense they can be said to project further outside the system than the sites of exposure. They acquire a distinctiveness and a versatility that the sites never afford. Besides, the sites are virtual; they only materialize when a character chooses or is forced to be exposed in them while, by contrast, the objects that we are going to describe provoke intense disturbance around them.

If we look at Donald Barthelme's balloon in the story bearing the same title,[1] we discover that, quite fantastically, although it hovers over a vast area of New York City, it is observed with equanimity as if it were one of the city sights:

> The balloon then covered forty-five blocks north-south and an irregular area east-west, as many as six crosstown blocks on either side of the Avenue in some places. That was the situation, then. But . . . there were no situations, simply the balloon hanging there . . . . (16)

The narrator adds humorously that people soon learned not to find any particular justification for its presence:

> There was a certain amount of initial argumentation about the 'meaning' of the balloon; this subsided, because we have learned not to insist on

meanings, and they are rarely even looked for now, except in cases
involving the simplest, safest phenomena. (16)

Yet, the impact of the freak balloon upon the population exposed to its
presence is immense:

> The ability of the balloon to shift its shape, to change, was very pleasing,
> especially to people whose lives were rather rigidly patterned, persons to
> whom change, although desired, was not available. (21)

The playful allegory that Barthelme's narrator puts into place is
unmistakable in its implications. The balloon could figure as a replica in
vastly magnified form of the New Yorkers' frustrated lives in the City. In
the end, it even boils down to a schizophrenic projection of the narrator's
own massive frustration at being left alone after his beloved's departure.
The whole story could finally resolve into an amusing skit about life in a
modern megalopolis, a realization that is poles apart from the destabilizing
effects that we associate with Othering. Yet, intriguingly this apparently
frivolous text places us at the center of the complex of relations that we are
analyzing.

The balloon is most conspicuously not a clearly delineated object, a
focal point or a center of attention. It is shapeless, "not limited, or defined"
(21) and it is apparently purposeless (18). It engages everybody that comes
into contact with it, though not in an interactive or significant manner. The
balloon conforms to everyone's tastes and intentions. Because of its
malleability and formlessness, it mimics the viewer's own existence—this
is the first paradox. It is as if referential reality needed to become
immaterial in order to become accessible. Thus the balloon offers an
occasion for viewers to express their opinions. Yet, far from fostering a
feeling of clarification, this regained power of expression promotes a
welter of contradictory views: "As a single balloon must stand for a
lifetime of thinking about balloons, so each citizen expressed, in the
attitude he chose, a complex of attitudes" (18). This is the second paradox:
from the moment reality ceases to be substantial it encourages expression,
but by acquiring complexity that expression loses pertinence. When reality
fails so does people's grip upon language. The balloon is a challenge to
expression but it is also an invitation to discover a fluidity in experience
that has no equivalent in language. Deprived of referential opposition,
people tend to dissolve and liquefy: "Others engaged in remarkably
detailed fantasies having to do with a wish either to lose themselves in the
balloon, or to engorge it" (19). No longer assigned to a fixed slot in the
system, the citizens enjoy existence not as a purposeful activity but as a

series of encounters or rather "intersections": "Each intersection was crucial, meeting of balloon and building, meeting of balloon and man, meeting of balloon and balloon" (20-21). Intersections, connections and chance encounters, these are what the characters—and vicariously the readers—are invited to experience when they come into contact with objects of disorientation.

These objects are in complete contradistinction with the well-known textual motifs that come under various designations such as symbols, icons, emblems or metaphors. All these figures have in common the property of synthesizing multiple, sometimes discordant features into unitary forms. They are productive literary devices that, out of the contradictions observed in the human predicament, create aesthetically accomplished constructions. Other familiar concepts could be brought forward to account for some of the disconcerting features that we have observed in connection with Barthelme's balloon. Symptoms as opposed to symbols do not signify in themselves but in relation to an outside system of coherence, either psychoanalytical or ideological. In that hermeneutic perspective, cleft or discordant motifs regain coherence in reference to explanatory systems. Following the well-documented logic of the "return of the repressed," the occultation of underlying patterns engenders the distortions observed at the textual level. Both symbols and symptoms partake of the same analytical and interpretive logic that the objects of disorientation deny.

Symbols and symptoms are densely present in Ann Beattie's story "Janus,"[2] that we intend to oppose to "The Balloon" in order to mark the specificity of the objects of disorientation. In "Janus," a real estate agent uses a bowl to attract customer's attention to the apartments that she offers for sale. As a result, she notices that her sales are inexplicably boosted. It later surfaces that an ex-lover had offered her the bowl as a love token. Two features in the bowl's definition immediately spring to mind that make it different from the objects that we'll review later: the bowl is a sophisticated artwork while most of the objects of disorientation are commonplace; moreover, its significance remains obscure to its owner: "The bowl was a mystery, even to her." (354), while objects of disorientation elicit intense reactions. Those in contact with such objects experience an increase in life's possibilities. They acquire an insight into the complexity of the most commonplace situations. Nothing comparable happens to the character in "Janus;" she is alienated by the object of her predilection and she fails to understand its appeal to her clients: "Alone in the living room at night she often looked at the bowl sitting on the table, still and safe, unilluminated" (355).

The character's absence of comprehension is an obvious invitation for the reader to take over. This is another striking difference with the Othering situation in which the character's confused perceptions are presented as an experience to be shared and expanded by the readers. Beattie's story, on the contrary, teases the reader into finding a plausible interpretation of the bowl on the two levels of pertinence that we evoked before. As symbol, the bowl could be considered as an image of the character's desire to live a self-enclosed form of existence eliminating commitment. In that reading, her existence would be "perfect" like the shapely bowl. In other words, she could catch everybody's fancy without being anyone's possession. Symptoms are like symbols' dark lining, they demystify what was perceived synthetically in symbols. The bowl's empty perfection could also be analyzed as the character's projection of her lack of sexual fulfillment. Whatever the interpretation we give to the bowl, two ideas come to the fore: the "bowl" motif is accessible to explication over and above the character's head, and the reader is given the final interpretive responsibility.

The situation is completely different when we come upon Othering stories like William Goyen's "The Enchanted Nurse"[3] or David Schickler's "Kissing in Manhattan."[4] In Goyen's story, a retired nurse relates the story of his relationship with a patient who came under his supervision after a mutilating war accident. The patient's restorative operation plunges him in a coma so that his body has to be manipulated in order to prevent paralysis. He is attached to a rehabilitation device made of ropes and pulleys that the nurse operates at regular intervals. This machine is surprisingly called a "loom." This insignificant slippage in designation creates an object of disorientation. A bizarre situation is put into place in which a medical machine becomes a loom on which the nurse can weave his patient's limbs into a sort of human textile. Othering objects are decontextualised to the point that, without ceasing to be recognizable, they become unintelligible within the cultural system. Though they remain fluid and changeable, from the moment they are redefined, they become the nexus of intense relationships. They are like blind spots from which intense networks of suggestions radiate. We are far from the symbolic or symptomatic situation in which the text converges upon compounds that encapsulate its ultimate signification. In the case of objects of disorientation, the center is empty although, like the eye of a maelstrom, it is endowed with a tremendous force of perturbation.

In "The Enchanted Nurse," because of the bizarre loom, the nurse's ostensible healing occupation deviates into a web of rapidly changing ambivalent relationships. We are far from the emphasis on consolidation and focalization that contributes to the proper economy of symbols or symptoms. By contrast, the Othering object is a center of intense instability. It is a horizon of dispersion rather than a progressively constructed objective. Thus, the nurse becomes more and more engrossed in his patient and progressively more confused about his role. Beyond the functional medical relationship, the nurse develops a growing fascination for the inert patient, which mutates into a form of depersonalization that almost verges on total absorption in the other—an absorption that engulfs his own life as well as that of his patient. The character is even conscious of the potential destructiveness contained in his attitude:

> There is something dreadful among us, I thought as I worked my loom with Chris upon it, a figure over the city we live in, to remind us...a creature within us that could murder or keep life (251).

Besides, in its repetitive operation, it looks as if the loom had generated a string of figures, ghosts or creatures extending beyond the relationship between nurse and patient to the whole hospital and even the city. Typically, instead of concentrating meaning, the Othering object tends to expand and mobilize all that it comes in contact with. As a matter of fact, the healing scene takes place in the middle of a hospital ward in which, although they remain dim, images of suffering seem to issue from the nurse's operation of the loom. One of the patients in particular, nicknamed Lord Bottle, careering through the ward in his wheelchair singing biblical verses, particularly those concerning the curse of Cain, places ambiguous overtones on the healing scene. In another but related register, when the nurse searches through the paralyzed person's belongings, he finds cryptic inscriptions associating him with Michelangelo's androgynous David. All these apparently unattached episodes, together with Chris's troubled former relationship with a couple of friends, are evoked evasively in the story while the nurse is himself thrown back upon childhood memories that tantalizingly appear to mesh with the preceding stories. It is as if the loom wove all these stories together and had become the only means to unravel them. The point, it seems to us, is not to reconstruct any hard and fast coherence between these stories—this would defeat the Othering purpose—but to experience the parallelisms or the intersections between them. These stories' marginal, almost fortuitous correspondences, like the various individual existences collectively affected by Barthelme's balloon, count more than the illusory clarification that could be expected from their interpretation.

Another story, Cheever's "The Enormous Radio,"[5] reveals a similar entanglement of human situations. For some unexplained reason, the radio that a couple has acquired to satisfy their musical tastes mysteriously happens to relay all the conversations that take place simultaneously in the adjoining flats. Whenever the young wife sits down to enjoy her favorite music pieces, she overhears the horrendous family scenes happening around her. The whole social world appears to be in jarring confusion and, as in "The Enchanted Nurse", the confusion spreads from the radio set to the staid couple's private life. They end up quarrelling like the rest of the couples around them. The relation between external commotion and personal disorder is carried a little further in Goyen's story. After being generalized the whole "weaving" situation is progressively internalized. Instead of simply relating his healing the nurse evokes the "mysterious double action, this marvelous reciprocity" (252) of his work. The loom is a double-action machine; it simultaneously preserves Chris's mobility and it also restores the nurse's psychological integrity: "Chris was bringing together lost parts of me" (252). The multivalence induced by the objects of disorientation is all the more notable as it contradicts the centripetal orientation of symbols and symptoms. They are centers of convergence whereas Othering objects create diffraction, dispersion and instability. Rather than promoting clarification, their action constantly verges on confusion. Even the storytelling process becomes uncertain. The narrator warns us that he will tell his story in a "crooked way" (241), he also reminds us that, "[he is] speaking of a connection, woven, as of threads and veins and vessels, through which human beings may communicate and tell each other everything" (253). The tale as fashioned by the loom does not proceed by logical increments to a conclusion, but in a constant slippage created by the proximity of different stories. In the end, it even seems that the story, as told, is just a provisional version destined to sensitize us to the complexity of the issues involved; the real story is still to come: "I was sure I saw him walking off the Ferry onto this Strait, come to tell me what I tell you. But no, not yet, it is not his time" (254).

David Schickler's story "Kissing in Manhattan" illustrates another original complication perceptible in the objects that we have examined so far. Rally, a young travel writer tries to find her twin soul in Manhattan. After various unfortunate adventures she finally meets a strange companion who, instead of satisfying her amorous expectations, places her in the most bizarre and frustrating of situations. At the end of each of their weekly encounters, after treating her to the most costly garments, he rips open the young woman's newly acquired clothes in order to expose her to their converging glances in a mirror. The situation is redolent of a prurient scenario, yet it soon appears that none of those that come to mind really apply. Although disconcerted, the young woman is content to renew the experience, though the man never tries to pursue his advances. Indeed, the mere suggestion of a lewd development to the scene suffices to infuriate him. The reader could very well share Rally's reflection, "She had obviously fallen in with a pervert, or a prophet" (93). This latter suggestion, fanciful and obscure as it may seem, opens other possibilities. What might be prophetic is the woman's transformation of her own body and of herself into an object of disorientation. From the moment her body is stripped, when her arms are pinioned behind her back and her dress has been tied like a scarf around her neck, Rally's body no longer belongs to her. She ceases to inhabit that body of hers and to control its semiology. No longer an object of desire, she becomes, in her own eyes and in her companion's,[6] an object of disorientation. Because her body has been so transformed the story does not fall into a lascivious scenario. The convergent gaze of the two characters determines the transformation of the girl's body into an Othering object. She evades classification, while her body escapes its boundaries: "She understood that she couldn't call herself Patrick's lover, but she felt unique, like she was modeling something intimate and perfect for him, something that could only be achieved by the mix of her body with the colors Patrick wrapped her in" (97). But progressively her relation to herself is changed from one of unproblematic intimacy to one of deep wonder, as if Patrick had changed her into a different person by exhibiting the factuality of her body: "When she dreamed at night, Rally saw herself as a nymph in a viny wood, all breasts and legs and psychedelic eyes" (99). Even if the contrived accents that color that vision inform the reader that the character is entering a world of illusion, we discover again the same dangerous confusion of relationships that we noticed in "The Enormous Radio" and above all in "The Enchanted Nurse." Instead of relating to the world, the young woman has fallen in love with what she imagines to be Patrick's perception of her body. Objects of disorientation dislocate our pre-constructed patterns in order to submit them to scrutiny.

Shortly after the preceding scene, the young woman finds herself in the Cloisters museum in exactly the same position that she adopts with her lover, but this time the situation is transferred to a work of art and the disorienting object given another twist. Rally is watching a hunt scene in a medieval tapestry in which a unicorn is being chased, and another man is looking approvingly in the same direction. At this point because of the double distantiation, the Othering object assumes its maximum force of suggestion. The young woman is no longer looking at herself but at the unicorn as a symbol of force and vulnerability through which the unknown young man guesses at Rally's fantasy. The somewhat ossified unicorn symbolism is revitalized by the two young people's involvement in a typical Othering encounter fraught with rapidly changing roles and relations:

> "It's terrible,' said Rally.
> The young man with the sleepy eyes studied Rally. He looked gentle, and doubtful.
> 'Is that really what you were thinking?' he said.
> Rally looked away.
> You're a stranger, she thought. I'm supposed to watch you.
> 'I like it,' sighed the young man. He gazed sadly at the unicorn. 'I—I probably shouldn't. Instead I should think it's awful. Right?'
> Rally paid attention suddenly to the sleepy young man, to the need in his voice. She reached out and touched his shoulder, just barely.
> 'No,' she said. 'Not right.' (99-100)

Looking at each other in front of the unicorn, captured and idealized in the other's glance, the two young people become for each other objects of disorientation, alternatively filling and rejecting the antagonistic roles of hunter and hunted.

The relationship induced by the act of becoming an object to oneself and to others leads to heightened perceptions but it is not devoid of danger. The shady side of the young woman's transformation is not long in manifesting itself:

> She couldn't see the nymph anymore. She opened [her eyes] again, saw what she wanted. It was an impossible, wavering trapped woman's body. (102)

Is this a return to another well-honed scenario—the inevitable day of reckoning after a moment's deviance? In the short story's conclusion when a Frenchman she encounters tries to makes advances to her, Rally's reaction is problematic: "she pulled herself away from the man, as if she'd betrayed a jealous, omniscient lord" (105). Are we supposed to imagine that Patrick, her tyrannical lover has left a debilitating imprint upon her? Is the straightforward relationship offered her too lacking in the complexity she is accustomed to? Has she become such a victim of her body's complete objectification that she can no longer experience love? All these questions and probably others point to another important attribute of the objects of disorientation; they delay closure and open out possibilities.

We have insisted so far on the peculiar structure and formation of objects; it is important at this point to probe their function more fully. Othering strategies do not bring instruction, knowledge or clarification;

nothing is, properly speaking, transmitted or acquired in Othering except perhaps perceptions, feelings or reflections *about* the experience of deriving knowledge, instruction or inspiration from texts. In the case of objects, we have chosen to gather that conglomerate of sensations under the notion of disorientation. "Disorientation" normally refers to an unpleasant situation in which people lose their sense of direction because of the absence of habitual landmarks. Yet, in keeping with the dissenting direction of Othering, we want to consider disorientation as referring also to a different experience in which the landmarks' disappearance does not foster bewilderment but coincides with the discovery of new forms of moving in space. The objects of disorientation that we have observed so far introduce delusive landmarks that force the characters not only to reconsider their actions but also to question their motivations and principles. The disorientation that these objects provoke has nothing to do with erring or deviating; they throw doubt upon ingrained notions such as origin, direction and destination. When these notions no longer apply what choices are left to the subject? Is total disorientation necessarily detrimental, or is it an occasion to discover new bearings in space? Perhaps objects of disorientation work to disqualify the very notion of movement, and their real function is to open new types of spatiality along with new ways of relating to them.

This is what takes shape in the three texts to which we now turn: two poems, Plaths's "Metaphors"[7] and Erdrich's "The Fence",[8] and a short story, L'Heureux's "The Comedian."[9] They all concern pregnant women placed in a situation in which their expected babies function as objects of disorientation transforming their lives. On the face of it, nothing could be less disorientating for a woman than the fact of becoming pregnant. Although anguish is always associated with this very common fact of life, the outcome is usually predictable and, generally, joyful. Yet, none of the three texts directly center on the outcome of the women's pregnancies. The expectant mothers seem rather profoundly perturbed by the unknown presence within their bodies. Again, there is nothing exceptional in these impressions. However, the three texts under consideration challenge "normal" assumptions by placing them in a situation of disorientation. Although neither of these heavy words is mentioned because never at any time conceptualized, these women experience pregnancy simultaneously as an aggression and a fulfillment. A veil of ambivalence is thrown over normal relationships: that between women and their bodies (as in the case of Rally's body in "Kissing in Manhattan") and between pregnant women and their unborn babies. The babies are at the same time inseparable and distinct from the mothers' bodies, an extension of their flesh and the promise of new lives. The conditions for the creation of an object of disorientation are gathered, placing these women in a position to confront, not necessarily to resolve, the perplexing opposition between inside and outside, intention and consequences, self and other. Yet, the simple mention of these weighty words suffices to classify the nature of an experience that resists conceptualization. Theirs is not a metaphysical or even a physical experience but a rapidly changing succession of tangled emotions and relations.

The three women—the speakers in the two poems and L'Heureux's heroine—go through three stages in disorientation. The first of these intense existential states concerns the evidence that normal definitions no longer apply and need to be fundamentally changed. In the two poems, this disconcerting impression translates into a spate of metaphors (actually the title of Plath's poem), which, through the rhetoric of excess that we have already observed in Chapter Four, attempt to approximate the chaotic complexity of the situation in which the speakers find themselves. Indeed, at times the incongruous accumulation of heterogeneous tropes defeats the very purpose of metaphor. Usual designations no longer apply and traditional means of evoking the unusual fail; the only recourse for these women is quibbling or equivocating, as Plath's poem announces in its first line: "I'm a riddle in nine syllables." L'Heureux's protagonist, Corinne is even more perplexed in her rendering of her situation: she imagines that her baby sings, significantly "slightly off-key" (5), apparently pursuing an existence of its own. As a consequence of its permanent intrusion, she comes to question her relationship with her husband and her own conception of life, and she even envisages an abortion. All the time her eyes hurt and she seems to be leading a double life (like Rally in "Kissing in Manhattan" or the wife in "The Enormous Radio") in which the baby plays a prominent part: "...she can see very little, and what she does see, she often sees double" (16). As a matter of fact, like the two other women she has entered a new life, perturbed and reoriented by her baby's singing: "For Corinne the singing is secret, mysterious. It contains some revelation, of course, but she does not want to know what the revelation might be" (17). Characteristically, the revelation materializes when she gives birth in an intensification of the light that restores her vision: "...and she reaches up and tears the light aside. And sees" (19), a situation which we recognize as the passage from blind sightedness to sighted blindness that we observed in Carver's "Cathedral" and Pollak's "Incident."[10]

The restored vision that the three women experience finds expression in a metamorphic flow of imagery. This irrepressible creativity is neatly represented in "The Comedian" by the unborn baby's joyful singing, while the two poems channel it through a tangled web of luxuriant images. Particularly noteworthy is the exuberance and even erraticism in the association of tropes, as if designation was no longer an objective but instead the observation of the transitions and transformations of one image into another. Plath probably gives the most intriguing form to that transformational process; her poem is a riddle in nine lines of nine syllables each of which eventually remains unsolved. Indeed, the abrupt juxtaposition between her various perceptions count more than the final resolution of the enigma. She has "[b]oarded the train there's no getting off" (43), which tends to indicate that the transit is more important than the destination and that the improbable succession of states that she describes is *her* answer to the riddle.

Transitions are also important in Erdrich's poem. Although as daring, they are more organically perceived than in Plath's poem. In a sustained construction combining metallic and vegetal impressions ("vine" and "fence"), the speaker contrasts in dual symbolism the sense of vitality and vulnerability that she perceives in her baby and the impression of agency and instrumentality that she senses in her own position. The whole poem is like a thick tress of words twisting metaphors in order to suggest the complexity and variability of her situation. In all these texts the language, denied its analytical function, resorts to a form of impressionistic transcription.

The last state in which the three women are plunged is related to the complexity and fluidity of impressions that was analyzed above. In this state, progression, continuity and logicality are no longer in order; various types and degrees of discontinuity between experiences replace them. The nature and the importance of the existential gaps thus created give a measure of the singularity of the feelings experienced by these women. Corinne's definition of her new mode of existence as a pregnant woman as a "sort of wandering way" (11) could be a description of what these poems are actually simulating through language. Nothing could be more abrupt than the conflation of the ideas of vegetable and human growth in Erdrich's announcement: "I see the first leaf already, the vined tongue/ rigid between the thighs of the runner beans," (61), yet it illustrates the effacement of the subject–object distinction that we noticed in connection with the sites of exposure. A similar baroque confusion of humans and objects, observation and sensation, pointing to a scattering of the self upon the world, is also evident in the first four lines of "Metaphors":

I'm a riddle in nine syllables,
An elephant, a ponderous house,
A melon strolling on two tendrils.

O red fruit, ivory, fine timbers!

Outrageous as this montage of images may seem, the last recapitulative line should be seen as a desperate attempt to seal them together into a very provocative invocation.

The complex states that the objects of disorientation elicit are not purely impressionistic fantasies. As we have already remarked, because of the presence of Othering objects, the system is destabilized, even discredited; as a consequence, new relations and conceptual frames have to be conceived in order to accommodate the perplexity in which the subject is plunged. This state could simply be corrected by replacing one set of concepts by another better adapted, and the system would be once again vindicated. Nothing of the sort happens in the texts that we have considered; the cultural system is maintained in spite of the evidence of its defection. This is the crux of the Othering experience. Subjects confront a multitude of contradictory stimulations while all the time conscious that they have nothing but the language of their culture to put their experience into words. We have named this paradoxical situation a stance,[11] hoping that the word's half passive, half active denotation might express the fragility and the strength of the existential situation that we are trying to define. In Othering stances a number of social and psychological themes are inevitably convoked, as we observed in Chapter Eight, for example in the different treatments that Jordan in "October 23, 1983" and Bishop in "At the Fishhouses" gave of the same theme. Yet these themes appear totally decontextualised, or rather the time frame or location evoked in the titles only serve to foreground the indeterminacy of the issues presented in the poems. What counts in the Othering stances is not the explication or the resolution of human issues but their projection as sets of vacillating options that the mind contemplates before deciding. The stances induced by the sites of exposure and objects of disorientation create privileged spaces of reverberation and speculation in which human issues are presented in a state of high visibility. They correspond to a specific way of signifying rarely distinguished from traditional intellectual processes. More than differences in comprehension, they should be seen as differences in kind. Just as in paintings where the referential nature of subjects proceeds from but does not exclude the intense stimulation of lines and colors that the observer's eye records straight away, stances present ideas and forms in a state of provocative indetermination that makes them sometimes logically intractable but that increases our apprehension of them.

The objects of disorientation create three specific types of stances. Although they are fairly well represented in the texts already studied, we

have selected a new set of poems in which they are particularly
conspicuous. Two poems can give an idea of the first stance of intensity.
In both objects, an apple in Gilbert's "Hunger"[12] and a mirror in
Ammons's "Reflective,"[13] are endowed with the capacity to concentrate or
rather violently compact notions that would have been considered distinct
or even opposite in the system. Such a degree of amalgamating intensity
paradoxically can be attained by a process of elimination, as in "Hunger,"
where the speaker's feverish hands tear ferociously into an apple. Yet the
poem reveals that desire is not satisfied in the consumption of its object:

> Getting to the wooden part.
> Getting to the seeds.
> Going on.
> Not taking anyone's word for it.
> Getting beyond the seeds.

The object initiates a frenzy of desire; desire reaches beyond satiety, even
beyond the means of its satisfaction, "beyond the seeds" where there is
technically nothing except the infinite affirmation of desire. Instead of
translating into verbal excess, as for example in the poems evoking
pregnancy that we considered above, the object's force of disorientation
brings about the rejection of language: "Not taking anyone's word for it."
Linguistic resources, because they are accessible to everyone, cannot
express that inexpressible "it." But whether by excess or by deficiency, the
same phenomenon is recorded: the impossibility of defining an intensely
paradoxical situation.

Ammons's very short poem "Reflective" combines condensation and
austerity in the curiously reversible relation that it envisages. Although the
"I" and the "weed" are presented as as two mirrors reflecting each other,
they appear to be inescapably affronted: both the "mirror/ in/ me" (the
speaker's reflective mind?) and the "weed that had a mirror in it'" (an
extraneous natural element?) capture the other's image in a kind of
circular stalemate recalling Patrick's and Rally's convergent glances in
"Kissing in Manhattan." But under its playful reciprocal form the poem is
far from being symmetrical; the concluding line opens the circle of
reflexivity:

> a mirror
> in
>
> me that
> had a
> weed in it.

It would be easy to bypass the Othering stance that the writer is opening and to consider as final the perfect circle of reciprocity between self and other induced by the two mirrors. This would certainly weaken the densification achieved by the final "weed" in the poem that can be interpreted as the persistence of the alien factor but also as the phonetic equivalent of "we'd." If that amalgam is accepted, *together* with the oblique form in which it is presented, then the "I" and the "you," so radically estranged in reality, can be perceived at the same time as coupled in language. The denial of the division between self and other is not asserted but overprinted through the specious logic of the poem's stance.

The second stance induced by the objects of disorientation concerns a feeling of entropy in which the affirmation of generalized randomness becomes a critique of the very notion of system. Well-known poems like Allen Ginsberg's "Sunflower Sutra"[14] and Jorie Graham's "Recovered from the Storm,"[15] both responses to eminent poetic predecessors,[16] give two opposed images of the same situation. While Ginsberg's sunflower becomes a scepter of ironic dominion over the chaotic American scene, Graham's broken branch recovered from the storm materializes the narrator's impotence. The sunflower is not simply the opposite of machinery ("You were never no locomotive, Sunflower, you were a flower!"), it is also the ironical emanation and emblem of the incoherence of the scene. In the flower's improbable growth, a new world of entropy is expressed:

all these
entangled in your mummied roots—and you there standing before me in
the sunset, all your glory in your form! (139)

In Ginsberg's poem chaos triumphantly prevails while, on the contrary, it remains traumatizing in Graham's. The speaker discovers, after the destruction caused by the storm, that the permanence she took for granted is destroyed. She realizes, and expresses in equivocating fragmentary sentences, that there is an unsuspected flaw in nature and even worse, in the intellectual means at her disposal to conceptualize it. The storm has wreaked havoc in her tidy, supposedly civilized, world. She cannot help observing, "[The] drowned heads of things strewn wildly through/ our singular, tender, green,/ clarifications" (107). A sense of responsibility for the world's coherence assails her, but the task that confronts her seems inhuman: "Am I supposed to put them back together—/ these limbs, their leaves, the tiny suctioned twig-end joints?" (107). Her vision is as apocalyptic as Ginsberg's is euphoric. Language cannot restore order to nature's confusion. In the end, the branch that she recovers from the storm is the opposite of Ginsberg's scepter, it is an image of human infirmity: "I pick up and drag one large limb from the path" (108). Both visions are tragic in different ways, but in both readers are left to ponder objects of disorientation, scepters of impotence that mirror our desire for order and our incapacity to realize it.

The final stance associated with objects of disorientation is a perception of ambivalence. We saw already that the experience of disorientation is not to be associated with notions such as plurality or polyvalence, in other words with diversity as a harmonious construction, but with ambivalence as the irreconcilable juxtaposition of opposites.[17] This is the kind of stance that is developed in Sydney Lea's poem "The One White Face In the Place"[18] and Norman Dubie's "Elegy to the Sioux."[19] Both poems, albeit in indirect ways, address sensitive political subjects: the coexistence between black and white communities for Lea, and the Indian massacres that followed the conquest of the West in Dubie's poem. However, these issues are treated through the mediation of objects of disorientation, which means that they are exposed rather than explicated or debated.

Lea's poem reminisces about the time when the speaker was the "One White Face" in the blues joints that he used to patronize in his youth. His attention is attracted to what in our terminology qualifies as an object of disorientation, a multiplicity of cobwebs discovered in the woods, that make him feel "trailed and tracked," but also "caressed by design and brilliance" (48). The representation of the blues is clearly superscripted upon this Othering object. The impression of disorientation he derives from this encounter should by now be familiar:

.... I fought
through them as I fight
through many reminders. Reminders
though, of what?
Well, maybe ambivalence if not
plain contradiction. (49)

This perception of generalized ambivalence in turn leads to the final assertion:

Dark blood pulses in the one
white face in the place
and will. (50)

A political agenda is unmistakably present in these lines, yet it should not be dissociated from the typical Othering indeterminacy produced by the line break after "one" and before "white face" ("one" possibly meaning the numeral "one," or suggesting qualities like "unique," or "undivided,") and the open-ended rebound of the last line: "and will" referring indifferently to a noun or a modal. This final assertion is not only a form of wish fulfillment; it is also largely fractured and vacillating in its expression, a characteristic that we associate with stances.

The disorientation produced by the Indian vase in Dubie's "Elegy to the Sioux" is even more uncertain in its implications. The Indian vase, which is the poem's center of attention, first appears as a crafted artifact evincing the white and blue areas created by the decorative technique used by a Native American potter. In the end it is returned to its utilitarian function as a flower vase placed on a window facing cherry trees, possibly at the White House. Between these two moments the vase is transformed into an object of disorientation, a sort of magic lantern producing visions depending on the type of attention it elicits. The greater part of the poem is devoted to the imaginary projection upon the blue and white designs of a series of events that took place in Montana during the Indian wars. The description of the historical scenes that hover around the vase is interrupted by another series of notations that concern its utilization in a different time frame. The disorientation introduced by both types of observations substitutes spatial suggestion for the chronological sense of history. In that spatial form of reasoning, the outside of the vase juxtaposes two improbably contiguous scenes: a party of Civil war-seasoned soldiers camp in the open field and a young Indian woman about to give birth lies in the adjacent wood. The proximity between the two scenes seems to imply that the war is suspended, but, on "the dark side of the vase" (167), the woman gives birth to a stillborn baby. A certain devious logic has been established that is corroborated by the poem's second sequence concerning the utilization of the vase: in the middle of the battle scene a man is consuming a bowl of cherries, "A general with white hair eats the fruit while introducing its color" (167). This inset scene and its avatars provide a plausible storyline: the "bowl of cherries" in winter signals the general's unconcern which parallels General Grant's, "drink[ing] bourbon from his boot," and the subsequent insouciance of the president who will "get his Indian vase/ And fill it with bourbon from his boot and . . . put flowers into it." (168). The disorientating logic induced by the vase shows historical events at cross-purposes in meaningless disarray. Images that are spatially related are in fact antagonistic, whereas images that seem totally disconnected suggest convincing causal links.

A third level of definition concerning colors contributes, as in Silko's "Storyteller," to further confuse the issues. The contrast between the blue and white sections in the vase's decoration in turn represents the opposition between the sky and the snow, and the blue coats and caps of the armymen. We expect the two colors to be symbolically pitted against each other but progressively, they are confused: the snow issuing from the woman's mouth invades the landscape, chasing the soldiers so that the scene becomes intriguingly "blue all over" (168). Instead of a stable color symbolism that would clarify the scene, we discover an ambivalent color scheme. The final impression left by the vase, more clearly than in Lea's poem, is definitely not political or polemical. It is one of perplexity because all the symbolic connections, the historical markers and the various usages of the vase are jumbled together, placed at cross-purposes and also somehow strangely related. Paradoxically this impression of kaleidoscopic confusion is not devoid of a certain inevitability that endows the scene with a great power of suggestion. The reader responds not with anger or revulsion, or even sadness, but with both fascination and anxiety. Just as the Indian vase conveys the complexity of "events in this wilderness," so the poem imprints its various layers of disorientation onto the reader's mind.

The Othering figures that we have described throughout this chapter as objects are in reality pseudo-objects since they remain misleading, erratic and chimerical. These are, as we indicated in our introduction, their distinctive features. Although none of these so-called objects are properly speaking "objective," the ideological assumption linking objects to subjects is difficult to eradicate. The objects of disorientation challenge that relation, destabilizing our conceptual preconceptions. In order to show how they cite and question pre-constructed relations, we have associated the word "object" with the notion of disorientation. Our objects are "objects of disorientation," which means that they are themselves subject to a process of destabilization and that they provoke a similar action around them. This problematic combination of words strongly differentiates these objects from symbols or symptoms such as we defined them initially. Although we describe them as Othering "nodes" in the network of Othering rhetoric, the objects of disorientation cannot be considered as foci of signification. They are not important in themselves but because of the disturbances they elicit. In them neither fusion nor concentration is achieved; only intersections and correspondences in which meaning is diffracted or decomposed into its various facets. Like an earthquake's epicenter, they are centers of disturbance from which tremors radiate. We saw that these tremors not only affect the situations in which the various characters or speakers are placed but, more deeply, they destabilize the very concepts and words through which they could be interpreted. Characters, speakers or narrators, and, indirectly, readers are confronted with situations of complexity in which values and norms are confused, complexified and distanced. The typical Othering situation that we analyzed in connection with the experience of pregnancy paradoxically combines feelings of fluidity and anxiety, creativity and incertitude. This particular situation is the foundation of what we call "stances." Although stances convoke ethical, political or psychological issues, they neither adopt nor reject any of these perspectives. The Othering stance tends rather to foster a state of conceptual perplexity that precedes and founds these ideological positions. Readers are faced with the relativity and the defection of the cultural system and, at the same time, with their responsibility as readers and human beings in sustaining it.

Notes

[1] Donald Barthelme, "The Balloon," *Unspeakable Practices, Unnatural Acts* (New York: Farrar, Straus and Giroux, 1964) 15-22.

[2] Anne Beattie, "Janus," *Park City: New and Selected Stories* (New York: Alfred A. Knopf, 1998) 351-355.

[3] William Goyen, "The Enchanted Nurse," *The Collected Stories of William Goyen* (Garden City: Doubleday, 1975) 240-254.

3 David Schickler, "Kissing In Manhattan," *Kissing in Manhattan* (New York: Dell, 2001) 83-105

[5] John Cheever, "The Enormous Radio," *The Enormous Radio and Other Stories* (New York: Funk and Wagnalls, 1953) 169-181.

[6] It surfaces later in one of the imbricated extensions to that story in Schickler's collection, that the exposition of his partner's bodies is for Patrick also a means of bringing a form of disorientation into his obsessive life blighted by his brother's death.

[7] Sylvia Plath, "Metaphors," *Crossing the Water, Transitional Poems* (New York: Harper & Row, 1971) 43.

[8] Louise Erdrich, "The Fence," *Baptism of Desire* (New York: HarperCollins, 1989) 61.

[9] John L'Heureux, "The Comedian," *Comedians* (New York: Viking Penguin, 1990) 3-19.

[10] Cf. Chapter Eight.

[11] The word equally applies to the characters placed in the othering situation and to readers trying to reneenact it.

[12] Jack Gilbert, "Hunger," *The Great Fires, Poems: 1982-1992* (New York: Knopf, 1994) 51.

[13] A.R. Ammons, "Reflective," *The Selected Poems*, Expanded Edition, (New York: Norton, 1986) 53.

[14] Allen Ginsberg,"Sunflower Sutra," *Collected Poems: 1947-1980*, (New York: Harper & Row, 1984) 138-39.

[15] Jorie Graham, "Recovered From the Storm," *The Errancy*, (Hopewell, N.J.: The Ecco Press, 1997) 107-108.

[16] Ginsberg takes up William Blake's "Oh Sunflower" while Graham replies to T.S. Eliot's "The Wasteland."

[17] This node concentrates and complexifies the ambivalence already found in some of the hybridizing motifs studied in Chapter Six.

[18] Sydney Lea, "The One White Face In the Place," *The Floating Candles* (Chicago: University of Chicago Press, 1982) 47-50.

[19] Norman Dubie, "Elegy to the Sioux," *The Mercy Seat: Collected & New Poems, 1967-2001* (Townsend, Wash. : Copper Canyon Press, 2001) 167-169.

CHAPTER TEN

MEDIATORS OF ESCAPE

The mediators of escape bring the last touch to the edifice of Othering. In Parts II and III of this study we examined the rhetoric of disruption in order to try to venture beyond the limits of conventional modes of interpretation. In the last two chapters we have observed the nodes that indicate lines of fracture in texts. Through their ambiguous revelations they help us recognize the limits of our systems and, at the same time, the vast areas of conceptual space that these limits place beyond the bounds of our perception. The mediators of escape share the distinctive duality of the nodes; like fictional characters they are recognizable human simulacra but they are also virtual and deceptive insofar as they behave in unpredictable ways. Moreover they help us take a final decisive step in our comprehension of the Othering excursion. Why do some literary texts relinquish conventional artistic completion in order to attract our attention to frustrating disorders? Why are these disorders given such prominence that we are induced to believe that they contain everything that is worth divulging in the text but somehow impossible to communicate? Is there for readers any specific gain to be derived from systematic disorientation?

The mediators of escape certainly constitute a major factor of perplexity that readers might be tempted to explain away by assimilating them to identifiable figures produced by our cultural systems, for example, alter egos, intercessors, doubles, secret sharers, or guardian angels. Represented as either a threat to or an ally of the self, these images have in common a core of reassurance that the mediators, on the contrary, serve to critique. They are all in varying degrees full-blown replicas of human beings, whereas the mediators only espouse that resemblance in order to call attention to the necessity that connects the self to something unknown outside itself. If we follow Levinas's very early analysis of the genesis of that connection in *On Escape*, we realize that, by fixing the self in time and space, social and cultural systems provide the indispensable frame that protects and encloses it. The system keeps us together in a dual sense—it affirms the integrity of the subject and regulates relationships with other fellow beings—yet it also founds the desire to escape the prison house of self: "L'expérience de l'être pur est en même temps l'expérience de son antagonisme interne et de l'évasion qui s'impose."[1] Through the vivid representations of experiences in self-division or self-projection that we are going to examine in this chapter, we will show how mediators provide insight into the complex developments of the subject's "internal antagonism." In contrast to most texts dealing with similar situations, the emphasis in the works we have chosen is not on the duplicates themselves but on the interaction between the questing self and its illusive replications. Like all the Othering experiences that we have observed, it is more important to participate in them than to comprehend and interpret them.

Michael Ryan's poem "Every Sunday"[2] offers a good introduction to the role of mediators:

> Psychotic homeless boy
> blocking our exit from the church
> straggle-haired, bloated,
> eyes shining like ice—
>
> doing his rooster-pecking thing
> with his hand made the beak
> into each of our faces
> as we file out—
>
> or is it snake striking
> or airhole-punching
> or just compulsive counting us
> one and one and one?
>
> He will not live long.
> He will allow the pastor
> to wrap his arm around his shoulder,
> and lead him to coffee and crullers.
>
> But to *be* him

The "psychotic homeless boy" standing outside the church entrance is a familiar late twentieth-century figure, easy to recognize and as easy to dismiss. Indeed, the poem might not immediately strike readers as an Othering text. The boy's obstruction of the church exit suggests predictable developments. While the poem's title excludes all radical solutions like police intervention or charitable rescue, we can expect that the parish pastor will perform some philanthropic gesture in the name of the community; the arm "wrap[ped] . . . around his shoulder" and the "coffee and crullers" are as foreseeable as they are ineffectual. The contrast between the pastor's charity and the parishioners' indifference could suggest an ironic perspective underlining the pathos contained in the boy's situation. Another reading might take the codified act of pastoral assistance as a reflection of the general absence of sympathy among the community at large. Other possible interpretations could be imagined that would situate the isolated straggler and the rest of the community in familiar relationships. Still, certain aspects of the poem deviate from recognizable situations and disturb ready-made assumptions. The discordant images clustered around the beggar could be seen as an alternative pattern of persiflage deriding available interpretations. If so, how can we reconcile into a coherent counter argument the references to a "rooster pecking," a "snake striking," or an "airhole-punching" or the boy's "compulsive counting" gesture? Are these images simply grotesque incrustations supposed to bring the character to life and emphasize his strangeness? Is this baroque imagery meant to reproduce the fantastic images or fear-induced fantasies in the stolid parishioners' minds? All these interpretations are plausible and it is precisely because they can be produced almost at will that they are obstacles to the perception of these intriguing images as possible Othering openings.

Since, as we mentioned earlier, the Othering and characterizing orientations work in opposite directions, the more we try to make sense of the characters as human analogues, the more we efface the features that give access to the Othering process. So doing, we are merely running the gamut of all the patterns generated by our culture to elucidate the situations that confront us. These predefined templates are meant to eliminate the feeling of strangeness that assails us when confronted with unexpected situations. Yet, a sense of incongruity persists in Ryan's poem even after we have more or less successfully decoded the scene. We cannot find a completely plausible solution because parts of the poem are not operating within the problem-solving format that underpins the diegetic situation. Besides the strange imagery, there is the compelling final line, set off from the rest of the poem by its structural and tonal difference from the preceding quatrains. The poem demands to be placed in and, at the same time, displaced from obvious interpretative schema; this is a basic feature of the Othering situation that we have observed all along. The boy's strangeness calls not, or not only, for assessment, but for a re-vision of cultural norms. If we refrain from placing the scene within predefined patterns, they cease to obstruct our perception of the Othering relation that the poem establishes. Reading the text in terms of characters and matching scenarios blocks our perception of the young man's provocative figure as the sign, or symptom, of a more global existential complex that his unusual posture only hints at.

The rooster's pecking and the snake's striking actions take another signification from the moment they can be imagined *in themselves* as summoning gestures directed at the churchgoers, and vicariously, at the readers. When the homeless boy is no longer perceived as a lifelike entity, we are free to envisage a multiplicity of modalities that no longer refer to one person in particular but to the various aspects of a relation. These aspects do not have to be coherent or convergent because the Othering relation is not stable in time and place; they are part of an unpredictable and incohesive process. If we abstain from conceptualizing the boy in thematic terms, giving him a name and place and role in society, we are able to respond to the suggestion contained in the final line. "But to *be* him" becomes an inescapable challenge. Nevertheless, in order to be able to comply with that projection of identity, formulated in the most forceful terms ("*be* him" i.e. not to mimic him or empathize with him but actually to become him), and directed at every one of us, we have to accept, at least in our imagination, being pecked and struck at, becoming at the same time the food that could feed and the intruder that has to be repulsed. The boy's indefinable gestures do not identify or accuse; paradoxically, they command attention, and at the same time, provoke dissociation. We are asked to distance ourselves *and* to wake up to the misery that this gesture indicates. The boy's gesture works to deflate protected lives, punching airholes in them, as well as counting them "one and one and one" in a simulacrum of Last Judgment. It addresses us, establishes a relation, and opens up a space of responsibility. We are clearly hailed, pointed at and assigned to play our part in the Othering relation that consists not so much in denying our own identities and stepping into another's shoes but, as the emphatic *be* makes clear, as in being oneself while accepting the other's identity, or more precisely, not imagining that we can continue being ourselves without admitting our connection with him. The peculiar mediator in Ryan's poem calls on the subject to see beyond the boundaries of the self, to become aware of the degree of subjection in subjectivity and to respond to the thrilling and terrifying attraction of other-than-self.

The mediatory role of the outsider in "Every Sunday" is to call into question not only our relation to the cultural system but also our mode of existing within the system. Up to now Othering rhetoric has been described as the exploitation or the creation of loopholes in the cultural system that enable readers to envisage alternative conceptions of existence. To a certain extent, Ryan's evocation of the homeless boy critiques the failure of institutionalized models of charitable aid. At a deeper level, it also reproves the very principles on which charity is founded, like, for example, the idea that it is a collective rather than a personal obligation, or that it consists in allocating material benefits instead of giving individual commitment. All this is certainly brought to our attention by the poem's oblique rhetoric; nevertheless, the feeling of malaise induced by the last line persists. Othering rhetoric can produce feelings of exhilaration, but also, as we see in this poem, of unease. The ludicrous vagrant projecting his hand like a rooster's beak claims another form of attention. The poem's poignant ending makes it urgent, if not perfectly clear, that we should break through cultural clichés, abandon moral certitudes and, in a bold performative act, directly identify with the vagrant and also the context in which he lives, that between him and us there should be no space or use for charity, because we are in the same world. Self and other are indissociably linked and co-dependent; the other does not so much offer an avenue of escape, as open a field of exploration in which the self can freely expand in order to survive.

Up to now, we have implicitly accepted the premise of a cultural system and a linguistic medium within which the subject functions. Discourse occupies the space between situation and system, and the relation between the two determines its relevance. The Othering factor comes into play when writers take advantage of the misfits and disorders in that space in order to manifest the system's relativity. Thus, we have shown, for example in the discussion of indexicals in Chapter Two, how writers interrogate both the construction of the subject and its relation to the system. However, we have not yet fully questioned our own position as readers. Instead, we may have seemed to adopt a privileged position at a distance from the system from whence to identify all the situations encountered in texts. The Othering characters or mediators that we are considering in this chapter force us to revise our assumptions. The mediators demand that as readers we switch from a Cartesian universe in which a potentially all-knowing subject converts the referential world into cognitive representations to a Heideggerian universe in which that conversion is no longer possible.[3] In that conception of the universe, one cannot "know" another being, converting him into an object of intellection, one can only "*be* him" or be next to him or her, because one occupies the same plane of existence, seen as *dasein* or being there, indistinguishable from him in commonly shared experience. In this vision of existence, we occupy the position suggested in the opening lines of Don DeLillo's *The Body Artist*[4]—the book that will be the backbone of our argumentation—like "a spider pressed to its web" (9). The mediators indicate a relation of being-in-the-world in which we can no longer think of ourselves as confronting the world, *res cogitans*, for the world is not conceivable other than through the phenomenal experience derived from our occupancy of it. Consequently, the cultural system is only a projection of society's preoccupations and not an absolute or unique means of access to truth.

Mediators of escape are not the alter egos or antagonists that we expect to find in diegetic scenarios but rather the shadows or flaws in the mirror of cultural appearances that reveal the illusory character of its reflections. In order to attract attention to the symptomatic function of mediators, we will not emphasize the factors contributing to character-definition; nevertheless, this aspect is never entirely absent. The characters that we are going to consider are both thematic constructs and illusory representations of the subject's aspiration to escape. In *The Body Artist,* Don DeLillo defines the heroine's special mediator, Mr. Tuttle, in a very pertinent way: "There has to be an imaginary point, a nonplace where language intersects with our perceptions of time and place, and he is a stranger at this crossing, without words or bearings" (101). Since Mr. Tuttle cannot be placed either in time or space, since he lacks the self-awareness to claim that space, he is a *tabula rasa*, open to Lauren's projection. Like all mediators, though, he offers the subject only a temporary release.

Mark Strand's poem "The Man in the Mirror"[5] and Charles Simic's "The Inner Man"[6] give us other visions of these ghostly forms of existence, hovering between the self and its imaginary analogues. In both texts it is easy and perhaps inevitable, as we have already admitted, to assimilate the mediators' dissociative disorders to psychological or social counterparts that challenge the self's unity. Nevertheless, although such explanations could be envisaged, the poems resist being fitted into preexisting cultural templates. In Simic's poem, although it so happens that the outer and the inner man "cast a single shadow," they still have to be seen as different persons, and the sometimes imperceptible contradiction of being two beings joined together in the same person has to be experienced:

If I'm quiet, he's quieter.
So I forget him.
A dog follows me about.
It might be his.

If I'm quiet, he's quieter.
So I forget him.
Yet, as I bend down

To tie my shoelaces,
He's standing up.

We cast a single shadow.
Whose shadow? (18)

The self divides not only in language between the first and third person,
between the uninflected adjective and its comparative form, but also in
space, as its gestures become dissociated (bending down and standing up).
Subsequently, that contrariety appears to come uppermost:

Shuffling the cards of our silence,
I say to him:

'Though you utter
Every one of my words,
You are a stranger.
It's time you spoke.' (19)

Paradoxically, at the very moment when the speaker is quoting himself in
the poem, asserting his identity through a first person statement, the
declaration that "you utter/ every one of my words" becomes either an
insoluble conundrum or the missing clue that should lead us beyond the
reassurance of grammatical categories. "You" is both "a stranger" and the
self. The final line of the poem is both an invitation to the other—your
turn to speak—and a peculiar admission of identification with someone
else—"you spoke" in me. Because of the difference between the verbs
"utter" (simple expression) and "speak" (solemn pronouncement), the
relation developed in the poem is not just shadow play with the double but
the anticipation of a vital revelation.

Strand's "Man in the Mirror" goes a little further in the exploration of
the intriguing relation between inside and outside, self and out-of-self. The
interval between the self and the other appears to be impassable because of
the mirror between them, which is paradoxically a reflection of self and
the suspicion of an other-than-self:

I remember how we used to stand
wishing the glass would dissolve between us
and how we watched our words

cloud that bland,
innocent surface (24)

In spite of the untraversable barrier, the self and the other outside it are
still joined here by the first person plural pronoun. Moreover, the subject's
relation with the rest of the world seems to be tied to the other's presence
reflected in the mirror. When it departs, it is as if the light of the world
vanishes with it:

> One day you turned away
>   and left me here
>   to founder in the stillness of your wake. (25)

Without his reflection the abandoned subject is bereft: "The mirror was
nothing without you" (26), until the moment when the "you" returns,
bringing with him the image of a changed self burdened and enriched with
the misery of the world:

> I go into the living room and you are there.
> You drift in a pool
> of silver air
>
> where wounds and dreams of wounds
> rise from the deep humus of sleep
> to bloom like flowers against the glass. (27)

The other's return is an occasion for the subject to discover his connection
with the world. Self and other are locked in a kind of life-sustaining and
life-threatening relationship, so that whether the reflection disappears or
remains the same, the self's integrity will be seriously affected:

> I stand here scared
> That you will disappear,
> Scared that you will stay. (28)

A similar process of self-preservation takes place in *The Body Artist*.
While the protagonist, Lauren Hartke, is undergoing a period of deep
sorrow following her husband's suicide, a mysterious houseguest arrives.
The stranger, whom she names Mr. Tuttle, after a ridiculous former
science teacher, offers no explanation for his presence. As a mime and
body artist, Lauren is prone to impersonating other people's lives, so Mr.
Tuttle could very well be one of her creations, or again, he could be a
figment of her tortured imagination, objectifying her obsessions. Mr.
Tuttle could also be a psychotic patient escaped from a neighboring
institution, a total stranger, who Lauren in her loneliness, has endowed
with exaggerated importance. The fact that all these scenarios are plausible

keeps Mr. Tuttle's presence ambiguous and unexplained to the end. The possibility of interpreting the novel thematically as a conflict between Lauren's tendency to yield to despair and various alternative options should never be excluded. Yet, in the Othering perspective, the mediator's intervention represents an alternative to these traditional motivations and scripts.

First, contrary to conventional projections of the subject, the mediator's relation to the protagonist is not an agonistic one of conflicts or alliances. The Othering text does not work toward the reduction or elimination of the space between the self and its other, but on the contrary to the elaboration of that space. As we saw in Simic's poem, the split within the self is almost foundational while in Strand's, the mirror-barrier separating the self from its reflection is both an unbridgeable division and a source of enrichment. Mediators can only function within a situation of isolation and multiple reflections.[7] Having little to do with referential space, a mediator is nearly always a product of inner space or, more exactly, of ambivalent spaces in which inner and outer coexist. In *The Body Artist*, Mr. Tuttle emerges from the several floors and rooms in the large beach house in which Lauren has taken refuge after her husband's death. This space of seclusion is rich in complementary and reversible "counter-surroundings" as she surmises in Mr Tuttle's simple summation of her situation—"Alone by the sea":

> Four words only. But he'd placed her in a set of counter-surroundings, of simultaneous insides and outsides. The house, the sea-planet outside it, and how the word *alone* referred to her and to the house and how the word *sea* reinforced the idea of solitude but suggested a vigorous release as well, a means of escape from the book-walled limits of the self. (50)

The mediator is not so much an antagonist, an alter ego, or a simple presence as an intersection or pathway between existential options, between inside and outside, between self as restrictedly conceived and self as thrown in with the rest of the world. The intersection that mediators occupy represents the field of experience, of life-as-experienced, in which all the characters contemplate and achieve mutations. Paradoxically, this focal point is also a blank space on which the mutating character projects his or her future integration in existence. The mediator is not an idealized or alternative image of self but the suggestion of an empty slot in existence pointing to a future evolution in life. As we will see in connection with *The Body Artist*, the ultimate objective of the mutation is not to acquire a new self but to keep open the possibility of change.

To emphasize the importance of the self's mutability, its open-mindedness rather than its fixity, *The Body Artist* pictures three highly contrasted images of existence. Periodically, Lauren watches a computer screen giving non-stop footage from an out-of-the-way place in Finland, called Kotka, "a live-streaming video feed from the edge of a two-lane road in a city in Finland" (40). This is one of the margins of Lauren's existence, the world of pure factuality, of absolute no-thing in which Lauren would like to lose herself. If the world can function without her in absolute materiality, then there is a chance that her pain might not exist. This can be considered as a form of defection from Othering in which the subject fantasizes relinquishing responsibility in confronting experience. Another fantasized evasion is the image of a Japanese lady whom Lauren has seen watering her garden. This alternative mode of existence would reduce life to a function: "Why not sink into it?" (118), she thinks for an instant. More inaccessible but always hovering in the background of the novel is a third option represented by the lively birds coming to the feeder placed outside the window. Although tied to the necessity of eating, they serve as the opposite of the other two options. They represent pure beingness: existence as lived in itself and for itself without the responsibility of assuming its burden, pure motility in space and time with "a shedding of every knowable surface and process" (24). The bird-watching moments are all the more precious for Lauren, both before and after her husband's suicide, as they are inaccessible and in part reconstructed:

> She wanted to believe the bird was seeing her, a woman with a teacup in her hand, and never mind the folding back of the day and night, the apparition of a space set off from time.
> ....
> She was making it happen herself because she could not look any longer. This must be what it means to see if you have been near blind all your life. (24)

These three impossible options precisely define the existential void in which Lauren seems to immerse herself in her relationship with her husband and that she is left with after his demise: "She looked into a space inside her head that was also here in front of her" (25).

It is that space set off from time, originally the space left by Rey's suicide, that she will have to recover through Tuttle's arrival. The mediator figures the exact middle term or middle-distance between the existential void of Kotka and the birds' existential plenitude—he represents the necessity to relate in order to continue in existence. After her husband's death, Lauren lapses into mourning but also paradoxically regains control of her existence. That regression provokes the half-real half-fantasized appearance of Tuttle. Tuttle represents the projection of the different modalities of existence that Lauren will have to visualize and experience in order to overcome her bereavement and regain control of her life. And control is directly linked to projection, not to intellection; she needs to extricate herself physically from her immersion in sorrow. The mediator helps her put in perspective what would otherwise remain mortally trapped within the confines of the self.

As opposed to the Japanese woman's two-dimensional fixation in her function, Lauren seems to be floating, unattached and diminished:

> She thought about broiling a cutlet, self-consciously alone, more or less seeing herself from the edge of the room or standing precisely where she was and being who she was and seeing a smaller hovering her in the air somewhere.   already thinking it's tomorrow.
> She wanted to disappear in Rey's smoke, be dead, be him . . . . (36)

She looks outside and sees a " twirling leaf", which could be an image of her state:

> There was no sign of a larva web from which the   leaf   might   be suspended, or a strand of some bird's nest-building material. Just the leaf in   midair, turning. (43)

Precisely when Lauren is hanging loose in this way, she discovers Mr Tuttle.

Mr. Tuttle is the screen of unreality, the "seem," the "somehow" or the "as if" on which Lauren projects her own pain, her past, and progressively her desire for recovery: "It was always as if. He did this or that as if" (47).[8] First, she has to confront a form of division in personality which, like that represented in Simic's and Strand's poems, far from being morbid or psychotic, is the first step toward expanded vision. She sees herself as dialoguing with "some third person in her mind" (65), a relation in which, for the first time, she ceases to be an omnipresent and obsessive "I" to become the objective interlocutor in the narration of her existence. Yet, although it is clear that she can only achieve personal transformation by preserving that vital distance from herself, the temptation is strong to lose herself in that projection, to switch from morbid self to compensatory out-of-self. Very soon she idealizes the timeless world in which Mr. Tuttle lives: "She thought maybe he lived in a kind of time that had no narrative quality" (67). Side by side with that desire for otherness coexists a powerful undertow of regression; Lauren tries at first to fill Mr. Tuttle's

non-narrative time with the story of her own past. She records Mr. Tuttle's
speech on a tape recorder, and his words are Rey's own words that she has
neurotically instilled into him. An obsessive relation with non-self obtains.

The relation is abruptly reversed from the moment when, no longer
forcing Mr. Tuttle to be the mute partner in a ventriloquist's act, she
discovers him in his bath and becomes conscious of his physical existence:
"the breathless shock of his being there" (71). From that moment, she
enjoys a different form of illusion; instead of immersing herself in her past
through him, she joyfully pours herself into his life. In spite of Tuttle's
incoherent yet clearly dissuasive words, "I will leave the moment from the
moment" (76) or "Because nothing comes between me" (76), she
experiences a new plasticity of self that authorizes a form of beatitude:

> He kept it going a while, ongoing, oncoming, and it was song, it was chant.
> She leaned into him. This was a level that demonstrated he was not closed
> to inspiration. She felt an easing in her body that drew her down out of
> laborious   thought and into something nearly incontrollable. She leaned
> into his voice laughing. She wanted to chant with him, to fall   in   and   out
> of time, or words, or things, whatever he was doing . . . . (76)

Her immersion in his chant takes her out of herself:

> The words ran on, sensuous and empty, and she wanted him to laugh with
> her, to follow her out of herself. This is the point, yes, this is the stir of true
> amazement. And some terror at the edge, or fear of believing, some
> displacement of self, but this is the point, this is the wedge into ecstasy, the
> old deep meaning of the world, your eyes rolling upward in your skull.
> (77)

The etymological sense of the word "ecstasy" pertains here, designating a
state of being projected out of the self. Ironically, though, Lauren escapes
the prison of self only to fall prey to the lures of immersion in the other.
When Lauren tries to immerse herself in Mr. Tuttle's world she simply
reverses the initial blocked position of grieving; she changes from self-
absorption to submersion in otherness.

Projection onto the other is the indispensable first step for the subject's
insertion in time and space. Once subjects perceive themselves as thrown
into the world they become aware of the self as inscribed in time and
affected by finitude. This is the main issue in *The Body Artist* and in some
of the poems that we are considering here. From the moment the subject
ceases to believe in a Cartesian universe in which his continuity depends
on the survival of the spiritual part of himself, he becomes involved in the
general drift of the world toward extinction. The realization can be

shattering. The temptation is strong to evade the responsibility that ensues, a last residual form of subject-induced misrepresentation. The subject can either escape from or, on the contrary, exaggerate his or her commitment to the world. The two forms of evasion are represented in the texts we are studying.

Texts such as Stanley Plumly's "November 11, 1942-November 12, 1997"[9] or Linda Gregg's "There she is"[10] present subjects irremediably shattered by the visitation of their mediators, caught rather than freed by their contemplation of otherness. The speaker in Plumly's poem cannot control his vision of his dead friend returning in his imagination to demand empathy but becoming instead a monstrously deformed visitor offering his organs and all his bodily fluids to him:

> And though he doesn't say so,
> because he never would, I'm sure he wants me
> to hold him, say his name, make him warm.
> But when I try he puts his hand inside
> his heart and offers me the stone,
> then the Armistice poppy, and then
> the bowl of bright arterial blood.
> And from where the scar is, where they
> saved his life and failed, the umbilical
> intestine, impurities and purities of kidneys
> and the liver, the two lungs out of breath,
> and breath itself, cupped till it runneth over. (6)

The allusion to the Psalms[11] and the "cup that runneth over" gives an ironic indication of the masochistic compensation that attends the contemplation of the other's suffering. The subject exaggerates its destructive power seemingly in order to attenuate his guilt as survivor. If the destruction is massive enough, even outrageously calamitous, there is a chance that he might be exculpated from his participation in the disaster. A similar feeling of exaggerated responsibility presides over the speaker's perception in Gregg's poem. The female mediator in the garden, reminiscent of Strand's mysterious man "stand[ing] in front of [his] house," or of Ryan's vagrant, appears affected by all manner of suffering, the pain inflicted upon her compounded by the wounds she has inflicted upon herself:

> There is blood on her face.
> I can see she has done it to herself.
> So she would not feel the other pain.

The "other pain" is no different from the other's pain, it is the pain of the world that the speaker is contemplating, and that she finds unable to face because she is unable to cope with the responsibility to herself:

> How can I live while she
> stands there? And if I take her life
> what will that make of me?

Maybe, when all is said and done, the difficulty of existence does not consist so much in placing oneself in front of the other, trading one's life for his or shouldering his burden as in Ryan's poem. Even if all these actions *are* generous transactions, these words are still redolent of the moralistic dealings of subjects negotiating existential issues instead of confronting them. The problem of existence cannot be resolved in transactional terms, it can hardly be conceived as a problem at all; life is a complex of perceptions and emotions that have to be experienced and processed in the act of living itself.

Another poem by Mark Strand, "The Tunnel,"[12] reverses these situations of identification and responsibility and thereby somewhat clarifies them. Instead of trying to identify with the mediator, like Lauren or like the churchgoer in Ryan's "Every Sunday," or remaining paralyzed before him or her like the speakers in Plumly's and Gregg's poems, the speaker in "The Tunnel," attempts to flee the silent visitation of a man standing motionless on his lawn. In desperation, he digs a tunnel under his house and eventually resurfaces in a neighboring yard, placed in exactly the same position as the man he is trying to avoid. Seeking to avoid the other, the tunnel digger only ends up in a blocked situation:

> I hear
> a man's voice,
> but nothing is done
> and I have been waiting for days. (14)

Avoidance, like immersion in the other, is the wrong kind of escape. Nonetheless, a new space of "waiting" seems to have been opened up at the end of "The Tunnel." The mediator's intervention sets in motion the self's transformation and, more importantly, makes possible the existential awareness of being exposed to its own mutations and hence ultimately to its own finitude.

For Lauren in *The Body Artist*, total absorption in Mr. Tuttle's life promises to afford protection from the erosion of time:

Time is supposed to pass, she thought. But maybe he is living in another
state. It is a kind of time that is simply and overwhelmingly there, laid out,
unoccurring, and he lacks the inborn quality to reconceive this condition.
(79)

Mr Tuttle represents a "walking talking continuum" (93), a kind of totality
in which things are not distinct from one another in space and time. They
form: "a continuous thing, a continuous whole, and the only way to
distinguish one part from another, this from that, now from then, is by
making arbitrary divisions" (93). This mode of existence that so fascinates
Lauren could be a perception of time and the world before the system
divides it up; as such it evokes the birds' state of pure beingness. It attracts
her because it promises to erase her husband's suicide, allowing Rey to be
reincarnated in Mr. Tuttle. Nevertheless, since it denies human existence
as an experience of time, it is a form of non-existence: "a kind of time that
is . . .. unoccurring" (79). Though this denial of the demands of existence in
favor of continuity promises release from time's destructive power, this is
an illusory hope.

Assiduously working with her body, Lauren comes to a new
realization:

But it can't be true that he drifts from one reality to another, independent
of the logic of time. This is not possible. You are made out of time. This is
the force that tells you who you are. (93-94)

As a mediator of escape, Mr. Tuttle presents a distorted image of the
human situation that paradoxically allows Lauren not only to see that
death is inescapable but also to survive that realization:

Time is the only narrative that matters. It stretches events and makes it
possible for us to suffer and come out of it and see death and come out of
it. (94)

Neither non-existent nor suffocatingly omni-present, time is a "narrative,"
a mode of structuring, containing and distancing reality.

As a mime and body artist, Lauren understands instinctively that the
true relation to her being-in-the-world and to the mediator in her life must
come from the bodywork that "made everything transparent." (59)[13] In a
very vibrant scene, she meticulously washes her visitor's body thus
creating a contact that she had failed to establish through language. The
very spastic dialogue that she attempts to establish with linguistically
deficient Mr. Tuttle is suddenly replaced by the sensuous intimacy
between hands and bodies that she forms with him. She discovers the pure

togetherness that brings solidity and continuity in existence, "the fact, the blur, whatever it was—the breathless shock of his being there" (71). This is the kind of feeling that she will eventually transform into the body act that she performs to private audiences after her visitor's disappearance. She systematically modifies her bodily shape, alters her appearance as a woman, even as a human being. Instead of avoiding or confronting time, she lets it unfold:

> Past, present and future are not amenities of language. Time unfolds into the seams of being. It passes through you, making and shaping. (101)

In a shift of focalization made evident by a new chapter heading that turns out to be the title of a magazine article, Lauren's best friend, a journalist, gives an account of her performance piece, significantly called *Body Time*. Through Mariella Chapman's article, "Body Art in Extremis: Slow, Spare and Painful," readers discover that the events and people that participated in Lauren's recovery have been fused and transformed into a sequence of bodily expressions: "She is acting, always in the process of becoming another or exploring some root identity" (107). The last of Lauren's expressions convulsively mimics the disappearance of her mediator as if she were birthing him into another world. But if Lauren's performance conclusively achieves the artistic projection of the whole story into lived and bodied forth time, the problem of selfdom remains unresolved. Lauren still fails to emerge as a consistent human being.

Apparently, for DeLillo, creation is not sufficient in itself; it places the artwork among the world of objects, body art included. The novel's final chapter marks the return of experience as lived in the present and the disappearance of illusions. Lauren extends the lease on the huge beach house she inhabited with her husband: "She has taken this action to fulfill the truth of [Mr. Tuttle's] remark [that she would return to the house] which probably invalidates whatever truth there may have been." (114), but Rey's presence is forgotten and so is Mr Tuttle's. In fact, it is as if a new lease on existence could only be obtained by erasing past events. Step by step Lauren reenacts the several stages in her previous ordeal and every time what strikes the reader is the mimetic power of her every move. After her successful performance she becomes an artist in life. She even mimics her husband's suicide, but it is in the bathroom with a spray-gun disinfectant. She meets the old Japanese woman again and notices that with her hands in her pockets she seems to have no hands—implying that the two-dimensional perfection that had attracted her attention offers no real compensation. She encounters a new visitor, but it is the house's owner who comes to recover a piece of property left behind after his removal. In his presence, "She began to feel she was fitting into something" (120). Rather than assigning him a role in the script of her past, as she had done with Mr. Tuttle, Lauren has to confront a new situation. As the man speaks to her, the process of unwriting and re-inscribing her story is in progress and she finds her place within it. The man wants to retrieve the chest of drawers in Mr. Tuttle's former room. This chest of drawers functions as a simulacrum signaling the end of Mr. Tuttle's usefulness in the house. When the man tries to describe the piece of furniture, Lauren reflects: "This is not what he was supposed to say" (121), implying that she expected an allusion to Tuttle or to Rey. Later, she barely notices the U-Haul truck when he comes to pick it up. Obviously a new scenario is in progress that demands completion.

She reenters the house and directs her footsteps toward the bedroom in which she is confident she will find her former husband. And, at the moment when she fantasizes a love scene, she discovers that the room is empty. What is important to notice is that the whole process of emancipation from the past is not the result of an intellectual process; it does not proceed from the young woman looking back at herself but from her moving forward into existence, erasing the past with acts of living. No mediator, intercessor or visitor is necessary for this kind of existential realization:

> The room was empty when she looked. No one was there. The light was so vibrant she could see the true colors of the walls and floor. She'd never seen the walls before. The bed was empty. She had known it was empty all along but she was only catching up. (126)

Curiously this form of instinctive knowing is a form of awareness that always precedes (didn't know) or exceeds (knew) the fact of understanding:

> She walked into the room and went to the window. She threw the window open. She didn't know why she did this. Then she knew. She wanted to feel the sea tang on her face and the flow of time in her body, to tell her who she was. (126)

The book comes full circle, marking Lauren's reentry into time not as "a spider pressed to its web," as in the beginning of the novel but as a responsible actor.

The form of Othering represented by the mediators in *The Body Artist* and in the other texts discussed in this chapter is doubly demarcated from the cultural system. It cannot take its place in terms of the systems' norms, and yet, unlike the Othering strategies we have considered up to now, it cannot be placed in contradistinction with them. Instead of inviting an excursion out of the limits of the system, the mediators demand a critical revision of the system itself. The mediators of escape occupy the very equivocal position of being at the same time full-bodied characters and Othering nodes, focal points and blank spots in the narration. This amounts to no less than a contradiction in terms since they are at the same time cultural constructions reinforcing our conception of the human subject and virtual projections denouncing its construction. Besides, we saw that the mediator's presence overprinted on the traditional character tends not only to discredit that diegetic category but also to fracture the notion of an ontological self. Mediators blur the system's categories and they open the possibility of a totally different conception of reality in which experience and relations replace concepts and categories. They call for immediate recognition and adhesion rather than understanding and interaction. As opposed to the other Othering tactics, they do more than offer an enlarged perspective; they require an ontological conversion.

As fictional characters, the mediators are like mirrors reflecting the protagonists' objectives; as Othering nodes, they are exactly the contrary, offering previously unseen images from the other side of the mirror. Just like all the Othering factors, they tend to background and relativize the cultural system insofar as they create an impression of disorientation that jars with the reassurance traditionally associated with fiction. Yet the mediators do not put the cultural system in question in the same way as all the Othering factors that we have analyzed before. They throw doubt upon the ability of human beings to relate to the cultural system and derive any enlightenment from the relation. In fact, they reject one of the pillars of culture, the foundational evidence on which the system rests: the conviction that any subject can take stock of his or her situation and give it a plausible interpretation in language. As phantom images of the questing subject, they suggest, sometimes through their vulnerability or improbability, the possibility of another form of knowing which lies beyond language, in the perception of one's commitment to existence in all its forms and modalities. The mediators of escape are the fleeting images of an existential subject supplanting the Cartesian self postulated by the system.

The mediators' greatest contribution to the Othering experience is that they offer the conditions for an escape out of self. That escape is not an escape from self or an evasion into the other but an ontological quest, the creation of an existential space of tolerance for the other-than-self. Mediators are not alter egos or images of otherness; they are suggestions of all that can be imagined that does not define selfdom but contributes to expand it. They provide a space of exteriority for an enlarged form of existence in which being a self ceases to be an objective and where all forms and modalities of otherness can find their just place.

Notes

[1] Emmanuel Lévinas, *De l'Evasion*, (Paris: Fata Morgana, 1982): 116. (The experience of pure being is at the same time the experience of its inner antagonism and of the escape that becomes imperative. [Our translation.])

[2] Michael Ryan, "Every Sunday," *New and Selected Poems* (Boston: Houghton Mifflin, 2004) 131.

[3] The few Heideggerian concepts that we cite are never consistently connected with each other or "applied" to the literary text. They are only used by analogy to clarify our conception of the Othering process.

[4] Don DeLillo, *The Body Artist* (New York: Simon & Schuster, 2001).

[5] Mark Strand. "The Man In the Mirror," *Selected Poems* (New York: Alfred Knopf, 1993) 24-28.

[6] Charles Simic, "The Inner Man," *Selected Poems: 1963-1983* (New York: George Braziller, 1990) 18-19.

[7] These spaces are evocative of the sites of exposure that we studied in Chapter Eight.

[8] These words are constantly associated with Lauren's perception of Mr Tuttle: cf. Delillo 80.

[9] Stanley Plumly, "November 11, 1942-November 12, 1997," *Now that My Father Lies Down Beside Me, New and Selected Poems, 1970-2000* (New York: Harper Collins, 2000) 6-7.

[10] Linda Gregg, "There She Is," *Too Bright To See* (Townsend, Washington: Graywolf Press, 1981) 15.

[11] Psalms, 23:5.

[12] Strand 13-14.

[13] This perception is in agreement with Lévinas's reflection that "Le corps n'est pas seulement un accident malheureux ou heureux nous mettant en rapport avec le monde implacable de la matière—son adhérence au moi vaut par elle–même." (The body is not only an unhappy or happy accident putting us in relation with the implacable material world—its conjunction with the self is a value in itself. [Our Translation.]) Emmanuel Lévinas, *Quelques réflexions sur la nature de l'hitlérisme* (Paris: Payot & Rivages, 1997) 18.

CONCLUSION

FROM CONFRONTATION TO COMPLEXITY:
THE OTHERING PROCESS
AS A RECONSIDERATION OF DIFFERENCES

As we explained in our preface, our research has been motivated by the desire to describe and explain differences in contemporary American literature. The current concepts based on either the confrontation between communities or on various versions of the concept of hybridity have proved inoperative for reading certain texts. Insofar as, to a greater or lesser degree, they demarcate the socio-political structures of American society, these approaches address already well documented phenomena. Some texts went beyond these surface characteristics, appearing enigmatic and difficult to interpret in terms of conventional reading grids. They seemed to escape the binaries of the socio-political field as well as the fusion or syncretism implicit in the concept of hybridity. Yet, far from being aberrant or deviant, the texts we have considered here could be seen as indicative of a major structuring principle in literature. In differing degrees and proportions, they represent both that which can be readily expressed through the cultural system and that which lies outside the conventional system of representation and hence remains largely inexpressible. We have identified this second orientation as the Othering factor.

Othering forms of expression are like cryptic traces inscribed or encoded within familiar, easily recognizable messages. They can be seen as attempts to relate experiences or worldviews inaccessible through the concepts of the cultural system. These experiences are beyond words not because they are unformulated or ineffable but because the cultural system as system cannot give them expression. Although these inaccessible experiences may be mistaken for psychologically or socially repressed drives, these correlations fail to account for the aesthetic impression that these texts produce. They seem to have an enduring newness, a lasting singularity, even though they frequently appear disconcerting. By flouting conventional formats they both replenish and renovate cultural forms.

Rather than being regressive or digressive, the Othering function opens new, unexplored areas of existence. Far from being deviant or even exceptional, these forms of expression are examples of a dynamic and necessary cultural phenomenon. Othering texts are at the same time reproductive of their context and prospective of other possible modes of living. Indeed, defined in this way, the Othering function certainly exists in numerous cultural productions through the ages. Rather than simply reproducing the concepts and forms available within their cultural world, artists and writers interrogate them and force them to express something other. Nevertheless, America provides a particularly fertile terrain for the Othering factor. Throughout its history it has been called on not only to affirm and define itself as a nation but also to question and redefine its ethos constantly in the face of difference. American artists and writers have had to assume the crucial cultural function of extending the boundaries of the representable through the Othering process.

In choosing to study a body of texts that clearly exemplify the Othering function, we incur the risk of being charged with attempting to create a new form of dualism by implicitly valorizing Othering texts over those that favor form. We may be seen as attempting to substitute an aesthetic of multiplicity and disruption for an aesthetic of unity and closure. If so, we want to insist that what matters in the Othering process is not the domination of one aesthetic principle over another, but the interaction of the two orientations. If we have underemphasized conventional thematic and structural values and given too much importance to obscure, deviant, neglected texts, our aim has nevertheless been to illustrate the relationship between what can be placed within the system and what lies outside. We do not conceive of literature as being divided between conservative and innovative texts. An ideal of formal perfection is only tenable if the work of art allows some space for the confusion that it displaces. In fact, terminology is once again misleading: form and de-form, as we have called them, should be seen as the two sides of the same entity. Texts are definitely not unified entities but fields of conflicting forces. We take dissonance to be the ferment of culture, not an obstacle or an impoverishment.

Hypothetically all literary texts have to negotiate their insertion within their cultural system. Texts could thus be described in terms of a ratio between the rhetorical structures confirming the system and those tending to destabilize it. If it is accepted that elements of form and de-form are constitutive of all literary texts, then all texts both reconfirm and challenge the system. On one side cultural signs are organized and structured, on the other, they are put into question and reshuffled. At the very least, the

Othering concept helps deal with the irreducible part in texts that is often overlooked or discarded as intractable. More radically, Othering could claim to be a fundamental structuring principle in literature. Rather than staging a confrontation between fully-fledged cultural universes, the Othering text has a double inscription in discourse: a rhetoric of disruption superscripted on a rhetoric of affirmation.

Even when it claims partisanship, the text is always double-faced or cleft. It depends both on what can be expressed within the system and what cannot be expressed. When we speak of what is "other" to the system we do not simply refer to the representations of minority or occulted communities but to everything that cannot be expressed (both the repressed and the inexpressible), as well as that which is confused or unintelligible in the cultural system. Because it is structural and concerns the foundation of signs and their relation to subjects, the Othering relation includes but exceeds by far group affiliations. It calls for a major revision of the concept of alterity. For lack of proper designations and because of the parasitic images that obstruct its comprehension, alterity is difficult to conceive. For us, alterity is not a concept but a conceptual space[1] outside the system and beyond the perception of subjects. This space of exteriority is the locus of intense cultural activity that can be divided into three different functions that in reality work in synchrony: it is a space of creativity activating innovation rather than reproduction; a space of awareness in which differences are magnified rather than obliterated; a space of experimental rather than formal textuality.

Indeed, our study demands more generally a rethinking of the cultural role accorded literature. Fundamentally, the task of literary texts is not to spearhead social struggles or to manifest psychological disorders— although we do not deny the importance of these factors—but to expose, organize and destabilize cultural signs. In positing that cultural signs are not automatically aligned in terms of the political power game, we have defined *stances* (spaces induced by texts and recreated by the act of reading) as intermediary sites in which signs can be exchanged, hybridized and reshuffled. Far from seeing stances as naïve enclaves of neutrality, we consider them as a necessary condition for creativity. Signs have to be unfastened from their underpinnings to become accessible to art; otherwise creation is only reproduction. Stances are places that permit observation of a culture's values, contradictions, and tensions. Places of specularity (exteriority rather than alterity or transcendence), they are characterized neither by aesthetic detachment nor ideological infiltration. Instead, like the Balinese cockfights described by Geertz, they are privileged locations in which social subjects can observe and exchange signs with others rather than passively submitting to their sociocultural context or actively defending their positions in it. In those liminal spaces, without ceasing to be themselves, they are given the opportunity, sometimes with the help of mediators, to envisage and respond to what lies beyond the self. They obtain access to a range of phenomena in which persons, objects and concepts cease to be recognized as such, where they begin to blur, exchange and circulate. In the interstices opened by the Othering process meaning loosens up, mutates and proliferates.

Our conception of the function of literature has dictated the orientation of our book. We have not sought to apply a theory but to conduct a three-pronged hermeneutical exercise involving first the selection of texts, then their interpretation, and finally the observation of the various modalities of the Othering principle. Rather than a conventional critical book it is an effort to put into practice a new attitude to texts.

The required attitude concerns, first of all, a new apprehension of texts as navigating between the search for signification and the recognition of the unattainability of meaning. Being fundamentally both accessible and enigmatic, texts question the very notion of comprehensibility. They simultaneously offer guided tours and open fields of exploration. Total comprehension is no longer even a distant objective; understanding only covers part of the way charted by the text, the rest calls for new forms of exploration that we have tried to put into practice. More than the act of seizing, suggested by its etymology, comprehension demands a releasing of meaning. The response induced in readers is not a sense of accomplishment and elevation but of angst and disorientation preparatory to a form of emancipating perception.

Second, in addition to conventional descriptive criticism, the Othering approach demands a form of creative criticism that explores the potentialities of texts. We realize that this more subjective form of criticism may not be considered as scientifically founded. Yet, we insist that it is the indispensable complement of all criticism if it wants to avoid being mere ideological reproduction. Critiques are not only texts about other texts but also ways of opening and amplifying their signification, sounding boards for creative texts.

Initially, we looked for an approach that would address difference in American literary production; we tended to define literary value in terms of distinctiveness and opposition. Our study of the Othering principle leads us to the conclusion that culture represents instead diversity, multivalence, and commutability. To study the Othering process is to submit to an experience in complexity. What we have identified as non-systemic or outside the system is in fact contained within a wider concept that we have evoked only marginally because it outreaches by far the empiric objective of our study. Complexity in all its forms and variants is the evident impression that even a cursory look at contemporary American culture discovers. Yet this complexity is not the original inchoate confusion of impressions that a Cartesian spirit confronts, but an enriched conception of reality that has to be recognized. Complexity contains all the unformulated, the obscure and the unspoken in culture, and, at the same time, it determines the various constructions and strategies that culture devises to counteract it. The system is at the same time an antidote to the general complexity and our only means of conceptualizing it.

Throughout this study we have tried to explore a paradox that has been forcefully stated by Edgar Morin concerning the more general domain of the social sciences:

> Il s'agit de voir clairement l'obscur, distinctement le complexe, d'aller du vague au précis, mais aussi de voir l'obscur dans le clair, le complexe dans le distinct, d'aller par le clair vers l'obscur, vers la bouche d'ombre que l'idée ne peut saisir, car toute idée porte en elle, dans sa rétine conceptuelle, une tache indélébilement aveugle.[2]

We have tried to follow Morin's exhortation in our approach. With each and every text that we have analyzed, we have tried to envisage its zones of obscurity not as flaws or dead ends but as invitations to decode the unexpressed and inexpressible meanings that they contain. Conversely, these semantically and semiotically rich zones do not exist separately from the text's conventional thematic and structural networks; paradoxically, they depend for their existence on the defection of the system. It is precisely when the system fails that it becomes suggestive of something else, and that something else can only be suggested through the system. Moreover that which is unexpressed and inexpressible in the system can only be decoded thanks to it. It follows that the systematic and non-systematic definition of texts is a false binary that obscures the intrinsic functional connection that binds and fertilizes the two. What lies outside the system is neither inferior nor superior to what is accepted as culturally relevant; instead, they both contribute to the definition of the cultural universe. They are the foundation of its complexity. In that perspective literary texts play a crucial role in the conceptualization of that complexity. They can be perceived as troublemaking agents in the conventionally agreed division between what is expressible and what is not. In the imaginary worlds they propose they either reinforce or fracture the boundaries that cultures have erected. Literature constantly redefines and displaces the limits between the structurally organized and the conceptually disorganized. The role of the critic could best be defined as reconciling and matching the values of both worlds that artworks tend to juxtapose sometimes dramatically, always problematically.

We have tried to privilege a reading attitude in which polyvalence, reversibility and ambiguity are given due recognition. We believe that analytical schemata, besides limiting or mutilating the experience of reading, only skim the surface of reality. By adopting the complexity paradigm we can more readily respond to the diversity of contemporary American culture. In order to access that complexified universe we used the Othering concept as a tool to rupture conventional critical templates in order to evoke other possibilities, other reading adventures. Othering is an aspiration to reach beyond commonly accepted interpretations and to confront the complexity that inevitably any literary text contains or tries to circumscribe. It is a heuristic tool that we have conceived to crack the system open and to address the complexity of literature by reforming our attitude to texts.

The risk involved in placing too much emphasis on the inexpressible and on texts that evince that orientation is evidently to fall into either subjectivism or confusion. Asking readers to look beyond the system is certainly to incur the risk of erraticism and bewilderment, but also to open up the possibility of discovering unsuspected realities that have been silenced or unaccounted for in the cultural system. That possibility certainly justifies occasional lapses into indecisiveness or idiosyncrasy.

After exploring various approaches to the multiple differences in American culture, we found that existing concepts were ineffective because not adequately formulated. Instead of differences based on oppositions and dualisms, we have discovered complexity, not as disorder or confusion (although it may appear as such if we approach it with conventional assumptions), but as something positive and seminal. The difference is crucial: complexity as we conceive it is not the opposite of clarity and simplicity, it is an attempt to approximate wholeness without relying on ideological constructions of totality. Instead of opposing or homogenizing differences, the complexity concept helps us to compare and combine without excluding. Seen in this way, the concept is in accordance with the etymology of the word in which the idea of intricacy is subsidiary to that of plaiting or weaving together or embracing.[3] We have tried to connect, confront and correlate instead of isolating, classifying and hierarchizing, or rather, we have aimed to show how these fundamental cognitive operations could be significantly correlated. We have tried neither to efface nor to underline the differences that we have observed in our selected texts, but to coordinate them into a multivalent, multifactorial web according to Morin's concept of the dialogic principle:

> Le principe dialogique consiste à faire jouer ensemble de façon complémentaire des notions qui, prises absolument seraient antagonistes et se rejetteraient les unes les autres.[4]

We have tried to show that these intricate cultural webs give support to literary universes in which, above or before ideological infiltration, society can explore its complexity. In the Othering process the role of the critic is no longer that of an elucidator or an arbiter of interpretations but that of a guide to the complexity contained in literary works. For the Othering critic there is not one reading corresponding to one literary text but a multiplicity of perspectives and sometimes conflicting reading experiences that (s)he must contribute to disclosing.

Notes

[1] A conceptual space does not refer to a compact notion encapsulating meaning but a field of dispersion in which meaning proliferates. The nodes that we have studied from Chapters Eight to Ten are examples of highly charged conceptual spaces.

[2] Edgar Morin, *La Complexité humaine* (Paris: Flammarion, 1994) 324. (It's a question of seeing the obscure clearly and the complex distinctly, of going from vagueness to precision, but also of seeing the obscure in the clear, the complex in the distinct, of going toward obscurity by way of clarity, toward the mouth of shadow that can't be grasped by the idea, for every idea carries within it, in its conceptual retina, an indelibly blind spot [Our translation.].)

[3] From the Latin "*complexus*, entwined round"; see Walter W. Skeat, *A Concise Etymological Dictionary of the English Language* (Oxford: Clarendon, 1882) 103.

[4] Morin 325. (The dialogic principle consists in allowing the complementary interplay of notions which, when taken as absolutes, would be antagonistic and mutually exclusive [Our translation.].)

BIBLIOGRAPHY

Literary Works

Fiction

Baldwin, James. "Sonny's Blues." *Going to Meet the Man*. London: Corgi Books, 1965. 87-124.

Banks, Russell. "The Blizzard." "Searching for Survivors." *Searching for Survivors*. New York: Fiction Collective, 1975. 21-33 and 1-5.

—. "My Mother's Memoirs, My Father's Lie, and Other true Stories." *Success Stories*. New York: Harper & Row, 1986. 30-39.

Barthelme, Donald; "The Balloon." *Unspeakable Practices, Unnatural Acts*. New York: Farrar, Straus and Giroux, 1964. 15-22

—. "The Rise of Capitalism." *Sixty Stories*. New York: Putnam, 1981. 204-08.

Beattie, Anne. "Janus." *Park City: New and Selected Stories*. New York: Alfred A. Knopf, 1998. 351-355.

Berry, R. M. "The Function of Art at the Present Time." *Dictionary of Modern Anguish: Fictions*. Normal, Illinois: FC2, 2000. 199-200.

Braverman, Kate. "Small Craft Warnings." *Small Craft Warnings*. Reno, Nevada: University of Nevada Press, 1992. 1-17.

—. "Tall Tales From the Mekong Delta." *Squandering the Blue*. New York: Ballantine, 1989. 35-60.

Butler, Robert Olen. "Fairy Tale." *A Good Scent From a Strange Mountain: Stories*. New York: H. Holt, 1992. 45-57.

Carver, Raymond. "The Calm." "Cathedral." *Where I'm calling From: The Selected Stories*. London: The Harvill Press,1998. 194-198 and 356-375.

Chang, Diana. "Falling Free." In *Charlie Chan is Dead: An Anthology of Contemporary Asian American Fiction*. Ed. Jessica Hagedorn. New York: Penguin, 1993. 60-75.

Chaon, Dan. "Falling Backwards." "Prosthesis." *Among the Missing*. New York: Ballantine Books, 200. 216-32 and 153-159.

Cheever, John "The Enormous Radio." *The Enormous Radio and Other Stories*. New York: Funk and Wagnalls, 1953. 169-181.

Cisneros, Sandra. "One Holy Night." *Woman Hollering Creek and Other Stories.* New York: Random House, 1991. 27-35.

DeLillo, Don. *The Body Artist.* New York: Simon & Schuster. 2001.

Dybek, Stuart. "Pet Milk." *The Coast of Chicago.* New York: Picador, 2003. 167-73.

Gass, William H. "In the Heart of the Heart of the Country." *In the Heart of the Heart of the Country, and Other Stories.* New York, Harper & Row, 1968. 191-223.

Goyen, William. "The Enchanted Nurse." *The Collected Stories of William Goyen.* Garden City, N.Y.: Doubleday, 1975. 240-254.

Hahn, Kimiko. "Afterbirth." In *Charlie Chan is Dead: An Anthology of Contemporary Asian American Fiction.* Ed. Jessica Hagedorn. New York: Penguin, 1993. 132-140.

Jones, Gayl. "Persona." "Your Poems Have Very Little Color In Them". *White Rat.* New York: Random House, 1977; Lawrenceville, N..J.: Northeastern University Press, 1991. 83-94 and 17-21.

Kingsolver, Barbara. "Extinctions." *Homeland and Other Stories.* New York: Harper & Row, 1989. 168-181.

L'Heureux, John. "The Comedian." *Comedians.* New York: Viking Penguin, 1990. 3-19.

Lopez, Barry. "Winter Count 1973: Geese, They Flew Over in a Storm." "The Woman Who Had Shells." *Winter Count.* New York: Vintage, 1999. 51-63 and 77-86.

Major, Clarence. "An Area in the Cerebral Hemisphere." First published in *Statements: New Fiction from the Fiction Collective.* Ed. Jonathan Baumbach. New York: G. Braziller, 1975. Reprinted in *The Norton Anthology of American Literature*, Fifth Edition. Ed. Nina Baym. New York: W.W. Norton, 1998. 2175-78.

Means, David. "The Gesture Hunter." *Assorted Fire Events.* New York: Context Books, 2000. 139-151.

Millhauser, Steven. "Beneath the Cellars of Our Town." *The Knife Thrower and Other Stories.* New York: Crown, 1998. 211-28.

Morrison, Toni. *Beloved.* New York: Alfred Knopf, 1987.

Paley, Grace. "A Conversation with my Father." *Enormous Changes At The Last Minute.* New York: Farrar, Strauss & Giroux, 1960. 159-167.

Salinger, J. D. "A Perfect Day for Bananafish." *Nine Stories.* Boston, Little, Brown, 1953. 3-18.

Schickler, David. "Kissing In Manhattan." *Kissing in Manhattan.* New York: Dell Publishing Co., 2001. 83-105.

Silko, Leslie Marmon. "Storyteller." *Storyteller.* New York: Arcade Publishing, 1981. 17- 32.

Walker, Alice. "Everyday Use." *In Love and Trouble*. New York: Harvest, 1967. 47-59.
Wallace, David Foster. "Everything is Green." *Girl With Curious Hair*. New York: Avron Books, 1989. 229-30.
Wetherell, W.D. "What Peter Saw." *Hyannis Boat and Other Stories*. Boston: Little Brown, 1989. 163-185.

Poetry

Ammons, A.R. "Gravelly Run," "The Quince Bush." *The Selected Poems: Expanded Edition*. New York: W.W. Norton, 1986. 11 and 68.
Anzaldúa, Gloria. "Cultures." In *Borderlands / La Frontera: The New Mestiza*. San Francisco: Aunt Lute Books, 1987. 120.
Ashbery, John. "And I'd Love You To Be In It." *As We Know*. Harmondsworth, Middlesex: Penguin Books, 1979. 89.
Baraka, Amiri. "An Agony. As Now." *Transbluesency, The Slected Poems of Amiri Baraka/LeRoi Jones (1961-1995)*. New York: Marsilio, 1995. 60-61.
Bishop, Elizabeth. "At the Fishhouses," "In the Waiting Room," and "O Breath." *The Complete Poems: 1927-1979*. New York: Farrar, Strauss and Giroux, 1983. 64-66,159-161, and 79.
Boruch, Marianne. "Grief." *View From the Gazebo*. Middletown, CT: Wesleyan UP. 19.
Carson, Anne. "Sumptuous Destitution," *Men in the Off Hours*. New York: Alfred Knopf, 2000. 13.
Clifton, Lucille. "perhaps." *New Bones, Contemporary Black American Writers in America*, Eds. K.E. Quashie, J. Lausch & K.D. Miller. Upper Saddle River, N.J. : Prentice-Hall, 2001. 150.
Creeley, Robert. "The Edge." *Selected Poems*. New York: Marion Boyars, 1991. 268-69.
Dickinson, Emily. "In many and reportless places." *The Complete Poems of Emily Dickinson*. Ed. Thomas H. Johnson. Boston: Little, Brown, 1997): 1382.
Donne, John. *Poems of John Donne*. vol I. E. K. Chambers, ed. London: Lawrence & Bullen, 1896.
Dobyns, Stephen. "Contingencies." "Refusing the Necessary." *Velocities, New and Selected Poems 1066-1992*. New York: Penguin, 1994. 38-39 and 49.
Dubie, Norman "Elegy to the Sioux." *The Mercy Seat: Collected & New Poems, 1967-2001*. Townsend, Washington: Copper Canyon Press, 2001. 167-169.

Erdrich, Louise. "The Fence." *Baptism of Desire*. New York: HarperCollins, 1989. 61.

Gibson, Margaret. "Burning the Root." *Long Walks in the Afternoon*. Baton Rouge: Louisiana State University Press, 1982. 30.

Gilbert, Jack. "Hunger." *The Great Fires, Poems: 1982-1992*. New York: Knopf, 1994. 51.

Ginsberg, Allen. "Sunflower Sutra." *Collected Poems: 1947-1980*. New York: Harper & Row, 1984. 138-39.

Glück, Louise. "Matins." *The Wild Iris*. New York: HarperCollins, 1992. 25.

Graham, Jorie. "Recovered From the Storm." *The Errancy*. Hopewell, N.J.: The Ecco Press, 1997. 107-108.

—. "I Was Taught Three." *The Dream of the Unified Field. Selected Poems 1974-1994*. Hopewell (NJ) : The Ecco Press, 1980. 6-7.

Gregg, Linda. ""There She Is." *Too Bright To See*. Townsend, Washington: Graywolf Press, 1981. 15.

Hass, Robert. "A Story About the Body." *Human Wishes*. Ontario, Canada: The Ecco Press, 1989. 32.

Hayden, Robert. "The Diver." *Collected Poems*. Ed. F. Glaysher. New York: Liveright Publishing Co., 1985. 3.

Hejinian, Lyn. "November, 13, 1986." *The Cell*. Los Angeles: Sun and Moon, 1992. 31.

Johnson, Denis. "The Rockefeller Collection of Primitive Art." *The Throne of the Third Heaven of the Nations Millennium General Assembly: Poems, Collected and New*. New York : HarperCollins, 1995. 141-142.

Jordan, June. "October 23, 1983." *Living Room: New Poems*. New York: Thunder's Mouth Press, 1985. 70.

Lea, Sydney. "The One White Face In the Place." *The Floating Candles*. Chicago: University of Chicago Press, 1982. 47-50.

Lee, Li-Young. "From Blossoms." *Rose: Poems by Li-Young Lee*. Brockport, New York: Boa Editions, 1986. 21.

Levertov, Denise. "Night on Hatchet Cove." *Poems: 1960-1967*. New York: New Directions, 1983. 15.

Lim, Shirley Geok-lin. "Brinjal." *Monsoon History: Selected Poems*. London: Skoob, 1994. 111.

McGrath, Thomas. "The Return." *Selected Poems: 1938-1988*. Ed. Sam Hamill. Port Townsend, WA: Copper Canyon Press, 1988. 118.

Merwin, William. "For the Anniversary of My Death." *The Lice*. New York: Atheneum, 1967. 58.

Moss, Thylias. "Remembering Kitchens." *Small Congregations: New and Selected Poems*. New York: Harper Collins, 1993. 49-50.

Nelson Waniek, Marilyn. "The House on Moscow Street." *The Homeplace*. Baton Rouge: Louisiana State U.P., 1990. 4-5.

Plath, Sylvia. "Metaphors." *Crossing the Water, Transitional Poems*. New York: Harper & Row, 1971. 43.

Plumly, Stanley. "Dove," "November 11, 1942-November 12, 1997." *Now That My Father Lies Down Beside Me, New and Selected Poems, 1970-2000*. New York: HarperCollins, 2000. 40 and 6-7.

Pollak, Felix. "Incident." *Tunnel Visions*. Peoria, Ill.: Spoon River Poetry Press, 1984. 18-19.

Rich, Adrienne. "Nightbreak." *The Fact of a Doorframe: Poems Selected and New, 1950-1984*. New York: W.W. Norton, 1984. 98-99.

Ryan, Michael. "Every Sunday." *New and Selected Poems*. Boston: Houghton Mifflin, 2004. 131.

Ruefle, Mary. "The Intended." *Life Without Speaking*. Tuscaloosa: U. of Alabama, 1987. 28.

Sanchez, Sonia. "for our lady." *The Norton Anthology of African American Literature*. Eds. Henry Louis Gates Jr. and Nellie Y. McKay. New York: W.W. Norton, 1997. 1904.

Simic, Charles. "The Inner Man." "The Stream." "Two Riddles" *Selected Poems, 1963-1983*. Revised and Expanded edition. New York: George Braziller, 1990. 18-19, 152-154 and 56-57.

Stevens, Wallace. "Anecdote of the Jar." *Collected Poems*. Boston: Alfred Knopf, 1954. 76.

Strand, Mark. "Another Place," "The Man In the Mirror," "The Tunnel," *Selected Poems*. New York: Alfred Knopf, 1993. 116, 24-28, and 13-14.

Twichell, Chase. "Japanese Weeping Cherry." *The Odds*. Pittsburg: University of Pittsburg Press, 1986. 27.

Wilbur, Richard. "A Hole In the Floor." "The Lilacs," *New and Collected Poems*. New York: Harcourt Brace, 1988. 189-90 and 118-19.

Williams, C. K. "The Gap." "Halves.*" Selected Poems*. New York: Farrar, Strauss and Giroux, 1994. 23 and 235-36.

Yau, John. "A Gargoyle in the Garden." *Sometimes*. New York: Sheep Meadow Press, 1979. 26.

Interviews

Graham, Jorie. "The Glorious Thing: Jorie Graham and Mark Wunderlich in Conversation." *American Poet,* 1996. Available online at the American Academy of Poets website (http://www.poets.org).

Critical and Theoretical Works

Adorno, Theodor. *Aesthetic Theory.* Trans. Robert Hullot-Kentor. New York: Continuum, 1997.

Anzaldúa, Gloria. *Borderlands / La Frontera: The New Mestiza.* San Francisco: Aunt Lute Books, 1987.

Attridge, Derek. *The Singularity of Literature.* New York: Routledge, 2004.

Austin, J.L. *How to do Things With Words.* Oxford, Clarendon Press, 1962.

Bakhtin, Mikhail. *The Dialogic Imagination: Four Essays by M.M. Bakhtin.* Ed. Michael Holquist, trans. Caryl Emerson and Michael Holquist. Austin, Texas: University of Texas Press, 1981.

Bataille, Georges. *Eroticism.* Trans. Mary Dalwood. London & New York: Marion Boyars, 1962 [1957].

Bernabé, Jean, Raphaël Confiant, and Patrick Chamoiseau. *Eloge de la Créolité.* Paris: Gallimard, 1989.

Bhabha, Homi K. "DissemiNation: time, narrative, and the margins of the modern nation." *Nation and Narration.* Ed. Homi K. Bhabha. London/New York: Routledge, 1990. 291-322.

—. *The Location of Culture.* London: Routledge, 1994.

Bloom, Harold. *The Anxiety of Influence: A Theory of Poetry.* New York, Oxford University Press, 1973.

Bonnefoy, Yves. *L'Improbable et autres essais.* Paris: Gallimard, 1992.

—. *La Vérité de parole et autres essais.* Paris: Mercure de France, 1992.

Brooks, Cleanth. *The Well Wrought Urn: Studies in the Structure of Poetry.* London : Dennis Dobson, 1949.

Culler, Johnathan. *On Deconstruction: Theory and Criticism After Structuralism.* Ithaca: Cornell University Press, 1982.

de Certeau, Michel. *L'Invention du Quotidien, 1.Arts de faire.* Paris: Gallimard, Folio: Essais, 1990.

de Man, Paul. *Blindness and Insight: Essays in the Rhetoric of Contemporary Criticism.* Theory and History of Literature, Volume 7. Minneapolis: University of Minnesota Press, 1983.

Deleuze, Gilles. "*Bartleby*; or, the formula." *Essays critical and clinical.* Trans. Daniel Smith and Michael A. Greco. Minneapolis: University of Minnesota Press, 1997. 68 – 90.

Deleuze, Gilles and Guattari, Felix. *Mille Plateaux.* Paris: Minuit, 1980. English edition: A *Thousand Plateaus.* Translated by Brian Massumi. Minnesota: University of Minnesota Press, 1987.

Derrida, Jacques. *L'Ecriture et la difference.* Paris: Seuil, 1967.

—. *The Truth in Painting.* Trans. by Geoff Bennington and Ian Mcleod. Chicago: University of Chicago Press, 1987.

—. *Acts of Literature.* Ed. Derek Attridge. London: Routledge, 1992.

Eliot, T. S. *On Poetry and Poets.* New York: Farrar, Strauss, Cudahy, 1957.

Emerson, Ralph Waldo. *Emerson's Essays.* Ed. Arthur Hobson Quinn. New York: Scribner's, 1920.

Fetterley, Judith. *The Resisting Reader: A Feminist Approach to American Fiction.* Bloomington : Indiana University Press. 1978.

Frege, Gottlob. "Thoughts." *Collected Papers on Mathematics, Logic, and Philosophy.* Ed. B. McGuiness, trans. P. Geach and R.H. Stoothoff. Oxford: Blackwell, 1984. 351-72.

Frey, Hans-Jost. *Interruptions.* Albany: State University of New York Press, 1996.

Freud, Sigmund. *Beyond the Pleasure Principle.* Translated and newly edited by James Strachey. New York : Norton, 1975.

Frost, Robert. "The Figure a Poem Makes." (1939). *Selected Poems of Robert Frost.* New York: Holt, Rinehart, and Winston, 1963. 1-4.

Geertz, Clifford. *Available Light: Anthropological Reflections on Philosophical Topics.* Princeton: Princeton UP, 2000.

—. *Selected Essays.* New York: Basic Books, 1973.

Genette Gérard. *Narrative Discourse: an Essay in Method.* Trans. Jane E. Lewin. Ithaca: Cornell University Press, 1980.

Glissant, Édouard. *Caribbean Discourse: Selected Essays.* Trans. J. Michael Dash. Charlottesville: University Press of Virginia, 1989.

Gumbrecht, Hans Ulrich. *Production of Presence: What Meaning cannot Convey.* Stanford: Stanford UP. 2004

Halliday, M.A.K. and Hasan, R. *Cohesion in English.* London: Longman, 1976.

Harding, Wendy and Jacky Martin, *A World of Difference: An Intercultural Study of Toni Morrison's Novels.* Westport, Connecticut: Greenwood, 1994.

Hejinian, Lyn. *The Language of Inquiry.* Berkeley: University of California Press, 2000.

Hoey, Michael. *Patterns of Lexis in the Text.* Oxford: Oxford University Press, 1991.

Iser, Wolfgang. *How To Do Theory.* Oxford: Blackwell, 2006.

—. "What is Literary Anthropology." *Revenge of the Aesthetic: The Place of Literature in Theory Today.* Ed. Michael P. Clark. Berkeley: University of California Press, 2000. 157-79.

James, William. *Principles of Psychology.* 1890.

von Kleist Heinrich. "On the Puppet Theatre." *An Abyss Deep Enough: Letters of Heinrich von Kleist with a Selection of Essays and Anecdotes.* Ed. and trans. Phillip B. Miller. New York: E.P. Dutton, 1982. 211-217

Lacoue Labarthe, Philippe. *La Poésie comme experience.* Paris: Christian Bourgois, 1986.

Lakoff, George and Johnson, Mark. *Metaphors We Live By.* Chicago : Chicago University Press, 1980.

Laplantine, François, and Alexis Nouss. *Métissages de Arcimboldo à Zombi.* Paris: Pauvert, 2001.

Lévinas, Emmanuel. Autrement qu'être ou au-delà de l'essence. Paris: Kluwer, 2001. English edition: *Otherwise Than Being: or Beyond Essence.* Trans. Alphonso Lingis. Boston: Kluwer, 1981.

—. *De l'Evasion.* Paris: Fata Morgana, 1982.

—. *Quelques réflexions sur la nature de l'hitlérisme.* Paris: Payot & Rivages,1997.

Lombardi, Marilyn May. *The Body and the Song: Elizabeth Bishop's Poetics.* Carbondale: Southern Illinois University Press, 1995.

Martin, Jacky. "La traduction éclatée: pourquoi et comment ne pas traduire la poésie." *"Traduire* ou *Vouloir garder un peu de la poussière d'or..." Palimpsestes* Hors Série. Paris, Presses de la Sorbonne Nouvelle, 2006. 77-88.

Miller, Joseph Hillis. *The Ethics of Reading.* New York: Columbia UP, 1987.

—. *The J. Hillis Miller Reader.* Ed. Julian Wolfreys. Stanford: Stanford UP, 2005.

Morin, Edgar. *La Complexité humaine.* Paris: Flammarion, 1994.

—. *Introduction à la pensée complexe.* Paris: ESF, 1980.

Morrison, Toni. "Unspeakable Things Unspoken: The Afro-American Presence in American Literature." *Michigan Quarterly Review,* 28 (Winter 1989): 1-34.

Nora, Pierre. "Between Memory and History: *Les lieux de mémoire.*" *History and Memory in African-American Culture.* Eds. Geneviève

Fabre and Robert O'Meally. Oxford: Oxford University Press, 1994. 284-300.

Orwell, George. "Politics and the English Language." *Collected Essays.* London : Secker & Warburg, 1961. 53-67.

Ricoeur, Paul. *Hermeneutics and The Human Sciences.* Ed. & translated by John B. Thompson. New York: Cambridge University Press, 1981.

Simic, Charles. "Negative Capability and its Children." In *Poetics: Essays on the Art of Poetry.* Eds. Paul Mariani and George Murphy. Tendril: Special Issue of Tendril Magazine, 1984.

Steiner, George. *Real Presences.* London/Boston: Faber & Faber, 1989.

Strand, Mark.*The Weather of Words, Poetic Invention.* New York: Knopf, 2000.

Winnicot, Donald W. *Playing and Reality.* New York: Basic Books, 1971.

Ziarek, Krzysztof. *The Force of Art.* Stanford: Stanford UP, 2004.

INDEX

communication, 6, 8, 10, 27, 34, 65, 67, 93, 133
commutability, 6, 160, 207
completeness, 83, 85
completion, 61, 85, 86, 95, 98, 185
complexity, viii, xv, 2, 6, 11, 15, 29, 52, 55, 56, 84, 86, 89, 109, 112, 129, 149, 150, 160, 163, 167, 168, 171, 173, 175, 176, 182, 183, 204, 207, 208, 209, 210
confrontation, viii, xi, xii, 120, 204, 206
confusion, xiv, 6, 24, 64, 79, 92, 117, 133, 143, 156, 163, 171, 172, 176, 180, 182, 205, 208, 209
conjunction, 49, 61, 159
context, 2, 3, 12, 15, 16, 19, 27, 34, 35, 39, 125, 130, 140, 189, 205, 207
continuity, xi, 11, 41, 42, 43, 51, 57, 61, 83, 112, 121, 127, 161, 176, 196, 199, 200
contradiction, x, 11, 17, 83, 86, 97, 98, 122, 125, 142, 156, 180, 190, 202
contradictory, 6, 11, 29, 60, 61, 88, 106, 112, 116, 117, 120, 122, 131, 136, 155, 167, 177
Creeley, Robert, 50-51, 77, 150, 153-154, 155, 162, 164, 213
creolization, 104
cultural interface, x
cultural system, viii-xv, 8, 9, 10, 12, 13, 24, 25, 82, 109, 119, 126, 135, 146, 147, 148, 163, 166, 169, 177, 183, 188, 189, 201, 202, 204, 205, 206, 209

D

dasein, 189
de Certeau, Michel, 216
de Man, Paul, 2, 19, 216
Deleuze, Gilles, 27, 30, 39, 49, 67, 217

DeLillo, Don, xv, 189, 190, 192-197, 198-202, 203, 212
Derrida, Jacques, 3, 9, 19, 20, 102, 217
destabilization, 139, 146, 182
destructure, 18, 123
deviance, 11, 128, 142, 173
deviation, x, 57, 121
dialogic, 50, 210
dichotomies, 85
Dickinson, Emily, 46, 47, 63, 213
diegetic, 187, 190, 202
difference, 6, 8, 12, 24, 57, 60, 97, 106, 116, 118, 120, 123, 128, 144, 169, 187, 191, 205, 207, 209, 217
differences, ix-xii, 5, 6, 26, 51, 140, 177, 204, 206, 209
diffraction, 10, 12, 20, 171
digression, xiii, 65, 72, 73, 79
discontinuities, 42, 46, 51, 127
discontinuity, 42, 44, 121, 146, 176
discrepancies, 24, 33, 82
disjunction, 13, 28, 41, 43, 56, 57, 64, 159
disorder, xiii, 7, 8, 64, 82, 153, 171, 185, 189, 190, 209
disorientation, x, xiv, 15, 18, 26, 104, 107, 125, 127, 140, 144, 147, 152, 166, 168, 169, 171, 172, 173, 174, 175, 177, 178, 179, 180, 181, 182, 183, 185, 202, 207
dispersion, xiii, 27, 41, 129, 137, 147, 170, 171, 210
disruption, xiii-xv, 13, 41, 49, 101, 105, 126, 146, 185, 205, 206
dissonance, 205
distancing, 70, 130, 133, 134, 199
divagation, xiii, 71, 74, 76, 79, 121
Dobyns, Stephen, 156, 164, 165, 213
Donne, John 41, 62, 213
double, 106, 185, 191
double vision, 44
dualism, xv, 2, 9, 205, 209

P

Q

R